MW01053327

Women in the Military

WOMEN IN THE MILITARY:

Flirting with Disaster

Brian Mitchell

Regnery Publishing, Inc.
Washington, D.C.

Library of Congress Cataloging-in-Publication Data

Mitchell, Brian (Brian P.), 1958–
    Women in the military: flirting with disaster / Brian Mitchell.
       p. cm.
    Includes index
    ISBN 0-89526-376-9 (alk. paper)
      1. United States—Armed Forces—Women. 2. United States—Armed Forces Operational readiness. 3. National security—United States. I. Title.
    UB418.W65M5723 1997
    355'.0082—dc21   97-43081
                                                        CIP

Portions of this book previously appeared in Brian Mitchell's *Weak Link: The Feminization of the American Military.*

Published in the United States by
Regnery Publishing, Inc.
An Eagle Publishing Company
One Massachusetts Avenue, NW
Washington, DC 20001

Distributed to the trade by
National Book Network
4720-A Boston Way
Lanham, MD 20706

Printed on acid-free paper.
Manufactured in the United States of America

10 9 8 7 6 5 4 3 2 1

Books are available in quantity for promotional or premium use. Write to Director of Special Sales, Regnery Publishing, Inc., One Massachusetts Avenue, NW, Washington, DC 20001, for information on discounts and terms or call (202) 216-0600.

This book is dedicated to

Charles B. Johnson,
Former Major, United States Marine Corps:

For rising generations it will become a real problem at what point the policies you are ordered to carry out have become so iniquitous that a decent man must seek some other profession....

—C.S. Lewis

CONTENTS

Introduction

THE G.I. JANE DECEPTION

*The greatest change that has come about
in the United States forces in the time that
I've been in the military service has been
the extensive use of women.... That's even greater
than nuclear weapons, I feel, as far as our own
forces are concerned.*

—GENERAL JOHN A. VESSEY
CHAIRMAN OF THE JOINT CHIEFS OF STAFF, IN A STATE-
MENT TO THE HOUSE ARMED SERVICES COMMITTEE

ON OCTOBER 26, 1997, Sara Lister, assistant secretary of the Army for manpower and reserve affairs, told a meeting of scholars, journalists, and military personnel, "I think the Army is much more connected to society than the Marines are. The Marines are extremists. Whenever you have extremists, you have some risk of total disconnection with society. And that's a little dangerous."

General Charles Krulak, commandant of the Marine Corps, told reporters her words "summarily dismiss 222 years of sacrifice and dedication" and "dishonor the hundreds of thousands of Marines whose blood has been shed in the name of freedom."

The Army, amazingly, defended Lister's remarks, saying that her words were "taken out of context."[1]

But the next day Lister was apologizing to General Krulak and "all current and former Marines" for words she admitted were "inappropriate and wrong." Defense Secretary William Cohen announced that he was "satisfied" with her apology, but many members of Congress were not. House Speaker Newt Gingrich fired off a letter demanding Lister's immediate dismissal, and the House quickly passed a resolution to the same effect. Within 24 hours Lister was history.

But Lister only said publicly what advocates of women in the military have long thought and often preached: that the Marine Corps's encouragement of "hypermasculinity" contributes to a hostile atmosphere. The Marines self-consciously train warriors, and compared to the new, more motherly Army, the Marines are indeed extreme.

As early as 1982 the Army was treating military police recruits at Fort McClellan, Alabama, to "the LaBarge Touch," a celebrated method of handling female trainees devised by a drill sergeant named LaBarge. The cardinal tenet of the LaBarge touch was "Be Nice"—no loud shouting or angry snarls for which drill sergeants had long been famous, but smiles and soft words and lots of encouragement.

Drill Sergeant LaBarge, who described himself as a "female chauvinist pig," taught his young female recruits that they were not equal to men but better than men because they had "no macho mentality" and had better communicative skills. LaBarge promoted "snobbery" among his women to make them feel psychologically superior to men. His "attitude check" (a motto shouted on cue by a formation of troops) for the women in his charge was: "When God created man, She was only joking." LaBarge encouraged his female MPs to use feminine charm "when it's to [your] advantage" and advised them to try breaking up a barroom brawl by "being sweet." He avoided unpleasantness in his training and refrained from telling his women that the M16 rifle would actually kill if used properly, telling them instead that the rifle was "made to wound people."[2]

That was fifteen years ago. Today, with many more women in the ranks and co-ed basic training, the LaBarge Touch has effectively been extended to all recruits. Drill sergeants still raise their voices, but not as often. They are forbidden to curse, call recruits names, or belittle them in any way. Harmless but humiliating punishments are no longer permitted. At the Navy's Great Lakes Naval Training Center, drill instructors carry laminated cards warning them not to apply any punishment that might cause a recruit "undue embarrassment," while recruits carry "stress passes" they can trade for a convenient time-out when the going gets too tough.

God forbid that a drill sergeant should ever actually lay a hand on a recruit. Instead, recruits are treated with dignity and respect, just as every mother in America would want her son or daughter to be treated. Problem recruits receive emotional support and counseling in stress reduction and self-

> Were it not for intense political pressure, there would be virtually no women in the military today.

esteem. A trainee is even "offered emotional support... and given a chance to explore his feelings by pasting cut-out magazine photos on a piece of cardboard." Discipline is out; communication is in. Physical demands are minimal, lower than many male recruits expect. As one young Navy recruit recently told the *Los Angeles Times*, "When you think boot camp, you think blood, sweat, and tears. But this was laid back."[3]

The truth is that after the various sex scandals at training bases across the country, drill sergeants are no longer trusted with their troops. "We used to be able to push them to the limits," says Army Sergeant First Class Garvin Gourie. "It's unheard of now. They call it trainee abuse. As a drill sergeant, you're always having to do a mental check. It changes your spontaneity, and in doing that it changes the way you think. It's like you are protecting your own interests."[4]

Drill sergeants are not the only men in uniform protecting their own interests. The profound changes occurring in our military today have all been implemented by military leaders protecting their own interests, obediently doing as they are told in the face of intense political pressure. Were it not for that pressure, there would be virtually no women in the military today.

The military has succumbed to the creeping influence of 1970s social upheaval. In fact, in the late 1960s the participation of women in the United States military was still following a long downward trend. A failed attempt to involve large numbers of women in the military during the Korean War convinced military planners that American women would not play a significant role in any peacetime force. By 1967 the participation of women in the American military reached its lowest point since World War II, with barely twenty thousand women in service, not including nurses. Women made up less than 2 percent of the total force.

But then in the early 1970s the trend was abruptly reversed. The shift to the All-Volunteer Force (AVF) and the political success of the American feminist movement combined to bring about a reversal of military manpower thinking and a rapid expansion of the military use of women. In just a few years, the number of women increased fivefold. Today, the American military has nearly 200,000 women in active service—almost 14 percent of its total force. Seventeen percent of first-year students at the nation's service academies are female, and one out of every five enlisted recruits is a woman. Women are still not assigned to infantry, armor, special operations, and submarines, but their assignment to combat aircraft, combat surface ships, and combat and combat-support ground units places them at the forefront of any United States military operation.

No other military in the world depends so heavily on women or has more women as a percentage of its total force. Israel and Canada tie for second, with 11 percent, followed by the United Kingdom with 6 percent. No other country has a military more than 3.5 percent female. Several European nations, including Germany, Spain, and Italy, have virtually no women in service. Russia's four-million-man armed force includes just 25,000 women (0.7 percent), who perform largely clerical and medical work. Israel drafts women, but the jobs open to them are more limited than the jobs that were open to American military women during World War II. A handful of small, secure NATO nations have opened combat units to women, but the numbers of women involved are very small, and expectations that they will ever actually see combat are even smaller.[5]

The U.S. Department of Defense clings to its official stance that the integration of women has proceeded without the slightest decline in the combat capabilities of the armed forces. According to the party line in the Pentagon, the modern volunteer force is far superior to any earlier force of volunteers or conscripts, and women, in official phraseology, are "an integral part." "We can't go to war without them," say the admirals and the generals; women are "here to stay." They perform "as well as or better than" men. They are promoted faster. They possess invaluable abilities that the services cannot do without. They add civility and wholesomeness to military service. Their effect on morale and readiness is positive.

> Nowhere in the U.S. military do women meet the same physical standards as men, nor are they a financial bargain.

In recent years, however, the services have struggled to maintain this stance in the face of the mountains of evidence that the presence of women is damaging our armed forces. The Persian Gulf War dramatized the problem of depending on soldier-mothers with young children. The trials of the Citadel and the Virginia Military Institute; the fatal crash of naval aviator Kara Hultgreen; the discharge of adulterous Air Force Lieutenant Kelly Flinn; and a rash of other celebrated cases have exposed the dangerous effects of sex-based integration and affirmative action on standards, safety, training, and discipline. These cases underline that nowhere in the U.S. military do women meet the same physical standards as men, nor are they a financial bargain. A presidential commission on women in the military in 1992 documented the problems of higher rates of attrition, greater need for medical care, higher rates of nonavailability, lower rates of deployability, lesser physical ability, and the growing number of single parents and dual-service marriages. More recently the Aberdeen sex scandal and other related cases have highlighted the persistent—and apparently ineradicable—problems of fraternization, sexual harassment, and the resulting breakdown of good order among the troops.

None of these problems can be dismissed as temporary difficulties. It has been twenty-one years since women first forced themselves into the federal service academies, where they have shattered tradition, fractured morale, and confused the academies' purpose—which is to train *combat* officers. It has now been nineteen years since the separate women's corps were abolished, and the services still have not proved that they know how to mix men and women together without suffering periodic outbreaks of embarrassing behavior, when men and women forget their oaths of office and their professional pretensions and behave toward each other not as soldiers and sailors but as males and females.

All of these problems were apparent when my first book on this subject, *Weak Link*, was published in the summer of 1989. But official pressure to ignore the manifold problems was overwhelming. *Weak Link* was the first—indeed, the only—book to cast doubt on the stock assurances of Pentagon officials that all was well with integration and that women were performing admirably.

But today, the problems have grown far worse. The bottom line is that with the exception of the medical professions there is no real need for women in the military. Every other soldier, sailor, and airman is a potential combatant, and, as the pages that follow will show, women are not up to that job.

Proponents of women in the military have failed to answer basic questions: Why, for instance, given the dramatic force reductions since the end of the Cold War, does the military need female recruits? Why should America be obligated to provide military careers for women if their effect is to hinder combat effectiveness? Why is America rushing forward when other countries with real experience of women in combat—like Israel and Russia—have pulled far, far back?

Library shelves groan under the weight of books praising the integration of women into the armed forces. *Women in the Military: Flirting with Disaster* is the only in-depth treatment that offers an alternative view of the revolution that threatens to leave the American military no more disciplined, no more efficient, no more fearsome, no more military than the United States Postal Service.

Houston, Texas
November 19, 1997

Chapter 1

MYTHS IN THE MAKING

War hath no fury like a noncombatant.

—C.E. MONTAGUE

THE FIRST AMERICAN WOMAN to serve in combat was Molly Pitcher. Few American schoolchildren escape the lower grades without hearing the story of Molly's heroism. They will not have heard of Alvin York or Audie Murphy, but the image of the petticoated heroine fetching water and swabbing gun-barrels for the hard-pressed Continental artillery stands clearly in their minds. In the minds of modern historians, however, Molly's image is much less clear. Was she Mary Hays or Margaret Corbin? Was she any one woman at all, or a legendary composite of hundreds of camp followers who lent a hand in the heat of battle? While the latter seems more likely, one thing is certain: Molly Pitcher made a good story.

Lately, good stories about women in combat are receiving greater attention. Feminist historians, eager to provide today's military women with a heritage of their own, are revising the history of every American military conflict to include women as soldiers, sailors, and secret agents. Male historians, say the revisionists, have heretofore neglected the role of women in war and habitually minimized the contributions of individual women. The revised history will correct this deficiency, while at

the same time magnifying the record of the few who did participate. It is history with a purpose. Every odd and improbable
inclusion is meant to prove that women can indeed be warriors.
Every legendary wonder-woman who defied convention and
credibility by masquerading as a man among men is supposed
to bolster the argument for mustering regiments of riflewomen.

Sometimes, however, the revisionists' enthusiasm for a good
story overcomes their natural skepticism. Fancy is often mistaken for fact when titillating tales of soft breasts beneath coarse
uniform tunics are accepted at face value. Most such tales
escape close scrutiny, but one that did not involved a prostitute
by the name of Lucy Brewer. Lucy's tale has come down to us in
a number of recent "histories" of fighting women, few of which
show the slightest inclination to doubt her incredible claim of
having passed herself off as a male Marine aboard the frigate
Constitution during the War of 1812. The revisionists seem to
accept Lucy's claim on faith alone, without explaining how Lucy
managed to conceal her sex for three years aboard the cramped
frigate. Conditions on the ship alone would have made her mas-
querade impossible. The ship had no toilet facilities and no private quarters for enlisted Marines. Marine Corps historians have
in fact discovered that Lucy was a fraud. Her published accounts
of her wartime exploits were lifted "almost verbatim" from official after-action reports filed by the *Constitution*'s commanding
officer. Officially, the legend of Lucy Brewer is a "mockery of the
bona fide traditions" of the Corps.[1]

The history of American servicewomen truly begins with
the establishment of the Army and Navy Nurse Corps in 1901
and 1908. By the turn of the century, nursing had become an
exclusively female occupation, so the need for nurses who could
be sent wherever and whenever there were troops made necessary the admission of women to the services as auxiliaries. But
nursing has little to do with soldiering. The first military nurses
held no rank and wore uniforms bearing no resemblance to
the men's uniforms, and no one seriously referred to them as
soldiers or sailors.

The same was true of the first nonnursing servicewomen inducted during World War I. In need of clerks, typists, and telephone operators, all of which were recently feminized occupations, the services avoided the chore of training men for such work by employing women for the task. The Navy enlisted some 12,500 "yeomanettes" in the Naval Reserve, circumventing a law requiring all sailors to be assigned to vessels by assigning the women, on paper only, to riverboats on the Potomac. The Army and Marine Corps also recruited women for work as secretaries and telephone operators, but the status of the Army's women has been a matter of debate. Some authorities say the women were never formally inducted as enlisted members. Others say they were. Either way, the participation of women in the American armed forces during the war is but a footnote in history. All of the 49,000 women who served in uniform during World War I were returned to civilian life when the war was over, except for a handful of nurses.

World War II brought more women to arms and into uniform than any event in human history before or since. Some 500,000 Soviet women are estimated to have served among the 7,000,000 Soviet combatants in the war. Great Britain employed more than 450,000 women in uniform. The United States ranked third in the world in the military use of women: 350,000 American women donned uniforms of khaki or blue from 1942 to 1945.

No doubt many women did serve well during the war and do not deserve to have their personal reputations deflated, but lately the wartime record of the women's corps has received such purposeful and elaborate praise that a critical appraisal of their contribution to the war effort is in order. The emerging myth about the use of women in World War II includes a dire shortage of American men and a stirring response from patriotic American women who supposedly turned out by brigades to "free a man to fight." Indeed, had the Army been able to recruit a million women as it had hoped in 1942, the creation of a women's corps might have made a dent in the demand for men. As it turned out, neither the manpower shortage nor the mass mobilization of American women materialized. At no time did women amount to more than 2.3 percent of all U.S. forces. Though 350,000 women donned uniforms, the combined strength of the women's components and both nurse corps never exceeded 266,000 at any one time.[2] The difference between the two figures reveals an astounding rate of personnel turnover for a force whose battlefield casualty rate was insignificant.

The truth about women in World War II is that, as soldiers, sailors, or Marines, they simply were not needed. Twenty-two million American men registered for the draft during the war; only ten million were drafted. The duties military women performed for the War and Navy Departments in Washington, D.C., where most military women were stationed, could easily have been performed by the men who were not drafted or by civilian men and women.[3] Their other uses hardly justified the trouble of establishing and maintaining separate women's components of the Army, Navy, Coast Guard, and Marines. In the end, the women's components served only to satisfy the ambitions of a handful of influential women and sympathetic men in Washington, among them First Lady Eleanor Roosevelt, Congresswoman Edith Nourse Rogers of Massachusetts, and Army Chief of Staff General George C. Marshall.

The establishment of separate women's components of the armed services was perhaps the most difficult legislative battle of the early war years. Marshall was an exception among the nation's military leaders, most of whom were not convinced they needed women's components. Most members of Congress were also reluctant to resort to the military use of women even after Pearl Harbor. Not until May 1942 did Congress, its arm twisted by Marshall's projected manpower shortage, authorize creation of the Women's Army Auxiliary Corps (WAAC). Two months later, pestered by Congresswoman Rogers and prodded by the First Lady, Congress authorized a women's component for the Navy, for which the Navy contrived a name to fit the acronym WAVES: Women Accepted for Voluntary Emergency Service. An unnamed component of female Marines was established shortly thereafter, followed by the Coast Guard's SPARS (short for *Semper Paratus*, the Coast Guard's motto). Last came the Women's Air Service Pilots (WASPs). Much mentioned today in any brief history of military women, the WASPs were technically not servicewomen but civilians contracted to perform routine flying duties until the services could train enough male pilots.

Once established, the women's components fulfilled no one's expectations. Female recruits were slow in coming, as the nation's women proved much less progressive than the activists in Washington. Many Americans could believe only that the kind of women who would join the Army were not the kind to take home to mother. As the first few women wandered in, rumors arose impugning the honor of the recruits. Tales of rampant promiscuity and lesbianism were met with indignant denials from the services. Official investigations found little to substantiate the rumors, but the damage was done nonetheless.

> **The truth about women in World War II is that they simply were not needed.**

The Army had both the highest hopes and the least success in attracting women. WAAC recruits, as members of an auxiliary, were not given full military status. Their simplified rank structure meant nothing to Army men, and their training and facilities were regarded as inferior to the other services. Worst of all, their uniforms were ugly and unfeminine. The Army's experience had taught it that soldiers complained about their uniforms only when they were too hot or too cold. It was surprised to learn that female recruits were much more concerned with their appearance and much more likely to join the WAVES, whose uniforms were more glamorous. Some of the WAAC's problems were solved when the auxiliary was reorganized as the Women's Army Corps (WAC) in 1943, but the search for more attractive, more feminine uniforms continued well into the war.

Just as the women's components were overcoming the pub-lic's initial disgust and enjoying some success in recruiting, their reason for being began to wane. By late 1943 the Army Air Corps had trained more male pilots than it needed, so the civil-ian WASPs were disbanded. The manpower shortage had always been a matter of having enough trained men in the right place at the right time, not a matter of there being too few men in America. In the summer of 1944 the Allies could not get enough infantrymen into France fast enough. Noninfantry reg-iments in the States were deactivated so the men could be retrained as infantry replacements. Boatloads of support per-sonnel disembarking at French ports were instantly reclassified as riflemen with the stroke of an adjutant's pen, an expedient not available to the modern integrated Army. Then, as the Allies tightened their grip on the European continent, the flow of troops through the manpower pipeline suddenly slowed. New recruits in the States marked time by repeating training cycles over and over again, being shipped overseas only after the war's end to replace combat veterans in the army of occupation. The supply of men had caught up with the demand.[4]

As the war reached its climax, the enthusiasm of the first women recruits began to waiver. The morale of the WAVES sank as the glamor of Navy uniforms wore off and the dreary tedium of military service made itself felt. WAVES began to complain about bad assignments, unrewarding duty, poor living conditions, and the lack of recreational opportunities. Some complained about not having enough to do. Others buckled under the strain of too much work.[5]

The WAC war effort also faltered. As early as 1943 WAC leaders noticed a surprising increase in the number of company-grade officers requesting transfer because they had "gone stale" and felt they had nothing left to offer their units. The WAC director, Colonel Oveta Culp Hobby, was able to persuade Marshall to order the establishment of "refresher training" for WAC officers, over the objection of the Army's chief of training, who argued that no such training was necessary or available for male officers; there was little else Hobby could do to boost morale. Some WAC leaders blamed low morale on a lack of gainful employment and respect for the corps, but the women in the ranks filed different complaints in letters to the director. Wrote one, "We don't want appreciation; we just want to go home."[6]

As morale crumbled, discharges for medical and other reasons soared. In January 1945 the rate of WAC medical discharges was twice that of January 1944. The rate of discharge under other than honorable conditions was many times that of the previous year. From January to December 1945 the WAC discharged 44,315 officers and enlisted women for reasons other than demobilization—almost twice the number demobilized that year. Other services experienced similar problems. Attrition among the elite WASPs had ranged between 36 percent and 40 percent, most of whom chose the alternative of getting married and going home over the opportunity for continued service. The experience of WASP leader Jacqueline Cochran led her to testify against admitting women to the Air Force Academy thirty years later.

At war's end all was forgiven if not forgotten. In the glow of victory only good things were said about the women who had served. No one had expected them to be anything other than ladies in uniform, anyway. No one noticed the high rates of attrition or estimated the cost-effectiveness of the women's components. No objective evaluation of the performance of the women's corps was ever done. Instead, the women got their share of exaggerated accolades along with everyone else. In a postwar interview with a senior WAC commander, Douglas MacArthur even dubbed the WACs "my best soldiers."[7] Today, some proponents of women in the military are quite willing to pretend that he meant what he said.

After the war, the heads of the women's components and their staffs expected and sought demobilization of all women and deactivation of the women's corps. But once their foot was in the door, they found it difficult to remove. First, the armed forces decided to keep many women in service to speed the demobilization of combat veterans. Then, as the leadership of the women's corps passed into the hands of the minority of those women who did not choose to return to civilian life, the services decided to retain the women's corps indefinitely. High-level staffs had come to depend on women in administrative and clerical roles, and no one wanted to give up their faithful and charming wartime secretaries for male draftees fresh out of clerk school.

Demobilization of women proceeded much slower than most women would have preferred, while the services did what they could to encourage women to stay on voluntarily and the War and Navy Departments petitioned Congress to establish the women's corps as permanent features of the new Department of Defense. In 1947 Congress authorized the integration of the nurse and medical specialist corps into the regular and reserve Army and Navy. In 1948 Public Law 625-80 allowed women veterans to rejoin the reserves, thus establishing a permanent place for women of other specialties. In the next two years, only 4,000 women with prior military service signed up for reserve duty, so in 1950 the law was amended to allow women without prior service to join. At the start of the Korean War, there were still fewer than 22,000 women on active duty, one-third of whom were nurses or medical specialists. The 15,000 women in the "line" components made up less than 1 percent of the total U.S. armed forces.

Though small to the point of insignificance, the women's components had friends in high places. General Marshall was then secretary of defense, with Anna Rosenberg as his assistant secretary of defense for manpower. Rosenberg quickly revived fears of another manpower shortage and began pushing for greater utilization of women by the services. At her urging, Marshall created the Defense Advisory Committee on Women in the Services, a blue-ribbon committee of prominent civilian women, known since as DACOWITS. With DACOWITS's assistance, the Defense Department mounted a massive publicity campaign to call American women to arms, shelling out large sums of advertising dollars. Slogans such as "America's Finest Women Stand Beside Her Finest Men" were trumpeted across the country by radio, television, magazines, newspapers, and billboards.

Aside from insulting the majority of American womanhood, the slogans did little else. Rosenberg and DACOWITS had completely misread the national mood and the ambitions of the nation's women. The campaign fell well short of its objectives, adding only 6,000 women in the time allotted to recruit 72,000. Many of the women it did attract were of the lowest category of recruits, as America's finest women apparently had other ideas about where to stand. Female strength peaked in October 1952 at 47,800, still less than 1 percent of the total force and well below the desired 112,000.

> Military service was once a privilege and an obligation, not a right or entitlement.

America's female population remained stubbornly unresponsive to recruiting through the end of the war. By 1955 female strength was down to 35,000. In 1956 Dr. Eli Ginzberg, a manpower expert with the National Manpower Council, told DACOWITS, "One cannot turn the country on its head in order to get a few more women into the services of the United States."[8] For many in the Defense Department and in Congress, the nation's second failure to mobilize significant numbers of women on a voluntary basis reinforced the experience of World War II and spoiled enthusiasm for women in the military for the next decade.

Bureaucratic inertia and the firm support of a small group of women in and out of uniform kept the women's components alive in the years following the Korean conflict, but the Defense Department no longer considered them a manpower advantage. The peacetime draft gave the services all the men they needed, and abysmal rates of attrition among women made the components more trouble than they were worth. Seventy per-

cent to 80 percent of first-term female enlistees in the late
1950s did not complete their initial term of enlistment. Most
left voluntarily to get married. Many others were separated
involuntarily for unsuitability, an avenue of exit always more
accessible to women than to men. Pregnancy in or out of wed-
lock was another cause for involuntary separation. The component directors still believed that motherhood took precedence
over military service and were extremely sensitive to charges of
immorality within the corps. Most staunchly defended the policy of discharging pregnant women as a means of protecting the
corps' honor.

Year after year the components atrophied, as women veterans hung on to serve out their time before retirement. To their
services, they were little more than window dressing. As such,
it was most important for the token force to look good. The services began requiring full-length photographs of potential
female recruits, taking only the best-looking among them.
Recruits were not instructed in marksmanship or combat survival, but they did learn how to apply makeup properly and to
conduct themselves as ladies. Their physical training was
intended to maintain trim figures, not to increase strength,
endurance, or coordination.

Appearance was always important, even in Vietnam. Jeanne
Holm quotes the WAC director writing to a senior WAC officer
in Vietnam in 1967:

> I am aware that conditions are bad and it must be difficult
> to maintain a neat and feminine appearance.... I do not
> want anything to spoil their image or standing as women.
> The matter of proper dress is very important to me.[9]

The director of the WAVES echoed the same sentiment,
reminding her charges that "WAVES are ladies first and
always."

While the civilian world was becoming increasingly feminized, the nation's armed forces were moving in the opposite

direction. Military jobs open to women shrank. In 1965, 70 percent of enlisted females were in administrative and clerical work, as opposed to 50 percent in World War II. Another 23 percent were in medical professions. Seventy-five percent of women officers were in administrative fields. Opportunities for promotion and assignment dwindled. The strength of the line components, not including medical women, dropped to 30,600 in 1965 and then to 20,000 in 1967.

The limited role of women in the services meant limitations on promotions and assignments for women officers. Until 1967 the highest pay grade or rank a woman could hold in any of the services was O-6.[10] Sometimes the only woman in a service to hold that rank was the director of the women's component. All other female officers held lesser rank, depending as much upon their assignment as anything else. As the directorship rotated among the most senior female officers, an outgoing director would sometimes accept a reduction in grade to remain on active duty in lieu of retirement.[11]

Though today such limitations on the careers of women are considered grossly unfair, twenty years ago it was assumed that the needs of the service came first, and the services simply did not need more high-ranking female officers. None of the services at that time promised equal opportunity for women; combat restrictions and the segregation of the ranks meant that opportunities were inherently unequal. Furthermore, the prevailing philosophy was that military service was both a privilege and an obligation, not a right or entitlement. Women, like men, served at the pleasure of the commander-in-chief and therefore had no grounds for grievance.

This philosophy of service was lost upon the civilian members of the once ineffectual DACOWITS. Since the Korean War, DACOWITS had concerned itself with recommending improvements in the "quality of life" of military women, which led in time to increasing opportunities for advancement. As early as 1960, when the size and the role of the women's components were shrinking, DACOWITS began arguing that the components had reached "a maturity which calls for re-examination of the structure with respect to the maximum career potential afforded new recruits." The committee focused its efforts on removing restrictions that prevented women from becoming admirals and generals and on promoting the women's component directors to O-7 (one star). DACOWITS felt that with a flag officer of their own, the women's components would receive the professional recognition they deserved and junior officers would have more toward which to aspire.

The services unanimously opposed the promotion of the component directors to star rank for a variety of reasons. First, they felt the responsibilities of the directors were too limited in scope to warrant stars. Second, the promotion of a director to star rank would automatically mean one less admiral or general somewhere else, since the total number of flag officers was limited by Congress. Third, promotion policies as applied to men meant that women would never truly qualify for star rank. Selection of officers for promotion to O-7 was based upon a variety of things, not the least of which was the assignment history and professional experience of the candidate for promotion. Combat service was naturally a big plus for an organization which existed for the purpose of doing battle. Candidates who had not served in combat but were especially qualified in non-combat fields were still expected to have a firm professional foundation in the business of war, as practiced by their branch of service.

Female officers lacked these primary qualifications. Not only had they never served *in* combat, they had never even been trained *for* combat. In the early 1960s few had ever supervised—much less commanded—men in any capacity, since most of them spent their entire careers within the women's corps. They were, in fact, the least "general" of officers, for their experience was limited to a small, vestigial appendage of the services. None of the women then on active duty had even enough years in service to warrant consideration for promotion beyond O-6, and many men felt that if the ceiling on female promotions were removed, the promotion of a few unqualified women as tokens would be inevitable.

But the services were on the wrong side of time. Political pressure was mounting against all governmental distinctions between men and women. Congress passed the Equal Pay Act in 1963 and the Civil Rights Act—with Title VII concerning women—in 1964. In March 1965 President Johnson ordered equal treatment, respect, service, and support regardless of sex for all employees of the executive branch of the federal government. Though the executive order was not aimed specifically at the military services, the civilian heads of the Defense Department could tell the way the wind was blowing. The same year, the Defense Department gave in to DACOWITS's demand and submitted legislation to Congress to remove the ceiling on promotions for women.

The Vietnam Memorial honors 7,500 women— less than one-tenth of 1 percent of all U.S. Vietnam veterans.

But the battle was not over. The proposed bill died in the Eighty-ninth Congress and was revived in the Ninetieth only after DACOWITS stepped outside its charter to assume a more active role. Until this time, DACOWITS's participation in the legislative process had been limited to recommending and endorsing legislation to the Department of Defense. Under the leadership of Chairman Agnes O'Brien Smith, the committee began to deal directly with Congress. According to Holm:

> From the time the DOD [Department of Defense] proposal was finally drafted until its enactment on 27 October 1967, committee members pulled out all the stops—soliciting support from women's groups, encouraging letter-writing campaigns, focusing media interest, and individually lobbying Congress.... Smith held regular strategy planning sessions with military women; after each DACOWITS meeting, the members fanned out over Capitol Hill, paying court to

whomever they knew, gaining support for the legislation.
Many had political connections in the White House and on
the Hill, others direct access to the media, which they used.[12]

Two former DACOWITS members testified before the
House Armed Services Committee in September 1966, urging
support of the bill, both mentioning their membership in
DACOWITS. Active members, however, were told that they
"are not lobbyists for DOD and are *not even to mention*
DACOWITS when they urge a congressman to support legislation."[13] (Emphasis in the original.)

Considering what they were up against, it should hardly
have taken so much effort. Lawmakers may have lacked enthusiasm for the bill, but there was no organized opposition. At the
time, Congress, the White House, and the Defense Department
had other things to worry about, and it was easier to give the
women what they wanted than to defend the silent services,
which were muzzled by the Defense Department.

Among those who contributed to the consideration of the
bill, only DACOWITS and its supporters understood the bill's
significance. If anyone else on Capitol Hill had any idea how
the bill would affect the military in the future, they were careful not to show it. Defense Department representatives naively,
if not deceitfully, minimized the bill's impact. The assistant secretary of defense for manpower, Thomas D. Morris, testifying
in support of the bill before the House Armed Services
Committee, said, "We believe that the Nation still adheres to
the concept that combat, combat support, and the direction of
our operating forces are responsibilities of male officers."[14] The
House report showed the same lack of foresight:

> *[T]here cannot be complete equality between men and*
> *women in the matter of military careers.... The Defense*
> *Department assured the Committee that there would be no*
> *attempt to remove restrictions on the kind of military duties*
> *women will be expected to perform.*

*Within the framework of this understanding, the
Committee believes that women officers should be given
equality of promotion opportunity consistent with the needs
of the service.*[15]

DACOWITS's seven-year campaign to improve the lot of
the most privileged military women culminated with the signing of Public Law 90-130. "Had it not been for DACOWITS,"
wrote Holm, "the struggle might have taken another seven."[16]
The somber service chiefs who were assembled for the signing
heard President Johnson remark, "There is no reason why we
should not someday have a female Chief of Staff or even a
female Commander-in-Chief."[17]

Two and a half years after the passage of PL 90-130, the
Army promoted Anna Mae Hays and Elizabeth P. Hoisington to
the rank of brigadier general. The Air Force followed suit in
1971 by promoting Jeanne Holm. The Navy waited until 1975
to promote Fran McKee to flag rank, and the Marine Corps did
not promote Margaret Brewer (no relation to Lucy) to flag rank
until 1977.

PL 90-130 did more for military women than open the way
to the stars, however, and other effects were more immediate.
The law also opened up promotions for women to other officer
ranks and repealed the 2 percent ceiling on the strength of the
women's components. At the time, female strength was at its
lowest level since the Korean War, again less than 1 percent of
the total force. But the Johnson administration was looking for
ways to lighten the burden of the draft on the nation's men, and
so it planned to increase female strength from 20,000 to 35,000
in two years, to reach the 2 percent mark in four or five years.

The first increase in female strength in fifteen years came
in 1968, when 6,500 women were added to the rolls. This hefty
boost for the women's components was nevertheless an imper-
ceptible addition to the mammoth wartime armed forces. The
participation of American military women in the war in
Vietnam was minuscule. The 7,500 women, mostly nurses, hon-

ored by the embellished National Vietnam War Memorial, accounted for less than one-tenth of 1 percent of all U.S. Vietnam veterans. The tribute, backed by many feminist supporters of women in the military, was late in coming. During the war, the needs of women veterans were ignored completely by the strongly pacifist American feminist movement. After the war, the fight to expand roles for military women further proceeded on other grounds, for other reasons.

Chapter 2

THE ALL-VOLUNTEER SURPRISE

The conscription calls out a share of every class—
no matter whether your son or my son—all must
march; but our friends—I may say it in this room—
are the very scum of the earth.

—THE DUKE OF WELLINGTON

THE EQUALIZATION OF PROMOTION POLICIES for male and female officers and the removal of ceilings on enlisted women achieved by PL 90-130 may have been the opening shots in the assault on the all-male services, but in themselves they were little more than stones thrown in the enemy camp. What was needed was a Trojan horse that would slip large numbers of warrior women into the citadel before the defenders knew what was happening. That horse appeared in the form of the All-Volunteer Armed Force.

By 1968 the draft had been an accepted part of American life for twenty years. Since passage of the Selective Service Act of 1948, the draft had provided the necessary manpower to back up the nation's global commitments and fostered patriotism, discipline, and civic responsibility among the nation's restless young men. Most American men who had served their time in war or in peace saw nothing wrong with conscription *per se* and were quite willing to allow younger men the privilege of serving, whether they wanted to or not. Proud veterans still outnumbered libertarians who saw conscription as inconsistent with civil liberty. Civil liberty, in the minds of many Americans, still entailed civic responsibility.

As a result of the Vietnam War, however, organized opposition to the draft grew rapidly. Antiwar activists portrayed the draft as an immoral means of supporting an immoral war. Hotheads like the Berrigan brothers responded violently by raiding, burning, or bombing draft board offices. Celebrity clerics like Bishop James Pike and the Reverend William Sloan Coffin, Jr., joined Dr. Benjamin Spock in publicly supporting civil disobedience to draft calls. A handful of draft-age men left the country. Many more marked time in college or avoided the draft by other legal means. The Supreme Court obligingly broadened defensible grounds for conscientious objection, and the number of conscientious objectors doubled between 1967 and 1970.

Those who obeyed the draft summons were disproportionately poor and poorly educated, and among the many good men drafted were many rotten apples—disgruntled, disillusioned, disobedient fellows who lacked the intelligence or the foresight to avoid military service before it was too late. They were the source of many of the problems that plagued the services during Vietnam: desertion (up 300 percent from 1966 to 1970), drug addiction, racial conflicts, disrespect toward superiors, and a general breakdown of discipline. Because the draft brought them in, the draft was sometimes blamed for the trouble they made. If we took only those who volunteered, thought some officers and NCOs (non-commissioned officers), we'd have only happy campers.

Of course, with a war on, ending the draft was out of the question. The best that President Johnson could hope to do was to make the draft more equitable. In July 1966 he created the National Advisory Commission on Selective Service, headed by Burke Marshall, former assistant attorney general in charge of the Civil Rights Division under President John F. Kennedy and author of the original version of the 1964 Civil Rights Act. The commission submitted its report seven months later, recommending that draft policy be "uniformly developed and centrally administered" through five hundred area centers instead of the much more numerous local draft boards. The report also recommended random, impartial call-ups and the elimination of student and occupational deferments. A single sentence in the report recommended that the services "broaden the opportunities" of women and civilians to reduce the number of men drafted, though no discussion of this option was presented.[1] The Burke Marshall report served as the basis for Johnson's 1967 draft reform proposals, but little became of the proposals in Congress and the report was soon shelved.

> The commission failed to consider the impact of women drawn into the All-Volunteer Force as substitutes for men.

Flawed though the system was, selective service itself was strongly supported in Washington. In 1967 only two votes were cast in Congress against a draft extension. Still, when a well-respected Republican suggested ending the draft, Washington eagerly submitted. The man to make that suggestion was Richard M. Nixon.

Running for president as the end-the-war-with-honor candidate in 1968, Nixon departed from the Republican Party platform by calling for an end to the draft to coincide with the end of the war. In a radio broadcast on October 17, 1968, Nixon told the American people that it was time to take a "new look" at selective service. He said that the draft was a relatively recent invention, that Americans were wrong to think of it as a natural part of life, and that the dignity of the individual should not be subject to the supremacy of the state.[2]

Once elected, Nixon created the President's Commission on an All-Volunteer Armed Force. Headed by former Secretary of Defense Thomas S. Gates, Jr., the commission included noted economists Milton Friedman and Alan Greenspan; two former supreme allied commanders; the director of the National Association for the Advancement of Colored People; various academicians and businessmen; a student from Georgetown University; and one woman, Jeanne Noble, New York University professor and vice-president of the National Council of Negro Women.

The Gates Commission initiated a number of studies on the relevant issues, whose conclusions were included in the final report. To maintain an all-volunteer force of 2.5 million men, the commission estimated that the services would need to attract 325,000 men per year; 500,000 men had volunteered for military service each year of the Vietnam War, and surveys of volunteers indicated that as many as 250,000 were "true volunteers" who would have enlisted had there been no draft. It seemed, then, that the services would need to attract only 75,000 more men each year to maintain an all-volunteer force. The commission was confident that higher pay and other improvements in service life would easily bring forth the extra men needed.[3]

Eight objections to an all-volunteer force were summarily dismissed. The commission's report admitted that while the "budgetary expense" of a volunteer force would be greater, the "actual cost" to the nation would be lower because the nation's young men would no longer be taxed in time and effort to subsidize the national defense. The report also argued that the savings from the low pay for first-term servicemen represented "discrimination" which needed correcting for reasons of equity alone.

Years later, the General Accounting Office (GAO) submitted a report to Congress on the additional costs of the All-Volunteer Force, or AVF, as actually instituted. According to the GAO, the Gates Commission had based its conclusions on several invalid assumptions and inaccurate estimations. The commission erroneously assumed that an AVF would have a lower personnel turnover rate, thus reducing both the number of men needed each year and the cost of training them. The commission failed to appreciate the differences between the Army and the other services and wrongly assumed that an all-volunteer Army would enjoy the same success in recruiting as the others. The commission overestimated the number of "true volunteers" by failing to consider the declining popularity of the military. It underestimated the cost of extra inducements for reservists and critical specialists. It also underestimated the cost of the more attractive benefits package offered to all new recruits and the total additional cost of the AVF. Its report claimed that an AVF of 2.5 million men would cost an additional $2.1 billion per year, but the GAO estimated that the AVF had actually cost an additional $3 billion annually since its creation, though its total strength never exceeded 2.1 million men.[4]

Two of the Gates Commission's errors were not mentioned by the GAO. One was that the commission had noted that the population of enlistment-age men would increase in the 1970s but had failed to warn that the increase would be short-lived and that the same population would begin to decrease by the end of the decade. The other not mentioned was that it had failed to consider the impact of large numbers of women drawn into the AVF as substitutes for men. In fact, the commission's report and supporting research barely mentioned women. Not only did it fail to consider that an all-volunteer force might become too dependent upon women, it failed even to recommend recruiting women to reduce the need for men. According to commission members, the subject simply never came up. Ironically, the oversight probably helped the commission make its case for an AVF. A recommendation to greatly expand the role of women would have strengthened the military's opposition to the AVF.

The Gates Commission delivered its report to the president in early 1970, having agreed unanimously that an AVF should replace the current mixed force of conscripts and volunteers as soon as the war in Vietnam was over. On April 23, 1970, in an address to Congress, President Nixon used the report to justify his decision to institute the AVF as soon as possible. For the rest of his first term, Nixon spoke often of draft reform to goad Congress into approving the necessary legislation and to remind the electorate, which for the first time included everyone over the age of eighteen, to thank the Nixon administration for the eventual end of the draft.

Nixon's decision to shift to the AVF in the early 1970s showed the worst possible timing. Never was patriotism in shorter supply throughout the fifty states, nor public confidence in the American military at a lower ebb. After an inglorious retreat from Indochina, the military came home to Watergate, women's rights, and a "zero draft" future. Still shaking the mud off its boots, it was ordered to pretty itself up for a recruiting drive.

Implementation of the AVF began with the appointment of the Central All-Volunteer Task Force within the Department of Defense. The task force quickly developed a twofold strategy to ensure success. First, it planned to increase enlistments by offering recruits higher pay, shorter tours, better living conditions, bonuses for special skills, veteran's benefits, allowances for dependents, and a host of other inducements. Second, it sought to decrease the need for men by making greater use of civilians and women, never considering that an all-male military might attract more men than a thoroughly feminized force.

The reason the task force did not consider an all-male volunteer military was the coincidence of the AVF and the Equal Rights Amendment (ERA). In March 1972, while the task force was still at work, Congress cleared the ERA for ratification by the states. Debate in both houses was light, considering the hard road ahead for the amendment. Most of the argument was not over the wisdom of the amendment itself, but over the need for special exemptions in the amendment to protect women from combat and compulsory military service. All such exemptions were rejected. Feminists feared that any exceptions to the amendment would weaken it. Senator Birch Bayh of Indiana argued, "If a woman wants to volunteer [for combat], should she be treated differently from a man?"[5] Senator Sam Ervin of North Carolina led the fight in the Senate against the amendment and for the combat and draft exemptions, but fifteen senators who had favored such exemptions when the amendment was first proposed in 1970 had changed their minds in two years. The final version of the amendment, approved by overwhelming majorities in both houses, called for nothing less than absolute equality between the sexes.[6]

Also in March, the House Armed Services Committee established the Special Subcommittee on the Utilization of Manpower in the Military, which published its report in June, flaunting the latest fashion of thought about the place of women in the military:

> *We are concerned that the Department of Defense and each of the military services are guilty of "tokenism" in the recruitment and utilization of women in the Armed Forces. We are convinced that in the atmosphere of a zero draft environment or an all-volunteer military force, women could and should play a more important role. We strongly urge the Secretary of Defense and the service secretaries to develop a program which will permit women to take their rightful place in serving in our Armed Forces.*[7]

In December 1972, with the ERA rapidly approaching ratification (so it seemed), the Central All-Volunteer Task Force published its own report, marrying the weakness of the all-volunteer military to the strength of the Equal Rights movement:

> *The pursuit of these two goals, equal opportunity and greater utilization, may well bring about the most revolutionary policy changes experienced in the history of military women.*[8]

The AVF's future dependence on the ever-expanding utilization of women was assured. The task force instructed the services to double the number of women in their ranks by 1977.

Only the Marine Corps, with its high ratio of combat troops to support troops, escaped with a modest, mandated 40 percent increase in its tiny female contingent.

At the start of 1972 the women's components composed 1.5 percent of the total force, with 12,600 women officers and 32,400 enlisted women. That year, before the end of the draft, the services enlisted 13,000 additional women, making them 3.3 percent of total recruitments. It was only the beginning.

On July 1, 1973, following the signing of the Paris peace accords and the expiration of the selective service authorization, Defense Secretary Melvin Laird announced the birth of the All-Volunteer Armed Force, a final step after hundreds of preparatory changes. The base pay of a first-term enlisted man had more than doubled, and life in the services had softened considerably. Open-bay barracks with rows of bunks were being replaced by dormitories with two- or three-man rooms, which the occupants were allowed to decorate as they pleased. Mess halls became "dining facilities," with carpeting and drapes and smaller tables with chairs instead of benches. Saturday morning fatigue duty and inspections were becoming less frequent. Sailors in port were allowed to live ashore. Soldiers were allowed to wander on and off post anytime they were not on duty. Many more officers and enlisted men resided off-post, and many more privates had wives and children.

But by the same summer, it had already become apparent that the services were not attracting enough of the right kind of men. Entrance exam scores plummeted, and the percentage of high school graduates among "true volunteers" fell from 60 percent in 1972 to less than 50 percent in 1973. The induction of college-educated enlisted men, fairly common during the draft, all but dried up. Personnel turnover, instead of decreasing as predicted by the Gates Commission, actually increased because of two-year enlistments and a doubling of the rate of early discharge for indiscipline and unsuitability. Medical and technical fields requiring special skills and extensive training were the hardest hit by low enlistments and high attrition, but the services also found it difficult to enlist men for the dirty jobs in the combat arms. The supply of men for reserve components slowed to a trickle, once the incentive of avoiding the draft by enlisting in the reserves disappeared.

To solve the problem, the Defense Department set aside $225 million in 1973 for various bonuses to attract doctors, nurses, technicians, and infantrymen. It then requested from Congress another $400 million over the next three years for the same purpose. The Defense Department also raised its requirement for recruits to 356,000 per annum to maintain a force of only 2.1 million, rather than the Gates Commission's 325,000 for a force of 2.5 million. Three years later, the department estimated it needed 365,000 to maintain 2.1 million Americans in uniform.

> The Pentagon saw that the only way—or the easiest way—to meet their enlistment quotas was to recruit more women.

Proponents of women in the services seized upon recruiting shortfalls and the "low quality" of enlisted men as an argument for enlisting more women. A report prepared for the Senate Armed Forces Committee in 1973 recommended raising the number of women as a percentage of the total force to possibly as high as 20 percent to make up for the lack of quality men. Historically, the women's components had maintained their integrity by carefully selecting their recruits, who were, on average, better educated, more articulate, and more intelligent (according to scores on entrance exams) than men. The Senate report stated in passing that its recommendation was based on the assumption that the quality of female recruits would remain constant as their numbers increased, an assumption that later proved invalid.[9]

Yet the services hardly needed to be told by Congress to recruit more women. Charged with making the AVF work one way or another, the manpower managers in the Pentagon saw that the only way (or at least the easiest way) to meet their quotas for enlistments was to recruit more women. With their very careers on the block if the AVF faltered, they wasted little debate on the matter. Contingency plans providing for an increase of 170 percent in the strength of the women's components were executed on order. The female share of total enlistments increased from 5 percent in 1973 to 9 percent in 1975. The Navy and Air Force women's components tripled in size.

By 1975 the armed forces were recruiting more women each year than the total strength of the women's components just three years earlier. In the fourth year of the All-Volunteer Armed Force, there were 109,133 women in uniform, making up more than 5 percent of the total force. A contemporary report by the Brookings Institution estimated that the United States had 44 percent more women in uniform than twenty other major nations combined, including the Soviet Union.[10] The trend would continue through the decade, to the alarm of the nation's warrior chiefs who were taken by surprise by the unexpected impact of the AVF.

While the women's components swelled with recruits and the Equal Rights Amendment gathered state ratifications, proponents of military women obtained another victory in the case of *Frontiero* v. *Richardson*. Lieutenant Sharron Frontiero was an Air Force physical therapist married to a veteran. Her husband had been denied status as an Air Force dependent under a federal law requiring female service members to prove that they provided more than half of their husband's support. The Frontieros sued the government and won. In May 1973 the Supreme Court ruled that the federal law in question was unconstitutional and that military women must receive the same dependent benefits as military men. Four justices sided with Justice William J. Brennan's opinion that sex, like race, was "inherently suspect" as a category of discrimination, requiring "strict judicial scrutiny." Three other justices agreed with the ruling of unconstitutionality but rejected the characterization of sex as "inherently suspect." Only Justice William H. Rehnquist dissented.[11]

Feminists were jubilant. Future Supreme Court Justice Ruth Ginsburg, then of the American Civil Liberties Union, who had argued for the plaintiff as an *amicus curiae*, was quoted by *U.S. News & World Report* as saying, "It is the most far-reaching and important ruling on sex discrimination to come out of the Supreme Court yet. It will spell the beginning of reforms in hundreds of statutes which do not give equal benefits to men and women."[12] She had every reason for such confidence. Justice Brennan had made perfectly clear in his written opinion where he stood on the subject: "There can be no doubt that our nation has had a long and unfortunate history of sex discrimination."

His opinion, however, did not stop the Court from turning around two years later and ruling in *Schlesinger* v. *Ballard* that the Navy could use sex as a discriminator for promotion policy—as long as it was used against men. Robert C. Ballard, a former Navy lieutenant, had sued the Department of Defense for discharging him after he failed to be promoted twice in nine years, as was required, though female Navy lieutenants were allowed thirteen years. Ballard's counsel argued the Navy's nine-year limit violated Ballard's right to due process under the Fifth Amendment of the Constitution. Writing for a five-justice majority, Justice Potter Stewart ruled that Ballard had not been deprived of due process because the Navy's different promotion policies for men and women served a legitimate government purpose. It provided for the needs of the service and compensated female officers for their limited military role.[13]

Just how limited that role was became open to question. In 1972 Senator Jacob Javits of New York nominated a woman to the Naval Academy. One week after Congress passed the ERA, Senator Javits and Congressman Jack H. McDonald of Michigan introduced concurrent resolutions to prohibit denial of admission to the service academies on the basis of sex. Javits argued that the services all had women officers, some of whom were on the academies' faculties, and that admission to the academies would improve the women's chances of promotion. He also argued that the ERA when ratified would accomplish the same thing, but not in time for his nominee to enter Annapolis with the next class. The Senate passed the resolution easily. The House referred it to the House Armed Services Committee, chaired by Congressman F. Edward Hébert of Louisiana, a strong ally of the Pentagon who had supported the war in Vietnam and opposed abolishing the draft. In his hands, the resolution died.[14]

In 1974 Congressmen Don Edwards and Jerome Waldie of California filed suit against the Defense Department on behalf of two women they had nominated for admission to the U.S. Naval and Air Force Academies. The plaintiffs argued that excluding women from the service academies violated constitutional guarantees of equal protection and due process under the Fourteenth and Fifth Amendments. The Defense Department countered that excluding women served a legitimate government purpose because the academies existed to train combat leaders for the Navy and the Air Force, and women were excluded by federal law from engaging in combat. The U.S. District Court in Washington upheld the exclusion of women from the academies, and an appellate court denied an appeal.

But the fight went on. Representatives of the National Organization for Women (NOW) and the Center for Women's Policy Studies successfully pressured DACOWITS to endorse integrating the service academies.[15]

Momentum was building. In two years, no less than six bills to admit women to the academies were submitted in the House, four of them by Congressman Pierre "Pete" du Pont of Delaware. In 1974 du Pont's bills were referred to the subcommittee on military personnel, which began hearing testimony that May.

Just before the hearings began, Undersecretary of Defense William P. Clements sent Congressman Hébert of the House Armed Services Committee a letter outlining the Defense Department's objections to the bills. The letter argued that the academies trained men for combat service and sea duty, from which women were barred by law. If not all graduates served at sea or in combat units, most did. Furthermore, limitations of funding and facilities would mean fewer men admitted if women were, and the services were receiving all the women officers they needed through the Reserve Officers Training Corps (ROTC) (opened to women in 1972), officer candidate schools, and direct commissions.[16]

At the hearings, fourteen representatives of the Department of Defense, including the three superintendents, a recent graduate of West Point, and a West Point senior, testified against admitting women, each one echoing the arguments of Clement's letter. Secretary of the Army Howard H. Callaway testified that 94 percent of West Point graduates entered combat arms upon graduation, the rest being physically disqualified from doing so. To dramatize the point, he submitted into the record General MacArthur's famous "Duty, Honor, Country" speech, which emphasized combat leadership as the reason for West Point's existence. Lieutenant General Albert P. Clark, superintendent of the Air Force Academy, testified that more than 70 percent of the academy graduates entered fields closed to women and cited higher attrition among female Air Force officers as a reason why integration was not cost effective.

Several Defense witnesses seemed most concerned about the disruptive effect the presence of women would have on the academies. Said Secretary Callaway:

> Admitting women to West Point will irrevocably change the Academy. And all the evidence seems to say that the change could only be for the worse. The Spartan atmosphere— which is so important to producing the final product— would surely be diluted....[17]

Lieutenant General Clark concurred: "It is my considered judgment that the introduction of female cadets will inevitably erode this vital atmosphere." He predicted that the academies would "inevitably find it necessary to create a modified program to accommodate the female cadet, or, God forbid, be required to water down the entire program."[18]

The Defense spokesmen were seconded by a single private citizen, Miss Jacqueline Cochran, famed aviatrix, test pilot, and veteran leader of the Women's Air Service Pilots (WASPs) in World War II. Miss Cochran strongly opposed the admission of women to the academies on the grounds that the academies trained men for combat and putting women in combat was "ridiculous." Her experiences in World War II convinced her that women "have no business" in combat. Members of the subcommittee pointed out that she herself was just the kind of woman to be admitted to the academies, but Cochran took a different view of her own example: "When I was a child I went to work twelve hours a night in the cotton mill before I was eight years old without shoes, and I became pretty hardened to the facts of life. I don't think that is the way women should be brought up. I certainly don't think I was properly brought up."[19]

On the other side of the issue, two representatives of the Maritime Administration testified that the Merchant Marine Academy, recently integrated, was experiencing no significant problems. Eight concerned citizens, most representing the Center for Women Policy Studies and the Women's Lobby, testified in support of integration. Nineteen members of Congress also expressed their support. Among them were Congressmen Pete du Pont, Don Edwards, and Patricia Schroeder of Colorado. Schroeder argued that "imminent ratification" of the two-year-old ERA made integration inevitable. Edwards accused the Defense Department of opposing integration for "essentially frivolous reasons and outmoded patterns of thinking." All of them reduced the argument for integration to a simple matter of equity. Most dismissed the largest stumbling block to integration—the issue of combat—by observing that not all academy graduates served in combat. One representative, Congressman Charles B. Rangel of New York, went so far as to call for the integration of the battlefield also. Rangel pointed to Israel and the Soviet Union, saying, "If fighting must be done, women should join men in doing it."[20]

The hearings concluded in August with the Defense Department thinking it had won, comforted by Hébert's private assurances that the committee would not report a bill for integration out to the full House. But other portents were not encouraging. Not a single member of Congress had dared to speak openly against integration in the hearings, and in June the Senate passed a resolution proposed by Senator William D. Hathaway of Maine in favor of integration.

The House committee had still taken no action by January 1975, when the Democratic Caucus, dissatisfied with Hébert's pro-Pentagon views, forced him from the chairmanship of the House Armed Services Committee and replaced him with Congressman Melvin Price of Illinois. There was another push to put a bill before the House. Early that spring, the new military personnel subcommittee chairman allowed the Defense Department to testify once more against integration, but the department declined, perhaps under the mistaken impression that integrating the academies was a dead issue.

Focusing on self-interest was the best way to recruit women into the military.

Activists who wanted to see women admitted to the academies in the bicentennial year were running out of time. So in April 1975 Congressman Samuel Stratton of New York bypassed the committees and introduced an amendment to a military appropriations bill before the full House for consideration. Again, debate centered on the issue of combat. Despite their enthusiasm for equal rights and the ERA, neither the House nor the Senate was ready to repeal laws restricting women from combat service, which the ERA would surely have done. The matter was finally resolved by drawing a line between the academies' responsibility to prepare officers for combat and their responsibility to prepare officers for careers in the armed forces. In the words of Judith Stiehm: "By making this distinction between combat and career training, Congress sidestepped having to decide whether women should enter combat; that, it reasoned, was not the central issue."[21]

Last minute suggestions that Congress establish separate academies for women went nowhere. Thus, left to themselves without the annoying arguments of military men, on May 20, 1975, Congress voted by a count of 303 to 96 to admit women to the service academies in the next calendar year. The Senate endorsed the amendment by voice vote on June 6. In an afterthought, Congress realized that it had overlooked the Coast Guard in the legislation. Reparative action proved unnecessary; the Coast Guard announced in August that it would admit women the following year.

On October 7, 1975, President Gerald Ford signed a massive appropriations bill into law, a small segment of which would radically alter the nature of the American military's most sacred institutions. Public Law 94-106 required the service secretaries to ensure that:

> (1) female individuals shall be eligible for appointment and
> admission to the service academy concerned, beginning the
> appointments to such academy for the class beginning in
> calendar year 1976, and (2) the academic and other relevant
> standards required for appointment, admission, training,
> graduation, and commissioning of female individuals shall
> be the same as those required for male individuals, except
> for those minimum essential adjustments in such standards
> required because of physiological differences between male
> and female individuals.

For feminists, the law's stipulation that admission would be "consistent with the needs of the services" left too much for the services to decide. For opponents of integration, the requirement that the authority of the service "must be exercised within a program providing for the orderly and expeditious admission of women" meant that there would be no "survival of the fittest" in the admissions process: the services were compelled to admit some women one way or another.

The passage of PL 94-106 was the high-water mark of the American feminist movement, the crest of a fifteen-year wave of legislative action. Along the way, feminists won for their flag a daunting array of campaign streamers: the Equal Pay Act of

1963, Title VII of the Civil Rights Act, Title IX of the Education Amendment of 1972, the Equal Employment Opportunity Act of 1972, congressional approval of the Equal Rights Amendment, and numerous other laws to protect and extend the rights and prerogatives of women in all areas of public and private life. They celebrated August 24, 1974, as National Women's Equality Day and all of 1975 as International Women's Year. In that year, the ERA was just three states short of the three-fourths needed to make it the Twenty-seventh Amendment to the Constitution of the United States. Few expected anything but ratification.

Meanwhile, the AVF limped along, inevitably falling back on the venal and illusory lures of money and easy living. The Volunteer Army wanted to join you—and to persuade you to let it, it offered short tours, fast cars, college educations, and off-post housing. One early recruiting commercial featured actor John Travolta as a new recruit behind the wheel of a Pontiac Trans Am. Later ads were equally ignoble. The focus was all on self-interest.

But self-interest *was* the best focus for military women. They discovered a new-found "right to serve." No longer were they merely support troops, freeing a man to fight. Now they had equal status, equal advancement, and equal benefits, and they were moving in large numbers into previously all-male units and specialties. Only the laws excluding women from combat remained, and they seemed doomed by the ERA.

But it was not to be. State legislatures were finding out that the ERA was not so popular after all. The very year that saw the first perfumed plebes enter West Point also saw the ERA sitting dead in the water, the victim of activist Phyllis Schlafly's STOP ERA counteroffensive.

The turning point came too late for the nation's service academies. Had they held out a year or two longer, they might not be integrated today.

Chapter 3

EIGHTY'S LADIES

The great thing about those first ten weeks [at Sandhurst] was that although one was being treated like mud it was at least grown-up mud. We were treated like men for the first time in our lives, and as men we were expected to react.

—DAVID NIVEN IN HIS MEMOIR
THE MOON'S A BALLOON

POETRY GREETS EACH YEAR'S CROP of young civilians entering the United States Air Force Academy at Colorado Springs, Colorado. As the ragged formation of new recruits marches down the ramp into the cadet living area, all eyes are affixed to three words proclaimed in stone from the granite roof overhead: BRING ME MEN. So begins the poem entitled "The Coming American" by Sam Walter Foss:

> *Bring me men to match my mountains,*
> *Bring me men to match my plains,*
> *Men with empires in their purpose*
> *And new eras in their brains....*

In 1976, when the entering class included not just men but women, the Air Force Academy rejected a suggestion that the offensive phrase be revised. The rejection was, however, a rare departure from the academy's policy of easing the process of sexual integration by thoroughly accommodating the first female cadets.[1]

The award for the worst performance by a service academy in the first year of sexual integration belongs to the Air Force Academy. It was the only academy where attrition rates for men exceeded those for women. The Air Force Academy Class of 1980, the first sexually integrated class, lost 23.5 percent of its male cadets in the first year alone, but only 19.7 percent of its female members. The same class graduated with barely half of its original men: 44.4 percent of those who started in the summer of 1976 did not finish, compared to 37.8 percent of the original women. Both men and women exceeded the average dropout rate of 35 percent among pre-integration classes. Today, the Air Force Academy remains the only academy where men have left in greater numbers than women, despite innovative attempts to reduce attrition.[2]

The Air Force Academy had been the one most enthusiastic about integration. It had begun planning for integration in 1972, when congressional passage of the ERA made integration seem inevitable to some academy administrators. By the summer of 1975, with the integration bill still pending, the Air Force Academy had already formulated a comprehensive plan for the admission of women.

Unfortunately, the academy's head start was in the wrong direction. Early on in its planning, it misidentified the chief problem of integration as making the academy attractive to women. A visit by the academy's planning committee to Lackland Air Force Base in 1974 reinforced fears that the sensitivity of the first women admitted would pose the principal threat to integration. At Lackland, female Air Force recruits responded better to encouragement, or "positive motivation," than to the harsh discipline applied to male recruits, yet even the comparatively relaxed atmosphere there was described by most female recruits as "stressful."[3] Convinced that the much more stressful environment of the academy's fourth-class system would be too much for most women, the committee incorporated in its draft plan several special measures to protect the women from the worst of cadet life.

The final plan differed from the draft plan in only one significant way. Instead of maintaining a separate women's squadron, the women were to be integrated into twenty of the forty squadrons of the Cadet Wing. For privacy, however, the women would be quartered together on the same floor of the same building, off-limits to all males during certain hours. To protect the women from the usual harassment endured by fourth-class cadets, upperclassmen were instructed to use positive motivation on the women.

In the fall of 1975, while scrambling to attract qualified young women for the class of 1980, the academy began its search for fifteen qualified female Air Force lieutenants or captains to volunteer to serve as Air Training Officers (ATOs), acting as "surrogate upperclassmen" and role models for the female cadets. Hundreds of records were reviewed, but only a handful of women who were physically and professionally qualified were also interested in the assignment. The following spring, fifteen female surrogates entered the academy as ATO candidates to undergo special training, including a three-week "mini-academy" to introduce them to life as an air cadet. Unaccustomed to intense physical exertion, the ATOs suffered an embarrassing rate of injury and fatigue. Two dropped out of the program before the end of training. The rest fell woefully short of academy standards.

Fortunately, the first female cadets were a different breed—younger, more athletic, with a somewhat better idea of what they were getting into and better reasons for being there. From more than a thousand applicants, the academy selected 157 of the most athletic, most scholarly women in the country.[4] Eighty-four percent were in the top 10 percent of their high school class; 79 percent were members of the National Honor Society. Their average SAT and ACT scores were slightly above the men's average in verbal skills, slightly below in math skills.

That year, 1,436 male cadets also entered the Air Force Academy. They too were among the most scholarly, most athletic young adults in the country. But they seemed nonexistent to the flocks of journalists who flew in and out of the academy that summer, clustering around the fledgling female cadets.

In addition to the journalists, the academy played host to several academicians who stayed for extended periods to observe the event. Among them were Dr. Lois B. DeFleur, professor of sociology at Washington State University, and Judith Stiehm, professor of political science at the University of Southern California. Dr. DeFleur would become a mainstay of the academy's efforts to monitor its progress, participating in nearly every official study of integration conducted at the Air Force Academy for the next ten years. Stiehm, a philosophical feminist, would later write a not-too-flattering book about the first year of integration.

An initial survey of entering cadets found that the only significant difference between the outlook of new male and female cadets concerned the role of women in society and in the military. On such issues, the male cadets were found to be "significantly more traditional" than civilian males at other institutions, while female cadets were found to be less traditional than civilian females.[5] These opposing attitudes inevitably inhibited assimilation, for which men regularly took the blame because their traditional opinions were officially out of favor. Years later, Dr. DeFleur would recommend easing the assimilation of women by recruiting "a wider variety of people," preferably fewer of the more traditional males, the very men who have historically shown the greatest interest in the academy.[6]

Though the survey showed the traditional cast of most of the male cadets, it also showed that the men of the Class of 1980 were initially neutral with regard to the presence of women at the academy, willing to wait and see before passing judgment. They did not have to wait long. By the end of the summer, the attitudes of male "doolies" had begun a long shift toward the negative.

Life as an air cadet begins long before the start of the academic year. While other recent high school graduates are working to save money for college or still cavorting about at the beach, cadet-recruits are beginning two months of military regimentation known as Basic Cadet Training, or BCT. Modeled after West Point's "Beast Barracks," BCT is designed to turn high school kids into air cadets.

There was nothing novel in the Air Force Academy's approach to this task. Throughout the ages, tribes of warriors have performed the same task with similar rituals, recognized as necessary by almost all societies. Only in our Western culture in relatively recent years have both the mechanics of the process and the rationale for the transformation been forgotten.

The Air Force Academy misidentified the chief problem of integration as making the academy attractive to women.

Neither was lost on the Air Force Academy after the first year of integration, however. A draft report produced in 1977 by the academy's Department of Behavioral Science and Leadership showed a clear understanding of the role of BCT in initiating young cadet-recruits into the Cadet Wing. "The Integration of Women into a Male Initiation Rite: A Case Study of the USAF Academy," by Dean H. Wilson and David C. Gillman, was perhaps the only official study of the academy's integration not heavily influenced by Lois DeFleur. Instead the authors followed the thinking of Arnold Van Gennep, whose work predated the feminist takeover of the field of sociology. In his 1908 book entitled *The Rites of Passage*, Van Gennep divided the initiation rites of aboriginal Australian and African tribes into three phases. Wilson and Gillman used the same phases to describe the process of BCT.

Van Gennep's first phase, the Rite of Separation, signaled the separation of the initiates from everything they had known until then—families, friends, all that was a part of their past life. At the Air Force Academy, it begins immediately upon arrival of the new cadet-recruits. The recruits lose much of their personal identity by having their heads shaved, donning uniforms, and marching for the first time in formation with other recruits. They are assigned rooms and roommates and are grouped into flights and squadrons under the complete control of the academy's officers and upperclass cadets. The rite of separation ends late the same day when the recruits are ceremoniously sworn in as air cadets.

The next phase, Van Gennep's Rite of Transition, begins after the swearing-in and lasts the duration of BCT. The first half of BCT is conducted in the cadet living area and consists of instruction in close-order drill, cadet regulations, military customs and courtesy, Air Force Academy traditions, and physical conditioning. The second half is conducted at the Jack's Valley encampment and consists largely of combat and survival training. Cadets learn land navigation, patrolling, marksmanship, weapons maintenance, tactical operations, and survival techniques. At Jack's Valley, new cadets are subjected to intense physical and mental pressure. The grueling experience involves demanding and sometimes dangerous assault and obstacle courses. The emphasis throughout this phase is on commonality of experience. Having put their personal lives behind them, the cadets must learn to live, act, and think as a group.

The last phase, the Rite of Incorporation, comes at the end of BCT, when the cadets who have not dropped out are awarded the uniform shoulder boards of full-fledged doolies and accepted into the Cadet Wing.[7]

These rites of passage are intended to impress upon new cadets three things: the irreversibility of their separation from their past, the significance of their transformation, and the value of their future status as cadets of the United States Air Force Academy and ultimately as Air Force officers. With these firm impressions, cadets will commit themselves utterly to the pursuit of an academy education, enduring years of repeated academic trials and demanding military training. But the impressions depend upon the seared memory of the initiation experience. The rites must be attended not only by stirring ceremony but also by the sharp experience of physical and mental pain. Without it, the rites will fail. The cadets will not feel the break between their lives before entering the academy and their lives after, nor will they think their status as cadets too valuable to give up.

These things the Air Force Academy knew instinctively prior to the summer of 1976. Twenty times since its founding it had successfully repeated the process. But with the first integrated class, Basic Cadet Training failed to achieve its higher purposes. It achieved neither the commonality of experience necessary to bind the integrated class together nor the intensity of experience to bind the new cadets to the academy. Its failure would forever curse the Class of 1980.

Behind the failure of BCT was a brazen double standard. That BCT was to be one thing for women and another for men was plainly evident on the very day the new class of cadet-recruits arrived. Flight by flight, cadet-recruits were marched into the base barber shop. Male recruits came out with stubble; female recruits escaped with neat and stylish trims. Women retained both their individuality and their femininity, while men suffered the embarrassment and dehumanization of fuzzy pates and radically altered self-images. There being nothing physiological about the length of one's hair, Congress's integration law would have required the women's heads to be shorn also, but no one dared ask that much of these daring women.

Next, the cadet-recruits were assigned rooms. All of the women were assigned to the sixth floor of Vandenberg Hall, off-limits to male personnel mornings and evenings. There the female cadets enjoyed the easy tutelage of their surrogate sisters, while real upperclassmen applied intense harassment to the bald-headed males on the floors below. Even if the ATOs had tried to match the male upperclassmen in ferocity, there were simply not enough of them to do so. Though male upperclassmen matched male recruits roughly one-for-one during the first summer, the ratio of ATOs to female recruits was one to ten.

Then came physical training. The academy's physical fitness test included push-ups, pull-ups, a standing broad jump, and a six hundred–yard run, but since very few of the women could perform one pull-up or complete any of the other events, different standards were devised for them. They were allowed more time for the run, less distance on the jump, and fewer pushups. Instead of pull-ups, female cadets were given points for the length of time they could hang on the bar; one pull-up earned them considerable extra credit.[8]

Though the female cadets performed somewhat better than the ATOs had earlier, their record was not impressive. They fell out of group runs, lagged behind on road marches, failed to negotiate obstacles on the assault courses (later modified to make them easier), could not climb a rope, and sometimes broke down in tears when confronted with their own limitations. The rate at which the female cadets sought medical attention could hardly have allowed them to keep up the pace of training. The women averaged eight visits to the medical clinic; the men averaged only 2.5 visits. Eighty-five percent of female cadets received medical treatment during the eight weeks of BCT, compared to 70 percent of male cadets. On the average, women suffered nine times as many shin splints as the men, five times as many stress fractures, and more than five times as many cases of tendinitis.[9] With time off for sick call and with their physical activity limited by medical restrictions, many female cadets must have *watched* a lot of BCT.

Such performance would have earned male cadets considerable harassment from upperclassmen, but because upperclassmen were enjoined to use "positive motivation" on female cadets, their abuse was concentrated on the males who were, for the most part, performing satisfactorily. Ironically, the men of the first integrated class received the brunt of the upperclassmen's disgust with integration. They were constantly derided as "Eighty's Ladies" and reminded that their BCT was easier than ever before. Upperclassmen felt that overall standards for men and women had been lowered and referred to the first integrated BCT class as the "coke-break BCT" and the "Burger King Basics" with "Have It Your Way" as their theme.

At the same time, some upperclassmen faulted the new males for not looking after their female classmates, though there was no real incentive for them to do so. Stragglers in earlier all-male classes tended to draw the fire of upperclassmen away from the rest of their class, receiving in return the support of the class, which had an interest in keeping the stragglers from falling out altogether. The women of the Class of 1980 provided no such relief for their male classmates and therefore received little support. When men did endeavor to pull the women along with them, they often found themselves not meeting performance standards. This no-win situation caused resentment among the men toward the women, and harboring such resentment, few men saw any reason for helping the women do what everyone (except the upperclassmen) said the women could do on their own.[10]

Most of the women did succeed in BCT, but largely because the academy overlooked their poor performance. Wilson and Gillman's survey of those who finished the summer revealed an increase in the women's confidence in their ability to survive at the academy. If BCT was not as hard on the women as it was on the men, it was still harder than anything the women had experienced before, and much more demanding than they had expected.

Their male classmates, however, were not impressed:

The male initiates, on the other hand, felt the physical and mental challenges of BCT were either easier or no different from what they had expected. The worth of the cadet status for the males had not been increased by the discomforts of BCT as much as for the females. The males' perception that

*BCT was easier led to a less established inner sense of iden-
tity and less pride in being a cadet.*[11]

Wilson and Gillman went on to conclude that the few experiences actually shared by both male and female cadets served
to diminish rather than increase the attachment of males to the
academy and to their class, particularly to their female classmates. Though shared experiences do serve to bond men
together when "the major social value of a military society is a
warrior image, particularly a masculine warrior image," at the
Air Force Academy "a new social value of an androgynous warrior was pressed upon the members of the institution." The
sharing of experience by men and women in order to mold
androgynous warriors would necessarily have made the women
more masculine and the men more feminine, had not the men
resisted this imposition on their inner self. Instead of growing
closer, male and female cadets grew farther apart.[12]

The Air Force Academy never acknowledged that the poor
performance of female cadets was the chief complaint of male
cadets against them. Indeed, the academy repeatedly insisted
that standards had not been changed and that the negative shift
in male attitudes was attributable to sexist upbringing and "negative emotional support" from faculty and upperclassmen. Nine
years after the first females struggled through BCT, however,
Dr. DeFleur, ever the accommodator, recommended that physical events in which women did not do well should be abandoned altogether.[13]

The start of the academic year did little to improve the
acceptance of women at the academy. One mistake was corrected. At the beginning of the second semester, the academy
decided to integrate all forty squadrons of the Cadet Wing to
eliminate the advantage of all-male squadrons in intramural
sports competition. Intramural sports are a chief means of
developing squadron *esprit de corps*, but the women's participation handicapped the integrated squadrons in competition
with all-male squadrons, causing male cadets to view female

cadets as liabilities on the playing field. Full integration of the Cadet Wing placed all squadrons on an equal footing, but it hardly improved the males' opinions of female physical abilities. Seven years later the Air Force Academy discontinued integrated intramurals altogether after discovering that neither male nor female cadets thought integrated sports conducive to the assimilation of women.

Many other mistakes in planning went uncorrected, most of which were intended to shield women from harassment. Harassment did not end with BCT, but the policy of "positive motivation" continued to protect women from the worst of it. Though some women complained to the academy and the press of sexual harassment in the form of insults and open opposition to integration, nothing came close to the fierce and sometimes physical harassment doolies traditionally faced

Upperclassmen felt that, because of women, standards for both men and women had been lowered.

throughout the doolie year. Insults had always been the daily fare of doolies, and every one of them had felt at one time or another that he had been singled out for persecution by some sadistic upperclassman who, for unknown reasons, had it in for him. Pain was the price one paid to belong. Positive motivation spared the women such pain, but it also barred their acceptance into the Cadet Wing.

Also inhibiting the assimilation of women was the mistake of concentrating the women on the sixth floor of Vandenberg Hall, instead of quartering them with their assigned squadrons. During the school year, doolies put themselves in harm's way anytime they entered their squadron area. They were often rousted out of bed at an early hour by screaming upperclassmen, who dogged them constantly during the five or ten minutes they had to prepare for the morning run. After the run, they had to hurry again to shower and dress before the breakfast formation. Harassment frequently interrupted these meager moments of personal time. Just as frequently, doolies were grabbed to form a detail to clean the day rooms, police the squadron area, or turn in laundry. Other details in the evening took them away from their studies.

The women, however, were spared such interruptions. Upperclassmen could not roust the women out of bed and send them scurrying up and down the halls in their skivvies, as they did the men. After a squadron run, the women returned immediately to Vandenberg Hall, escaping further harassment as well as the morning details. Out of sight and out of mind, they were usually left alone in the evenings. This arrangement produced the academy's intended result of making life easier for the women, but also the unintended result of making their male classmates resent them more.

The task of supervising the women in their own area was left to the fifteen female Air Training Officers, but none of the male cadets trusted the ATOs to do the job properly. To upperclassmen, the ATOs were not and had never been cadets and therefore had no business training doolies. The Air Force Academy had used surrogate upperclassmen before in its first few years of existence, but those surrogates had all attended other military academies and had acted in the absence of upperclassmen, not in their stead. The female ATOs, on the other hand, had no valid academy experience and were entrusted with duties that could have been performed by male upperclassmen, as indeed was the case at the other service academies. To upperclassmen, the ATOs were intruders, whose poor performance in training only proved that they did not belong at the academy.

Through the year, the ATO program caused more harm than good. Though the ATOs struggled to show that they were as hard if not harder on the women as the upperclassmen were on the men, most male cadets suspected that it was all an act. Indeed, Stiehm recounts one incident in which an ATO and a female cadet deliberately staged a dressing down, complete with tears, to impress male onlookers.[14]

If the ATOs were not easier on the women, they made sure that male cadets were. When ATOs were present, male cadets took care not to treat female cadets too roughly, and having ATOs present whenever possible was standard policy. For their own protection, the cadets began including their squadron's Air Officer Commanding (AOC), an Air Force officer who shepherds cadets through the academy, in any event in which women were likely to be subjected to harassment or physical stress.

Fostering an atmosphere of distrust was another effect of the ATO program. Their very existence was proof that the academy did not trust the Cadet Wing with the task of initiating the first female cadets. The cadets in return distrusted the women and altered the way they conducted training to protect themselves. Where once it was common for upperclassmen to take the time to work one-on-one with a doolie on some point of performance, group instruction became more and more common, as male cadets were uneasy dealing with female cadets in private.

One unacknowledged good the ATO program did accomplish, from the academy's standpoint, was to lower male expectations of female ability prior to the arrival of the Class of 1980. Thus, when the first female cadets performed somewhat better than the ATOs, upperclassmen were impressed. This of course did not improve the ATOs' reputation among male or female cadets. And the academy discontinued the program a year earlier than planned, pretending for the press that the program had met its objectives ahead of schedule and was therefore "successfully concluded." Dr. DeFleur was more candid. "There was an abortive attempt to bring female officers to the academy as ATOs," she wrote, eight years later, "but this turned out to be an untenable role and both male and female cadets rejected them."[15]

Some inequities of integration were unintentional, such as the different experience of male and female doolies in the cadet dining facility. Every infamous "square meal" in Mitchell Hall was an ordeal for doolies. After reciting the menu and serving the upperclassmen at their table, doolies sat stiffly on the edge of their seats, chin up, back straight, eyes always level. When they were not responding to questions or requests from upper-classmen, they ate in a mechanical manner, conveying food to their mouths via right angles above their plates. The amount of food a doolie was able to ingest under these conditions was gov-erned by the whim of upperclassmen and reflected the doolie's performance of the required tasks. Doolies who performed poorly went hungry.

Most female doolies escaped this torture by joining one or more of the academy's many women's athletic teams. With more slots on teams than female cadets to fill them, women who had never participated in organized sports in their lives became instant collegiate athletes. One advantage was that it frequently took them away from the pressures of the academy for weekend games or meets. Another advantage was that it permitted them to sit with their teammates at separate "jock ramps" during meals, where harassment was forbidden and even doolies ate like normal people. The women therefore rarely went hungry. Many developed what the cadets called "CHD," or Colorado Hip Disease, caused by the high caloric value of meals in Mitchell Hall. (West Point cadets noticed a similar phenomenon and dubbed it "Hudson hips.") At least one member of the women's cross-country team was enrolled in the academy's weight-control program.

Other persistent inequities were deliberate results of the academy's policy of special protection. Those charged with making integration work were not about to risk their careers by taking seriously their own boasts about equal treatment and able young women. To guard against failure, they devised a number of ways to uphold the appearance of success and keep the female attrition rate down. Double standards on physical tests hid the poor female performance compared to male per-formance. Higher ratings for women from AOCs made up for the lower scores they received in peer ratings and military stud-ies, thus ensuring that women ranked as high as men on the Military Order of Merit. Even in academics, where they hardly needed it, women were allowed special protection. In class, women as a group performed nearly as well as the men, slightly less well in the hard sciences. Even so, male doolies with low grades were dismissed and sent home, whereas similar female doolies remained.

The academy's reluctance to let women leave contrasted sharply with its lack of concern about men, later much regretted. The custom had always been that doolies who wanted to leave were sent packing with little effort by the academy to change their minds. Traditionally, the very act of quitting revealed a weakness of character that confirmed that a doolie did not belong at the academy. For males, this custom continued, but for females indicating a desire to leave, the academy required mandatory counseling in the hope of persuading them to stay. In one unprecedented exception, a female doolie who voluntarily left the academy before the end of the first year was allowed to return the very next year as a sophomore.[16] Such exceptions made men of the Class of 1980 feel that the academy considered it more important for a woman to graduate than for a man.

Individual acts of insensitivity further irritated the Cadet Wing. According to Stiehm, male cadets were offended by the inclusion of females in the squadron selected to march in President Carter's inaugural parade. The squadron that won the honor during the first semester was originally all-male, but by the time of the inauguration, the squadron had been integrated. When a number of cadets were cut from the squadron to reduce the size of the formation, not one of the new female squadron members was among them. Knowing that the new commander-in-chief was keen on women in the military, academy officials rearranged the formation to place women conspicuously in the front rank and on the left flank, contrary to military custom and Air Force regulations, which require the shortest in a formation to march in the rear.

The unkindest cut of all, in the eyes of male cadets, was the academy's dishonesty on the subject of integration. Many inequities would have been more tolerable if the academy had been willing to admit that they existed. Instead, the academy consistently denied the use of double standards or the serious difficulties of integration. The official line was that, yes, a few cadets were having a hard time accepting the change, but they would adapt, and, no, the essential nature of the academy was not in the least affected by the integration of women. Changes to academy standards were "insignificant." The academy needed only a little more time to modify a few outdated or misconceived policies, and everything would work out fine. And of course, the women performed superbly.

The worst offender was the academy superintendent himself, Lieutenant General James R. Allen. Stiehm quotes upperclassmen saying, "The guys at West Point and Annapolis *knew* their 'supe' didn't want girls, but our 'supe' didn't back us."[17] Allen repeatedly annoyed cadets with public proclamations of the integration's success. In October cadets were shown an Air Force promotional film that included scenes of female cadets in BCT, with Allen saying, "The women are undergoing the same training program that the men are undergoing... with some insignificant changes." Later in the year, Allen told the *Denver Post*, "The only problem we've had is finding that there's no way to hold the women back to equal effort.... They've been working harder than the men all summer."[18] Male cadets were outraged by what they read as both a lie and an insult. Attempts by the academy cadre to explain away the affront did little good. What was needed was a confession and an apology from the superintendent himself.

Cadets were limited in the ways they could express their disgust at the academy's hypocrisy. The December issue of *The Dodo*, a cadets-only humor serial, mocked the policy of positive motivation and the public relations line that "all is well." A later issue poked fun at the academy's crackdown on squadron nicknames that eliminated the sexually suggestive and otherwise unsuitable. The official reading of the Wing's pulse was taken by Dr. DeFleur, whose surveys showed male approval of integration dropping throughout the academic year. By spring, the attitudes of male cadets, particularly upperclassmen, were "significantly less positive" toward women at the academy and in combat and significantly more traditional toward women in general.[19]

Some male cadets, however, did grow to like having women around. By the end of the first year, there was one wedding, one engagement, and an unknown number of romances, many of which were violations of the rule forbidding fraternization between doolies and upperclassmen. Some cadets avoided discovery by exchanging letters through the mail or, in one case, communicating by two-way radio. Others were less careful. Seven percent of the commandant's Disciplinary Boards dealt with fraternization, and seventeen frat offenders were on conduct probation.

Academy officials would not risk their careers by taking seriously their own boasts about equal treatment of women.

The first female cadet to leave the academy due to pregnancy was apparently not the victim of a ramp-side romance, however. She probably entered the academy pregnant, for, according to Stiehm, she planned to have the baby during spring break and to return to the academy afterward. Six days before the cadet was to go on leave, she went swimming, acted in a school play, and ran several miles. Her condition was discovered when she was admitted to the hospital later the same day. This remarkable story was reported only in the *Denver Post*, which gave none of the details but noted that the academy had officially admitted to what the paper called an "inevitable first."[20]

As a rule, the nation's media ate up everything the academy fed them and regurgitated nothing but hurrahs for both the bastion-breaching women and the breached academy. The serious press was committed to heralding a feminist triumph. The not-so-serious press was infatuated with delightfully boyish coeds in their spiffy little uniforms. Both saw everything about the first year of integration through rose-colored glasses provided by the academy. "So Far, So Good," said *U.S. News & World Report*'s headline. The story beneath it quoted a female air cadet testifying, without contradiction, that male cadets were finally growing warm to the idea of women at school.[21] It wasn't true, but everyone who wanted to believe it, did.

At least one article did report that integration had been less than satisfactory at the Air Force Academy. *Science News* called it "a rough start" and linked the high rate of male attrition to the presence of women.[22] Wilson and Gillman were right. Basic Cadet Training failed to foster sufficient pride and a strong sense of belonging among many male doolies, and the rest of the year only made things worse by undermining the cadets' respect for both the academy and the Air Force. As a result, when things got tough many male doolies saw little reason to stay.

Ironically, because the academy never openly admitted its mistakes, the blame for high attrition rates, for the failure of the women to assimilate, and for much of the difficulty with integration fell upon those men who stayed to graduate. For not "going along with the program" in the beginning, the Class of 1980 never quite earned the full confidence of the academy staff. Eighty's Ladies were branded a troubled class, to be used later by academy cadre as a negative example for later classes not to follow. "Don't be like the Class of '80," they counseled. "It's got problems."

By its own narrow measure, the academy's plan for integration was a success. It got what it wanted: the percentage of women to finish the first year was the highest of any defense academy. The academy's success, however, was the Air Force's loss. The women who finally graduated did not make up for the loss of men. The Air Force got far fewer pilots, navigators, missilemen, science officers, and administrators for the increased trouble and expense of educating the Class of 1980.[23]

But the real losers were the men of the first integrated class. All of the men who entered the academy in the summer of 1976 were cheated out of much of the pride they might have felt in their status as air cadets. Those who finished the first year were betrayed by some of the very officers who talked to them of honor and integrity. Those who finally graduated were so burned by the bungling of integration that it is hardly likely they share with earlier classes the same fondness for and devotion to the Air Force Academy. At least one graduate of the Class of 1980 was so embittered by the experience that he applied for and received, upon graduation, a service-transfer to the United States Army.

Chapter 4

"THE LAST CLASS WITH BALLS"

Your mission remains fixed, determined, inviolable—it is to win our wars. Everything else in your professional career is but corollary to this vital dedication. All other public purposes... will find others for their accomplishment; but you are the ones who are trained to fight; yours is the profession of arms.

—GENERAL DOUGLAS A. MACARTHUR TO THE
WEST POINT GRADUATING CLASS OF 1962

THE U.S. MILITARY ACADEMY at West Point and the U.S. Naval Academy at Annapolis avoided some of the early mistakes made by the U.S. Air Force Academy, but after the first year of integration none of the academies could resist pressure for greater accommodation of women. In a very short time, the academies were converted from "bastions of male chauvinism" to institutions officially dedicated to the feminist principles of equality and androgyny. Those principles were pushed upon the men at the academies with little success. Though opposition to integration outside the academies had been routed and scattered, inside the conquered and occupied academies resistance went underground.

One difference in the first year of integration at West Point and Annapolis was that male cadets and midshipmen believed academy officials were opposed to integration. They knew that some academy officials had opposed integration before the congressional mandate, and those who now supported integration somehow managed to avoid offending the cadets and midshipmen with exaggerated public pronouncements of integration's success. West Point and Annapolis intended to make as few adjustments as possible to accommodate women and adopted a policy of equal treatment, in contrast to the Air Force Academy's policy of special protection.

This is not to say that the first women at Annapolis or West Point experienced the same torture that men traditionally endured. A survey of male and female midshipmen at Annapolis showed that less than 5 percent of both sexes thought female plebes were treated the same as male plebes. Almost two-thirds of the male midshipmen said upperclassmen showed favoritism toward women. Three-quarters said women received favoritism from physical education instructors (a third of the women agreed), and half said the same about company officers, academic instructors, and executive department officials. Most of the women thought men received favoritism, especially from upperclassmen. Certainly some upperclassmen deliberately harassed the women more than men, hoping to make them quit the academy. But most found it difficult not to be gentlemen. "It's tough to discipline a soldier when she blinks her baby-blue eyes or slips you a dimple," explained an Army colonel at West Point.[1]

Women performed less well academically and suffered higher rates of attrition than did men at West Point and Annapolis. At Annapolis, the first year's attrition rate for women was 22.2 percent, twice the rate for men. At West Point, it was 28.6 percent, compared to 23.8 percent for men.

Despite the disparity between the attrition rates of men and women, many believed the first year of integration had been a success. Proponents of integration were relieved that the women's attrition rates were not higher. The Carter administration publicly praised the Air Force for its "success" and kept criticism of the Army and Navy quiet to avoid giving the impression that integration had failed. To many critics of integration, the results of the first year were a psychological defeat. Underestimating both the kind of women admitted in the first year and the academies' willingness to accommodate them, many old soldiers and sailors had expected most if not all of the "ladies" to wither like roses in the desert. When that didn't happen, and life at the academies seemed to go on as before, some gave up and joined supporters in proclaiming integration's success, while others retired in silence, privately bemoaning the brave new world.

Of course, nothing short of mutiny among male cadets and midshipmen would have stamped the first year of integration as a miserable failure. The question answered by the experience of the first year was not whether integrated academies would succeed or fail, but how the presence of women would change the academies. Male students at all of the academies registered overwhelming disapproval of the changes. Surveys of midshipmen at Annapolis showed that 81 percent of upperclassmen and 74 percent of plebes still opposed integration. The survey also showed a slight shift toward a less traditional view of women in society among male midshipmen, but the report of the survey warned "the more the situation touched these men personally, the less likely they were as a group to endorse equal opportunity for women."[2]

The most common complaint heard from male cadets and midshipmen was that integration had lowered the academies' physical standards. Physically, the women simply could not keep up. The dropout rate on morning runs during West Point's "Beast Barracks" was 23 percent for women and less than 3 percent for men. In the seventh week of training, 26.3 percent of female cadets reported for physical "reconditioning" instead of the morning run, compared to 5.6 percent of men. Women reported for sick call an average of 6.8 times per female cadet, compared to the male average of 1.7 times. They suffered more than ten times as many stress fractures as men. Attrition during the first summer was 16 percent for women, 9.7 percent for men. Even after a year of regular physical training, West Point women in the first integrated class suffered five times as many injuries as men during field training. The following year, the injury rate for women in field training was fourteen times the rate for men.[3]

Even when the women were healthy, they could not perform to male standards. On their first timed two-mile run, 85 percent of the female plebes at West Point received a score of D or lower according to the male standard. When 61 percent failed a complete physical test, compared to 4.8 percent of male plebes, separate standards were devised for the women. Similar adjustments were made to other standards. At Annapolis, a two-foot stepping stool was added to an indoor obstacle course to enable women to surmount an eight-foot wall. At West Point, women carried M16 rifles for rifle-runs and bayonet drills, while men continued to carry much heavier M14s. On parade, West Point women were initially allowed to brace the M14 on their knee when drawing back the bolt for inspection. Later, the bolt springs were shortened to reduce tension, making the bolt easier to draw.

Like the Air Force Academy, West Point and Annapolis also made allowance for some differences between the sexes that were not based on physiological differences, as the law required. Women were thought to require more privacy than men and so were issued shower curtains though men were not, and of course none of the women had their heads shaved. Likewise, the substitution of classes in karate and self-defense (and "interpretive dancing" at the Coast Guard Academy) for classes in boxing and wrestling had more to do with what the academies thought becoming of women, than what physical risks the sports presented to them. It didn't seem to matter that the purpose of training men to box and wrestle was to develop physical courage and aggressiveness, neither of which was achieved by most of the alternatives offered to women.

These differences were not missed by the male cadets and midshipmen. In her book *Mixed Company*, Helen Rogan explains how men at West Point felt:

> *The separate grading scale on the obstacle course and the three-mile run meant that a female cadet could get a low score and pass, while a male who got the same score had to go to summer school to make up—and this in an institution that was making so much triumphant noise about equality.... Furthermore, since the women learned neither to box nor to wrestle, and their close-quarters training emphasized self-defense, they never had bloody noses. The men were outraged, since deep down they knew war was about bloody noses.*[4]

To combat the "misconception" among male cadets that separate standards meant lower standards, the academies tried to point out that standards for men had not changed since the admission of women. Later, they developed the doctrine of "equivalent training," which held that physical training was intended to elicit from each cadet "equal effort rather than equal accomplishment."[5] Since women were often frustrated by their failure to meet male standards, "dual standards" were established as attainable levels of performance.

Male cadets saw little difference between dual standards and double standards, a term never used by academy officials, and they overwhelmingly rejected the doctrine of equivalent training as another strained attempt to accommodate women. It applied only to physical requirements and only to differences between the sexes. Short males were still expected to meet the same standards as tall males. Effort mattered only if one were female. Otherwise it was performance that counted.

Some requirements still embarrassed and frustrated women despite the double standards. In those cases, it was easier to eliminate the requirement than to manipulate the standards. One such requirement was West Point's Enduro run. The Enduro run was a timed event requiring a cadet to run 2.5 miles wearing combat boots and a helmet and carrying a rucksack, rifle, canteen, and poncho. Coming near the end of summer training for third-class cadets, the run was the last event a cadet was required to complete successfully to be awarded the Recondo patch.

Since the run was viewed as essentially a combat task and women were not being trained for combat, the West Point cadre debated over whether to devise a double standard for the Enduro run or simply excuse female cadets from the requirement. For the Class of 1980, they decided that women would participate in the event but their performance would not be used to determine who received the Recondo patch. Only 42 percent of the women completed the run on time, but 73 percent were awarded the Recondo patch, whereas 89 percent of the men passed the run, but only 75 percent received the patch. Naturally, the men were not happy with the devaluation of a once-coveted award.

The next year, the academy sought to avoid the outrage of male cadets by requiring female cadets to complete the Enduro run to the same standards as the men. Forty-two percent of the women of the Class of 1981 passed the Enduro run, but only 32 percent qualified for and were awarded the Recondo patch. Ninety-seven percent of the men passed the run, and 82 percent received the patch.

In the third year of integration, the academy changed its mind again, this time to spare female cadets the stigma of failure by eliminating the Enduro run altogether, for both men and women. The final official report on integration at West Point hailed this as a good example of "the academy's attempt to normalize physical requirements."[6] Dual for double, normalize for lower—anything could be fixed to accommodate women if only a suitable euphemism could be found.

The doctrine of equivalent training was bound to undermine the importance of physical activity at the academies. It held that men (but not women) were required to perform pull-ups, not because pull-ups were of any value in themselves, but ssaaa...........

because the academy wanted the men to exert themselves physically—it wanted to see them sweat. Sooner or later, cadets would have asked why they should sweat over something that was not itself important.

Thus, before the doctrine's effect could be fully felt, officials were pushing for the preeminence of academics over all else. Defenders of integration insisted that nothing had changed. "Academics have never taken a backseat to military education at the academy and certainly never should," wrote Rear Admiral William P. Lawrence, superintendent at Annapolis.[7] But critics like James Webb, a 1968 Naval Academy graduate and later Reagan's second secretary of the Navy, charged that making men combat leaders had been the academies' central concern right up until the admission of women. In 1979 Webb wrote, "Harvard and Georgetown and a plethora of other institutions can turn out technicians and intellectuals *en masse*; only the service academies have been able to turn out combat leaders *en masse*, and they have ceased doing so."[8]

> Each superintendent felt free to dismiss long-established traditions and make his academy what he wanted it to be.

The new emphasis on academics coincided with the liberalization of the academic curriculum—more electives, more courses in the humanities and social sciences, fewer courses in military science, fewer required courses in the hard sciences, and academic majors in fields other than engineering. At all three academies, it also meant the end of the Order of Merit, the age-old practice of ranking each class by academic record. "We want to recognize that each individual has his own academic profile," explained West Point's second superintendent after integration, Lieutenant General Andrew Jackson Goodpaster. "It is no longer possible to reach a high level of competence across the board... I do not want to stereotype or categorize a man according to a single number. Everyone has more dimensions than that."[9]

Liberalization was a boon for women, who usually performed less well in the hard sciences than the men, but it was not initiated merely to accommodate them. The trend began after World War II, proceeding with stops or starts for thirty years with each change of superintendents.[10] The admission of women, however, accelerated the process precipitously by allowing superintendents to make whatever changes they desired. Unbound by respect for the way the academies had always been, each superintendent felt free to make his academy what he wanted it to be, without regard for traditions.

Goodpaster had replaced Lieutenant General Sidney B. Berry as West Point superintendent after the first year of integration, ostensibly to restore integrity to the academy's educational program after the 1976 cheating scandal. Berry had publicly opposed integration but accepted the task of integration with soldierly stoicism. "We have our orders, and it is our responsibility to implement them to the best of our ability," he told the academy's alumni in 1976.[11]

Goodpaster was another kind of soldier. Second in his class at West Point in 1939, with two master's degrees and a doctorate from Princeton University, he had retired as a four-star general in 1974 after serving as supreme allied commander in Europe and returned to active duty to assume the superintendency in 1977. To some, he was a scholarly intellectual in the mold of Maxwell Taylor, an ideal choice to lead the academy through coming changes. To male cadets at West Point, he was the kill-joy dean of the movie *Animal House*.

Goodpaster initiated the most sweeping reforms in West Point's history, many of which had little to do with academics. To West Point alumnus James Salter, writing for *Life* magazine, it was "a ruthless pruning of outmoded traditions."[12] There were fewer parades and formations. Gym shoes replaced combat boots on morning runs, and rifle runs were much less frequent. Plebes were sent home for Christmas and were no longer required to recite a litany of useless trivia about the academy before being allowed to eat their fill at mealtime.

Breakfast was made optional for upperclassmen. Shouting in plebes' faces was replaced with "eyeball to eyeball instructing in a firm voice." Mental pressure at the academy should be academic, not abusive or demeaning, explained Goodpaster.

Academy officials passed many of these reforms off as fallout from the 1976 cheating scandal, in which ninety-four third-class cadets were expelled and forty-four resigned after a cadet honor board found them guilty of cheating on a take-home engineering examination. The scandal prompted a thorough review of the cadet honor code, which critics said was unrealistically rigid. Changes were made to the code, and those who were forced out were allowed an opportunity to reenter. Still, the breadth of reforms instituted by Goodpaster far exceeded expectations. Even critics of the academy's harsh discipline thought it was over-reacting. Cadet Timothy Ringgold, a central figure in the scandal who had filed suit in U.S. district court to get the honor code ruled unconstitutional, told the *New York Times* in 1978, "The academy may have gone overboard on easing military discipline."[13]

The same thing was happening at the other academies, without a cheating scandal as an excuse. At the Air Force Academy, the doctrine of positive motivation was extended to all cadets, not just women. At the Naval Academy, traditional forms of harassment were losing their sanction among the officer staff. Many were outlawed entirely. Plebes no longer "braced up" anytime they entered Bancroft Hall, nor reported to upperclassmen for "come-arounds."

The common denominator among the academies was the presence of women. Some reforms were intended specifically to help them. Peer ratings were discontinued at the Naval Academy when it saw that women consistently received lower ratings than men. Without peer ratings, the selection of midshipmen for leadership positions depended entirely upon the evaluation of the officer cadre and was thus susceptible to manipulation to advance women. Many male midshipmen felt that women needed only "good grades and a modicum of professionalism," in James Webb's words, to make rank at the academy. One middie told Webb, "The academy has used a lot of pressure to establish women as stripers. Women are groomed from plebe year. The scary thing is that it's creating the presumption that women can command troops."

Other reforms were the result of a growing feminine sensibility among academy officials. Female cadets and midshipmen had shown little sympathy for the practice of hazing and even less understanding of its purpose. To the women, hazing was either a deliberate attempt to drive them from the academy or a childish and unnecessary display of malicious *machismo*. As upperclassmen, the women never indulged in the more severe forms of hazing. As plebes, they sometimes tearily reported incidents of relatively mild harassment to the academy cadre. Webb tells of one such incident in which a senior at Annapolis ordered a female plebe to eat with oversized utensils as punishment for poor table manners. The woman cried to her roommate, the roommate complained to her company commander, and her company commander reprimanded the senior for harassing the woman. At West Point, two third-class cadets, a man and a woman, resigned after the woman was goaded by her classmates into biting the head off a live chicken. At a press conference, they denounced the sexist nature of hazing at the academy.

Actually, biting the head off a chicken was a routine event during survival training at West Point. After demonstrating any of the various ways to decapitate a chicken, the instructor, usually a noncommissioned officer, would offer a bird to the class. In the absence of volunteers, the class often pushed forward the most squeamish among them to do the deed. In this particular case, the woman claimed she had been selected because her classmates disapproved of her romantic relationship with the cadet who later joined her in resigning.

To the press, such an event was sensational, and when accompanied with charges of official toleration for sexist harassment, it was scandalous. "West Point Concedes Some Hazing

Tactics Have Become 'Sexist,'" read the headlines. Goodpaster relieved anyone's doubts about the academy's official line. He denounced such "sophomoric antics" as no longer appropriate, saying "the time for foolishness over the matter of women at West Point is long past."[14]

For the academies to side regularly with plebes against upperclassmen was a serious blow to the fourth-class system. "The whole place has been pulled down to the level of the women," a midshipman told Webb.

It was bad enough when the academy cadres began interfering in what were traditionally student affairs. It was worse when uninitiated outsiders began second-guessing the decisions of duly appointed student committees. In 1978 a federal judge in Brooklyn issued an injunction to stop the expulsion of a West Point senior accused of fraternization with a female plebe and lying. The following year, Secretary of the Army Clifford L. Alexander intervened on behalf of a sophomore also charged with fraternization and lying. Upon the recommendation of a cadet honor committee, Goodpaster had ordered the cadet dismissed, but Alexander countermanded the order and had the cadet reinstated, an unprecedented act which incensed the corps of cadets, as well as many officers at the academy.[15]

Like hazing, fraternization was an issue over which male cadets and the rest of the world seemed hopelessly at odds. A minority of men considered any social contact between male and female cadets fraternization. Many more thought romantic relationships between members of the same company or squad inappropriate. Most supported a conservative interpretation of the official policy, which defined fraternization as social or romantic contact between upperclassmen and plebes, and between cadets or midshipmen and members of the academy staff.

Female cadets and midshipmen were decidedly more liberal on the issue than the men. More than a third of West Point women favored relaxation of the ban on fraternization, while almost none favored tighter restrictions. Those who favored the status quo did not consider fraternization a serious offense. Male cadets complained that women often failed to support the ban fully by neglecting to enforce it.

Women had much more to gain from relaxing the ban on fraternization than men. With a male to female ratio of better than nine to one, many more women than men could expect to start both a career and a family upon graduation. Half of the women graduating with the first integrated class at West Point were married within a year or two of graduation, the great majority to other academy graduates. At the Air Force Academy, 90 percent of the women of the Class of 1980 had been romantically involved with someone at the academy (officer, cadet, or civilian) during their four years there. Of the first twenty-five women to drop out of the Naval Academy Class of 1980, twenty married former midshipmen.

The academies gradually accepted the view that social relations between the sexes were further proof of integration's success. Marriage had always had a stabilizing effect on male officers, and everyone assumed that it would have the same effect on the women. Romance in the ranks was thus seen as a healthy social development.

The academies were looking on the bright side. As everyone knew, unhealthy social developments were impossible to prevent as long as men and women lived in close quarters. The best the academies could do was to keep them quiet. The number of times a cadet walked into his room to find his roommate in bed with another cadet cannot be counted. But between 1977 and 1981 the Naval Academy punished twenty-nine midshipmen of both sexes for sexual misconduct. The worst offense was committed by five men and one woman who videotaped themselves having intercourse in Bancroft Hall, while a crowd of middies cheered from outside the window. A 1984 study at the Air Force Academy found an "exceptionally high rate of pregnancy among women cadets" and widespread concern for what the cadets derisively called "the USAFA dating game."[16]

Originally, all of the academies dismissed women for becoming pregnant. West Point and Annapolis also dismissed men for causing a pregnancy. But the Air Force Academy, as early as November 1977, changed its policy to allow a pregnant female to take a leave of absence, have the baby, and then return as a cadet in good standing. Subsequent recommendations by the Air Force Academy staff have shown the same willingness to do anything but discourage sexual promiscuity. One report recommended the following: a liberal dorm-room visitation policy for both sexes to stop cadets from "sneaking around"; mandatory courses in human sexuality; "assertiveness training" that must "clearly address 'date rape' from both the male and female perspective"; an assault and rape hotline; widespread dissemination of information on hospital and clinic services; readily available "contraception, rape management and counseling, and sex education." Such information "must be common, firsthand knowledge to *every* cadet.... There is no way we can oversaturate this information (original emphasis)."[17]

The thoroughly feminized service academies continue to live by a double standard.

What no one addressed was the effect of fraternization and sexual promiscuity on the cadets' respect for the academies. "All summer we were lectured about the high standards we were expected to meet," one midshipman told Webb. "Our squad leaders talked about honor, performance, and accountability. Then before you knew it, they were going after the women plebes, sneaking some of them away on weekends." When the academies were unable or unwilling to deal effectively with such violations, the cadets turned cynical. Sometimes it seemed as if only the male cadets were willing to defend their academy's honor by prosecuting other male cadets.

But aside from fraternization and sexual immorality, the integration of women had a much more general effect on the social nature of the academies. A new factor had entered the equation. A force more powerful than the call of duty, the pride of honor, or the bonds of comradeship completely reversed the social relationships at the academies. Even self-disciplined men could not remain indifferent. Wrote Salter:

> *There were women in the barracks. There were cadets with beautiful, boyish hair, like that of a shipmate on a cruise. It was an appeal that touched fantasies—on a clear autumn morning or in the winter dusk, the image of a tender cheek beneath a military cap, the trace of a smile, the womanly figure in rough clothes....*[18]

The men were charmed. They could never see the women as just cadets, and they could never treat women as they treated men. Men who remained critical of women in general could not be so critical of individual women they had come to know. The women were just too hard to hate. Some men could bluster threats and insults from a distance, but when they came face to face with the enemy, they quailed out of natural affection and decency. If they were sticklers for equal treatment and especially careful of themselves, the men could succeed in bringing pressure to bear on a female plebe, but not without careful scrutiny of their own feelings and actions, and they were never sure if they had been too tough or too easy.

The academies were also charmed. They were no longer the strange and cold conclaves of unsentimental militarism, where young men first learned the pain of separation, where love was delivered in sealed envelopes at distant intervals, where alienation made plebes on leave feel like strangers at home, where cadets could prepare for lives of sacrificial hardship and deprivation, where they could learn leadership and gain confidence without the fearful disruption of suddenly running into someone with whom they were falling in or out of love.

Women brought the world into the academies—the world with all its mystery, romance, jealousy, and pain, with its flirting, and with its fumbling in a private darkness. Women were not just one part of the world hitherto excluded, as black males had once been; women were the world itself, they were what life was all about. In comparison, the ancient military glory of the academies seemed parochial and quaint, and the traditions that attended that glory purposeless and anachronistic. Their virtue and distinction were gone. They would never again mean as much to those who went there. Never again would a graduate's last conscious thoughts be of "the Corps, and the Corps, and the Corps."[19]

"The plebe experience, in particular, was not modified in the slightest because of women and remains as intensive today as during my time as a plebe thirty years ago," wrote Admiral William P. Lawrence, superintendent of the Naval Academy, responding in 1980 to James Webb's charges to the contrary.[20] It was the standard, official response: nothing of consequence had changed, the women were doing everything the men were doing, and they were doing it as well as or better than the men.

Still, those embarrassing attrition rates had to be explained. Attrition rates for women at graduation exceeded those for men for all classes at all of the academies, except for the Air Force Academy classes of 1980 and 1986. No one knew why. Surveys of those who quit revealed little, as women gave the same answers as men. Some suggested that maybe the academies were recruiting the wrong kind of women, or maybe women came to the academies without an accurate expectation of what life would be like there. West Point proposed to seek new sources of qualified women and advise female candidates to expect the worst.

The only other possible answer given by academy officials was that the lack of acceptance by the men drove the women out, and if so, "then strong negative sanctions must be enforced to discourage this from happening."[21] Sanctions included punishment for cadets (and officers) who voiced opposition to integration or whose words or actions revealed sexist tendencies.

But it wasn't enough for cadets to keep their opinions to themselves; they had to become believers. The academies became fervid propagandists for the very beliefs they had so staunchly resisted only a few years before. West Point's "Institutional Plans to Overcome Sexism" called for tighter controls on the gathering of data related to integration to "avoid research activities which have sexist consequences." It also called for stopping publication of all documents and manuals containing such words as "gentlemen," "star man," and "he." Air Force Academy cadets were taught the supposed "male penalties of sexist behavior (heart attacks, repressed emotions)." At all of the academies, classes on sexism and sex-role socialization, taught solely from the feminist perspective, were mandatory. Feminism was the official orthodoxy, the measure of morality, and if cadets or cadre were not among the faithful, "then they're in the wrong line of work," warned General Goodpaster.[22]

These campaigns showed a crusader's contempt for whatever beliefs the men already possessed. Like barefooted boys from the backwoods of Borneo, cadets were assumed to be ignorant, superstitious primitives. They were not allowed opinions, only "attitudes." If they did not support the doctrine of equivalent training, it was because they did not "understand" it. If they were "helped to understand the women's perspective," they would be more "open-minded" to "pluralistic beliefs" and therefore more accepting of integration. No study produced at any of the academies suggested that women needed to understand the male perspective, except, as mentioned earlier, on the subject of "date rape." Only the men needed to have their minds changed. If they resisted, they were considered morally defective.

It was all for naught. It only succeeded in suppressing overt expressions of opposition to integration. The absurdities of dual standards and equivalent training were too obvious, and the defense of such absurdities only incited resentment, disrespect, and cynicism, though of course cadets were smart enough to keep such things to themselves, at least most of the time. The Naval Academy Class of 1979 chose *Omni Vir* as its class motto.

The West Point Class of 1979 proudly professed to be "the last class with balls." A picture in *The Howitzer*, West Point's yearbook, showed members of that class holding a variety of balls: footballs, baseballs, basketballs, and balls for golf, tennis, and billiards.

Opposition to women at the academies did not end when the Class of 1979 graduated, as many integrationists had predicted. When Kristine Holderied received her diploma as valedictorian of the Naval Academy Class of 1984, there was only polite applause from the crowd and the class, nothing to compare with the ovation Dean Miller received as salutatorian. The midshipmen knew and the spectators knew who should have been first in the class. That same year, surveys of cadets and midshipmen revealed widespread opposition to women at all of the academies. Administrators were shocked. Three out of five midshipmen said women were not accepted at Annapolis. A study group at the Air Force Academy admitted that many preconceived notions of the success of integration were "inaccurate, unfounded, misguided and/or shallow."[23]

But the grip of radical feminism on the academies was too strong for any hope of redress. The response of the Air Force Academy was reflexive. It was interested only in redressing the grievances of female cadets, and the solution for that was even greater accommodation. "Are certain tasks in basic training or some of the athletic competitions really central to the primary goals of the academy?" one academy researcher asked. If not, then those tasks should be eliminated because "as males observe and 'learn' that young women do not perform well in some areas, there is an immediate decline in favorable orientations towards women." Other suggested solutions included admitting more women to the academy, recruiting a "wider range of people" with fewer traditionally-minded males, and making "the entire academy milieu" less military, "less discontinuous" from the rest of society.[24]

The results of an eight-month investigation by a committee of academy faculty members came up with similar recommen-

dations. The committee called for: a standing watchdog committee to meet monthly to discuss the status of integration;
classes on "power relationships" and "powerless to power broker" to assist the "sociosexual development" of "well-adjusted
human beings"; the segregation of integrated intramural sports
to prevent men from learning the wrong things; an expanded
definition of combat that would include duties to which women
are assigned; greater emphasis in the classroom on Air Force
support functions and less emphasis on its mission to "fly and
fight"; and a crackdown on "expressing 'anti-woman in the military' feelings." The committee's report stated, "The intent is for
everyone to be aware of potential anti-woman feelings and to
insure people do not *consciously or unconsciously* contribute to
it."[25] (Emphasis added.)

None of these recommendations is likely to change things
at the academies. Men and women are essentially different
both physically and psychologically. And the purpose and
nature of the academies only highlight sexual differences.

The biggest difference is that men and women do not come
to the academies with the same interest in the military. Their
higher attrition rates, both before and after graduation, and
their consistently poorer performance in history and military
science prove that women at the academies simply do not want
to be soldiers or sailors or airmen as much as men do. Nothing
can explain why women score lower in history except that history does not much interest them. Nothing can explain why
60 percent to 70 percent of the women at West Point score
below the mean in easy military subjects like map reading, military heritage, and tactics, except that they do not much want to
be soldiers.

Surveyed after graduation, many male West Point graduates said the academy should have required more courses in
military history; none of the women made the same recommendation. Because the academies now teach less military history, officers learn most of what they know from what they have
read on their own. Because few young girls grow up reading

Landmark Classics about D-Day or the Battle of the Bulge, and few develop such an interest later, female academy graduates are likely to be dangerously ignorant of the history, art, science, and psychology of war.

When the first of these women graduated from West Point, 20 percent of them had decided already that they would leave the Army after serving their initial commitment, as opposed to only 2 percent of their male classmates. Six years later, the attrition ratios for the women and men of the classes of 1980 were 40 percent to 25 percent for West Point graduates, 23 percent to 11 percent for Air Force Academy graduates, and 32 percent to 24 percent for Annapolis graduates who had entered the Navy. Of the first women to enter the Marine Corps from Annapolis, more than half (57 percent) had left the Corps by 1986, as opposed to only 27 percent of similar males.

The benefits of sexual integration of the service academies are few.

Academy officials have minimized the import of these statistics, which they say may not reflect significant trends. The Class of 1980 was not typical of other classes because they bore the scars of blazing the trail. Fewer men were eligible to resign in 1986 because of extended service commitments for flight training and other assignments. And lastly, the first women were encouraged to expect too much from the services and may have become disappointed as the years passed when they found their opportunities limited by combat exclusion laws.

But ample evidence shows that differences between male and female graduates will persist in all classes of all academies for the foreseeable future. Interviews and surveys of West Point graduates found that women rarely listed any positive aspect of their West Point education except physical training; they were more likely to say that there should be less infantry training at West Point, and that they had more trouble as cadets dealing with noncommissioned officers; and they were more tolerant of unethical behavior at the academy, preferring to live and let live in most cases.

Of life in the Army, the women were less tolerant of adverse conditions like long hours and unpleasant surroundings and much more concerned about the imposition of work on their personal lives. When asked to talk about their jobs, three-quarters of the male graduates interviewed mentioned positive aspects of their jobs as sources of satisfaction, but less than a quarter of the women mentioned any source of satisfaction. Men were most likely to list "successfully completing a job, seeing a job done right, completing a mission, doing a good job" as their primary source of job satisfaction. Women were much less likely to agree. The number one reason for job satisfaction among women was "working with troops, helping troops."

Asked about sources of "life satisfaction," most men and women cited marriage and family as primary sources, but in varying degrees: 26 percent for men and 18 percent for women. Men were next most likely to list their job (12.5 percent), women to list travel, sports, and their job (all 7 percent). Thirty-five percent of women officers felt negative about their Army careers, while only 2 percent felt positive.

Marriage, which had a stabilizing effect on male officers, had the opposite effect on female graduates of the academy. Of those who were married within five years of graduation, almost all married other officers. Problems with joint-domicile assignments, conflicting work schedules, and family priorities made married life much more difficult for the women than for the men. "Problems of spouses' commitment seem to be much more severe among females than males," the surveys found. One-third of the husbands of female graduates of West Point did not want their wives to stay in the Army.[26]

Not surprisingly, children also increase dissatisfaction with military life among women. One 1981 graduate of the Air Force Academy had five children within five years of graduation. Generally, the families of female graduates had fewer children than the families of male graduates, but even one child is enough to alter a woman's desires for the future radically. Many resign. Others accept less demanding assignments in order to be with their families. "When Rebecca was born, I knew I could never go back to sea," said Liz Belzer, now Liz Semcken, a 1980 graduate of the Naval Academy. According to her male class-mates, Belzer was one of the women who were "groomed for stripes" by the academy staff. After graduation, she married a Navy pilot of the Class of 1978 and became a surface warfare officer because officers at the academy had convinced her that she would excel there. She left the Navy in 1987. "To the world, being in the first class was probably the most significant thing I've done," she said in 1985. "But in my own life, there's no question—it's Rebecca."[27]

A report by the U.S. Military Academy on the post-gradua-tion beliefs of male and female graduates recommended a more sophisticated joint-domicile assignment system to relieve the stress of family separation for "dual career couples," and greater career opportunities to prevent women from becoming dis-couraged with their careers. Some would add expanded military child-care to the list. The report contained an admission that was unremarkable for its truth but astounding for its frankness. The services rarely say things so plainly:

> *All of these [suggested] changes are in the direction of accommodating the Army to the officer, rather than the other way around. Changes in the other direction, requiring accommodation by female officers, are likely to accentuate the negative aspects of an Army career and drive more women out.*[28]

The thoroughly feminized academies continue to live by a double standard. Wherever necessary, allowance is made for the unsuppressed girlishness of female cadets. There was a time when uncontrollable fear was called cowardice by military men, but now "intellectual discipline" is more important at the acad-emies than physical courage or discipline of any other sort. A female first-class midshipman can flatly refuse to complete a mandatory requirement for graduation because of her fear of a thirty-four–foot jump into the water, which simulates abandoning ship. One woman who did so was granted a waiver, allowed to graduate, and commissioned as an unrestricted line officer in the United States Navy.

The benefits of sexual integration of the service academies are few. "The place looks quieter," one observer has said. Others have spoken of an improvement in the quality of students. Today's cadets and midshipmen are cleaner, better behaved, and more refined than the brutes of yesteryear. "If there was one thing that was irrelevant to my preparation for combat it was refinement," Webb wrote. As secretary of the Navy, Webb directed that Naval Academy graduates on orders to the Marine Corps will attend "Bulldog" training, formerly required only of Marine officers from other sources of commission. His concern was that Marine officers needed to develop a certain toughness they no longer develop at the Naval Academy.

There were women at the academies who, like Webb, wished the academies still prepared cadets and midshipmen for combat. They were ambitious women who were not happy with the combat exclusions. In 1981, when an admiral at the Naval Academy, speaking to an assembly of midshipmen, told a female middie why women were excluded from combat, the woman interjected, "Maybe women shouldn't be here at all!"[29] The mostly male assembly responded with vigorous and sustained applause. The Class of 1979 was not the last class with balls after all.

Chapter 5

DAMN THE SERVICES, FULL SPEED AHEAD

The first quality of a soldier is the ability to support fatigue and privations.... Poverty, privation, and misery are the school of the good soldier.

—NAPOLEON BONAPARTE

ON AUGUST 18, 1976, a detail of American soldiers was pruning a tree in the Joint Security Area separating North and South Korea when they were suddenly attacked by a truckload of axe-wielding North Korean guards. Two American officers were killed. Nine other soldiers were wounded.

An appropriate response to the attack was hotly debated at all levels. "There was no question in the minds of anybody in Korea that we had decided to take limited military action," recalls Major General John K. Singlaub, then chief of staff of U.S. forces in Korea. Neither was there any doubt that a military response, however limited, might be misinterpreted by the North. While the White House weighed the risk of provocation with the necessity for some show of force, United Nations forces in South Korea prepared for the worst. Ground units assembled and moved forward into battle positions, and air forces were called in from Alaska and Japan. On the night of

August 20, UN forces in Korea stood at DEFCON 1, with B-52s winging their way toward the North Korean capital, fighters warming their engines on the runway, and helicopter gunships hovering above the border. "We had rounds up the spout and hands on the lanyards, and every weapon had a target," says Singlaub. For all that anyone in the ranks knew, they were going to war.

Early on the morning of August 21, American soldiers cut down the half-pruned tree and dismantled a few unoccupied shacks built by the North Koreans in the Joint Security Area. The timid response provoked no one, and the emergency soon passed, but not before U.S. Army commanders observed a disturbing reaction among their troops. As soon as it became clear that the alert was no ordinary training exercise, commanders throughout Korea were flooded with requests from female soldiers for transfers to the rear. War was more than these women had bargained for when they had joined the Army. Most fully expected to be evacuated in the event of hostilities, but when the question was raised at higher headquarters, Singlaub nixed the idea immediately and ordered all soldiers to their posts.

Later, when the emergency was over, Singlaub learned that his order had not been strictly obeyed. Many women had abandoned their posts near the border and headed south on their own. Some turned up later in units well to the rear. Others reported for duty with dependent children in tow, since their arrangements for child-care did not cover the event of war. In some instances, male noncommissioned officers had left their posts temporarily to tend to the safety of their wives and girl-friends in other units.

The Korean emergency dramatized the growing concern among commanders in the field about the presence of women in the ranks. Four years after the marriage of the All-Volunteer Force (AVF) to the Equal Rights Amendment (ERA), the honeymoon was over and the debilitating effects of integration had begun to show. Social and sexual relationships between male and female service members defied bans on fraternization between ranks. Marriages between service members were on the rise. Incidents of sexual assault soared. For the first time ever, commanders and supervisors throughout the services were confronting problems with sexual harassment, dating, pregnancy, single parenthood, in-service couples, and joint domicile. Most had never served with women and were just beginning to learn the vastly different art of managing women. Their knowledge and experience as leaders of men were of little use.

In December 1976 the Army completed the first of several studies of the problems relating to integration. The report, entitled simply *Women in the Army*, drew much criticism from proponents of integration, for while it identified and explored most of the problems caused or aggravated by the presence of women in the ranks, it did not compare the advantages and disadvantages of women versus men. One whole chapter discussed problems caused by pregnancy among Army women, but there was no discussion of the disciplinary problems caused by men, though it was widely known that men presented much higher rates of indiscipline.

Worse was the report's timing. Jimmy Carter had just defeated Gerald Ford in the race for the presidency, and no study, however valid, would have altered the president-elect's commitment to the feminist movement. "I am fully committed to equality between men and women in every area of government and in every aspect of life," declared candidate Carter in July 1976. As president, he recited the same oath of commitment to securing for women "every choice" and an "equal role" whenever the occasion, and the women around him called for him to do so.

The Carter administration vigorously supported any program that White House feminists thought would advance their cause, from special federal grants to schools that provided "nonsexist" education and girl's football teams, to programs under the Comprehensive Employment and Training Act (CETA) that trained and encouraged women to become plumbers and welders instead of secretaries or nurses. The president and First Lady also took a very active role in pushing the states to ratify the stalled ERA, so much so that Phyllis Schlafly accused the Carters of violating the constitutional doctrine of separation of powers. The Carters personally telephoned pro-ERA state legislative leaders to offer encouragement and sometimes to dangle federal funds as a lure for ratification. When these efforts failed and time ran out on the proposed amendment, Carter met monthly with pro-ERA leaders to plan strategy to win an extension.

Feminists could not have asked for a more loyal president, but they might have asked for a more effective one. Carter's biggest help to their cause was his personal program of affirmative action whereby he appointed women, always ardent feminists, to high-level government positions. Of his 2,110 political appointments, 22 percent went to women, including twenty-eight federal judges, four cabinet heads, three undersecretaries, twenty assistant secretaries, five heads of federal agencies, and thirteen ambassadors. Heading up this network of federal feminists was Sarah Weddington, special assistant to the president for women's affairs, chairwoman of the Interdepartmental Task Force on Women, and publisher of a newsletter touting administration achievements for women and of a network directory, *Your Guide to More Than 400 Top Women in the Federal Government*.

The Defense Department was by no means exempt from the infiltration of feminists. Those near the top in the Pentagon included: Kathleen Carpenter as deputy assistant secretary of defense for equal opportunity; Deanne Siemer as Defense Department general counsel; Antonia Handler Chayes as undersecretary of the Air Force for manpower, reserve affairs, and installations; Jill Wine Volner and Sara Elisabeth Lister as general counsel of the Army; Mitzi M. Wertheim as deputy undersecretary of the Navy; Patricia A. Szervo as deputy general counsel of the Navy; and Mary M. Snavely-Dixon as deputy assistant secretary of the Navy for manpower. None of the above had ever served in the military. Most had no connection with the Defense Department before 1977. All were committed to expanding opportunities for military women even if it meant drafting women for combat.

Not all feminists in the Pentagon were women, however. Both Secretary of Defense Harold Brown and Secretary of the Army Clifford J. Alexander, Jr., distinguished themselves by expanding the prerogatives and privileges of military women. One week after taking office, Secretary Brown ordered an appraisal of women in the services. The task fell to another man much impressed with modern women, Navy Commander Richard W. Hunter. In the course of his study, Hunter consulted Martin Binkin and Shirley Bach, who were already at work on an independent study of the same issue. Binkin was a fellow at the Brookings Institution, a liberal think tank in Washington, D.C., for which Hunter had worked in the early 1970s while on loan from the Navy. Bach was a lieutenant colonel on loan to Brookings from the Air Force. Their study, though unfinished, had piqued the interest of the new civilian chiefs in the Pentagon, for they already knew that the study would conclude that the services could make greater use of women.

> The honeymoon was over, and the debilitating effects of integration had begun to show.

Based largely upon the findings of Binkin and Bach, Hunter's report, entitled *Use of Women in the Military*, reduced the entire issue to a simple matter of cost and quality. High-quality female recruits were less expensive to attract than high-quality male recruits, wrote Hunter, and were more desirable than low-quality males. So, to save money and improve the quality of the enlisted force, the services should recruit more women and fewer men. Hunter figured the services could save $1 billion annually by 1982 by doubling the number of women in service. Only two factors might limit the number of women the services could employ: women were physically weaker than men and were excluded from combat. All other arguments against employing more women were dismissed as "centered on emotionalism" or "supported by unsubstantiated generalities, or isolated examples."[1]

The Hunter study gave the Defense Department the green light to expand the number of women in the services, but the study that laid the foundation for all future arguments for women in the military was Binkin and Bach's *Women and the Military*, published by the Brookings Institution later in 1977. The study invalidated a crucial assumption of the Gates Commission—that the population of enlistment-eligible men would increase through the 1970s. Binkin and Bach showed that it had already begun a long decline which would continue into the 1990s. The post–World War II baby boomers were moving out of the ages of eligibility. If the AVF needed to attract one in eleven eligible males in 1977 to maintain a force of two million plus, by 1992 it would need to attract one in eight. On that fact alone, the study concluded that the AVF would be forced to make greater and greater use of women to sustain current levels of manning.[2]

Another important contribution of Binkin and Bach to the integrationist argument concerned the issue of how many women could be absorbed by the services without degrading their ability to accomplish their missions. Given that the military was becoming increasingly dependent upon technology and that the ratio of combat troops to support troops was shrinking, Binkin and Bach figured that women could fill more than 600,000 positions—almost a third of all military jobs—without harmful effect. On the other hand, the statutory ban on women in combat and at sea and the number of women interested in military service made that level of participation unattainable. Binkin and Bach suggested 22 percent as a more realistic level.

Binkin and Bach also argued that women were cheaper to attract, more intelligent, and better behaved than most men. Female recruits scored higher on entrance tests and were more likely to have finished high school and to have had some college. They were also generally older and much less prone to disciplinary problems than men. All of which, argued Binkin and Bach, made them a better investment of defense dollars and better qualified for many of the more technical jobs in the modern military, in which brains were assumed to be more important than brawn.

But the Binkin and Bach study did have its faults. The authors wrongly assumed that the mental quality of female recruits would remain the same no matter how many women were recruited. Later studies would find that as the number of female recruits increased, their "quality" dropped precipitously. When the services were forced to equalize entrance standards for men and women, the advantages of recruiting women over men evaporated. Four years after publication of the Brookings study, women were still older, better behaved, and more likely to have high school diplomas, but test scores had evened out, and dramatically higher rates of attrition among low-quality women made men the better investment.

Naturally the study gave short shrift to all objections to integration. A single chapter handled the problems of attrition, pregnancy, menstruation, physical strength, fraternization, emotional and psychological differences, effects on group performance, and the military's prestige abroad. The study did not touch on the impact of single parents and in-service couples on the services. It did not substantiate the assumption that technology had alleviated the need for physical strength in the many jobs that women were supposed to fill. It ignored evidence that the greater aggressiveness of men is rooted in biology and not solely the product of socialization. It doubted that women interfered with male-bonding in groups, noting that terrorist groups enjoyed intense camaraderie despite the inclusion of female terrorists, a worthwhile observation only if the minds of Carlos the Jackal and G.I. Joe were more similar.

Most problems mentioned in the study were dismissed simply for lack of documented evidence that they actually existed. Again and again the authors confronted the limitations of social science: "Virtually no information is available... evidence is far from conclusive... largely unknown... inadequately researched and poorly understood." An exclusive reliance upon the work of other sociologists led to absurd admissions of ignorance when common sense would have sufficed. "Precious little is known about the effects of combining men and women," the authors wrote. But such holes of knowledge did not prevent Binkin and Bach from drawing optimistic conclusions about the use of women by the services. Though Binkin now insists the study was meant to determine how many women the services *could* employ given the combat exclusion policies, not to recommend how many women the services *should* employ, most of those who used the study never made that distinction.

In the years following the publication of the Binkin and Bach study, the Carter Pentagon tried to "paper over" the holes of knowledge with tests and studies showing the apparent ability of women to perform all kinds of tasks without degrading unit performance. The Army led the way in 1977 with two tests of women in combat support units in a field environment. The first test, called MAX WAC, lasted only three days, hardly enough time to evaluate any unit for any purpose properly. The second test, called REF WAC 77, lasted ten days and employed fifty "observers" to evaluate the effects of integration during RE-FORGER operations in West Germany. A number of difficulties were observed during the test. First, 29 percent of the women assigned to units scheduled to participate in the test were excused from going to the field for "personal reasons," as opposed to 15 percent of the men. Many of the women who did participate were not required to perform much of the physical labor of loading and unloading trucks and setting up and tearing down equipment. The women complained about the absence of shower facilities and disliked using field-expedient slit-trench latrines. Some refused to leave their tents at night for fear of the dark. Male coworkers resented doing the women's share of heavy lifting and dirty work, and most supervisors identified eighteen support specialties as being too physically demanding for women. Still, the official bottom line of both MAX WAC and REF WAC was that no evidence had been found that women worsened the performance of units in the field.

Another test designed to support the Carter administration's policy of expansion was the Army's Female Artillery Study conducted in 1979. Thirteen handpicked female volunteers, all over 110 pounds, were given extensive physical conditioning and additional training and were then tested on their ability as gun crews to meet standard rates of fire for 105mm and 155mm howitzers. The study's conclusion, as summarized later by the Department of Defense, was that the women "showed the ability and aptitude to perform all the artillery assignments *given them*."[3] (Emphasis added.) In other words, the women achieved the standard rates of fire.

If achieving minimum standard rates of fire were all that gun crews are required to do, the Army's artillery study might have served a legitimate purpose. But gun crews are tested on their ability to do much more. One common task is called a "hipshoot." A battery on the move is suddenly ordered to stop and fire a few rounds down range. Each crew must hurriedly emplace the gun, unload the ammunition, fire the mission, and pack it all back up. Speed is essential, and physical strength is a must. The women were not required to emplace or move their guns, or even to unload their ammunition. They were tested only on their ability to adjust elevation and deflection by means of a handcrank, load a round into the breech, close the breech block, and pull the lanyard. The test was conducted under ideal conditions, without the strain of combat or fatigue or simple boredom. Even so, only pairs of the tallest women were able to perform the test's most difficult task, loading the ninety-five pound projectile into the breech of the 155mm howitzer.

The artillery test's limited scope enabled the Carter Pentagon to marvel at yet another demonstration of female ability and to help persuade Congress to repeal the combat exclusion laws. Armed with a battery of such studies, Secretary of Defense Harold Brown, in 1978, ordered the services to double the number of women in uniform to 200,000—11 percent of the total force—by 1983. The following year, 1979, the goal was raised to 236,000 by 1984 and 265,500 by 1987. This meant 99,000 women for the Army, 53,700 women for the Navy, 9,600 for the Marine Corps, and 103,200 for the Air Force. The Air Force would have both the most women and the highest percentage of women: 18.7 percent.

The Air Force presented the least resistance to expansion. Only 10 percent of all Air Force personnel billets were closed to women under Section 8549, Title 10, U.S. Code, which prohibited Air Force women from flying combat missions. Fewer jobs in the Air Force than in the other services involved physically demanding work, and most jobs had a relatively pleasant work environment. Not surprisingly, it had the least difficulty attracting female recruits. From 1977 to 1980 the Air Force added twenty thousand women to its rolls, a 50 percent increase. By 1981 women made up 11 percent of the Air Force's enlisted force and 9 percent of its officer corps.

Most advances for Air Force women under the Carter administration affected only officers. Since women were barred by Title 10 from flying combat missions, the Air Force had not trained women for flight duty. The Carter administration quickly persuaded the Air Force to change its mind and begin training female officers as both pilots and navigators. The Air Force also began assigning women to all-female Titan II missile crews and was under pressure to open Minuteman crews to women.

In the rush for expansion, the Air Force disappointed the Carter administration only once. In 1979 it closed the security specialist field to women after a three-year test program showed exceptionally high rates of attrition among female security specialists. Less than half of the women admitted to the field remained after one year, compared to 71 percent of the men. The closing brought howls of protest from administration feminists, but the field was not reopened until 1982, by the Reagan administration.

Unlike the Air Force, the Navy presented formidable obstacles to increasing its number of women. From 1972 to 1977 the number of enlisted women in the Navy had already more than tripled. Since Section 6015, Title 10, U.S. Code, barred Navy women from serving aboard ship, they were concentrated in the Navy's "rotational base" of shore billets. This meant fewer billets open to Navy men when they returned from sea duty and therefore more time at sea. The Carter administration's solution was to open sea duty to women.

The Navy had experimented with women aboard ship before. In 1972 the unconventional Admiral Elmo R. Zumwalt, then chief of naval operations, authored the notorious "Z-grams," which ordered sweeping changes in the Navy way of doing

As the number of female recruits increased, their "quality" dropped precipitously.

things. The promulgation of Z-gram 116 would open the door for Navy women to a host of opportunities in the civil engineers' corps, the chaplains' corps, naval ROTC, and command of shore units. Z-gram 116 also initiated an experiment involving 424 Navy men and 53 thoroughly screened volunteer Navy women aboard the hospital ship *Sanctuary*. Publicly, the Navy claimed the test went very well, but press reports and the Navy's own official report told another story. The ship was under way for only forty-two days of the four hundred-day test, and while the women performed most of their shipboard duties well, they often required the assistance of men to perform physically demanding tasks. Romantic relationships developed between crew members, several women became pregnant, and public displays of affection, or PDA, were demoralizingly common. "The situation was becoming serious and was definitely detrimental to the good order and discipline of the ship's company," reported the ship's commanding officer. A ban on PDA was announced, and the ship's company assumed a more professional appearance, which satisfied the commanding officer that all was well.[4]

The Navy itself, however, was not so easily satisfied. Many senior officers, including the director of the Women's Naval Reserve, doubted whether the *Sanctuary* experiment proved anything except that putting women on ships would cause problems that the captains could very well do without. A commanding officer also had to consider the reaction of Navy wives, many of whom were opposed to women on ships for obvious reasons. It seems that everyone, except Martin Binkin and Shirley Bach, knew enough about men and women to predict what would happen on a sunny cruise through the South Pacific. The *Sanctuary* spent most of its time in port as a floating dispensary before being quietly decommissioned in 1975.

To the Carter administration, however, no inconvenience justified limiting the opportunities of a handful of women. In 1977, to make room for more women, the Department of the Navy sponsored an amendment to Title 10 to permit women to serve permanently aboard noncombat ships such as hospital, transport, and supply ships, and temporarily (up to six months) aboard all other ships. In 1978 the amendment was added to the Defense Authorization Act of 1979, which was still under consideration by Congress when a federal district court in Washington, D.C., threatened to preempt the democratic process by judicial fiat. In the case of *Owens* v. *Brown*, a group of Navy women seeking assignment aboard ship brought a class-action suit against the Department of Defense. In July 1978 Judge John J. Sirica of Watergate fame ruled that the statutory ban on women at sea wrongly denied women their right of equal protection under the Fourteenth Amendment of the U.S. Constitution. The ban, wrote Sirica, "tends to suggest a statutory purpose more related to the traditional way of thinking than to the demands of military preparedness." His assumption was that traditional ways of thinking about the sexes never justified democratic legislation and were always unconstitutional. Sirica dismissed all practical reasons for wanting to keep women off ships, saying, "whatever problems might arise from integrating shipboard crews are matters that can be dealt with through appropriate training and planning." He stopped short of ordering the Navy to integrate its ships, however, noting imminent approval of pending legislation.

In the summer of 1978 Admiral James L. Holloway, Chief of Naval Operations, issued a call for Navy women to volunteer for sea duty, and in November, the first female sailors were piped aboard the repair ship *Vulcan*. Within a year, the *Vulcan* was christened the "Love Boat" by the press, when three pregnant sailors were returned to shore before the ship had even put to sea.

The Navy's female enlisted strength increased 53 percent from 1977 to 1980. Very few of them volunteered for sea duty. Later, when the call for volunteers failed to provide as many enlisted women as the Navy had hoped, the Navy was forced to send women to sea involuntarily.

In the same three years, the Marine Corps' female enlisted strength almost doubled, though the number of women Marines remained relatively small. Since a greater proportion of Marines were considered combat troops and Marine units went to sea aboard combat ships, the Marine Corps was better able to defend its desire to keep down the total number of women. By 1980 women still made up only 3.7 percent of enlisted Marines and 2.7 percent of officers, the lowest levels among the services.

The Army, however, was in some ways more vulnerable to expansion than even the Air Force. No law excluded Army women from combat. When the exclusion laws were written in 1948, the authors could easily keep Navy and Air Force women out of combat by keeping them off ships and aircraft, but they could not decide where to draw the line with the Army. That task was left to the secretary of the Army, with the understanding that Congress intended combat to be off-limits to women. For twenty-five years, the Army had lived by the understanding, making sure women were kept as far as possible from the battlefield.

The influx of women into the Army in the early 1970s forced women into many jobs and units previously closed to them, so that by the time of the Korean emergency in 1976, women were already serving in units which operated regularly within the wartime "combat zone," defined by Army doctrine as anywhere forward of the rear boundary of a corps in the field. But when the Carter administration proposed further increases in the number of women, Army leaders balked, raising the issue of combat. Soon calls came from Carter appointees in the Department of the Army and the Defense Department for a new definition of the word *combat*. War had changed, said many who had never known it. There were no more friendly lines or enemy lines, they argued; the modern battlefield was much more fluid.

Did this mean that the Army needed a broader, more inclusive definition of combat? Or that units which once operated safely behind friendly lines should be closed to women because they were now endangered by the fluid nature of modern combat? On the contrary, the same civilians who argued that war was now more fluid also argued that war was now more technical, more tidy, and thus more suitable for women. Modern war meant pushing buttons in an air-conditioned bunker. Since decades of typing orders had proved that women could push buttons as well as men, the new definition of combat, said the activists, must allow for expanding the role of women in the Army.

To do so, the definition of combat was narrowed drastically. It no longer made any reference to boundaries or distances. It had nothing to do with where one was in relation to the enemy or how close to the fighting. The single definitive factor of the new term *combat* was an individual or unit's primary duty or mission. If a soldier's primary duty was to engage the enemy with lethal force, he was considered a combat soldier; a unit with the same primary mission was designated a combat unit. As for women, the Army's new combat exclusion policy stated: "Women will be excluded from units and positions which have as their primary mission or function crewing or operating direct or indirect fire weapons."[5] This policy allowed the Army to make the widest possible use of women while still pretending that congressional intent and the will of the American people protected them from combat.

The only issue remaining concerned the size of the unit to be included in combat. Infantry and armored divisions could have been considered combat units, as indeed they always had been, because they exist only to maneuver against and engage the enemy. On the other hand, the Army's 1978 Evaluation of Women in the Army (EWITA), interested primarily in expanding opportunities for women, defined a unit as any element company-size or smaller and recommended opening thousands of positions in maneuver battalions, excluding women from only 20 of the Army's 350 Military Occupation Specialties (MOS). The Army ultimately decided to bar women from combat units battalion-sized and smaller, a policy so liberal that if it had been in effect in World War II, women would have parachuted into Normandy.

During the Carter years, the Army's female enlisted strength increased 40 percent. At the end of 1980 the Army had more women than any other service, with 61,351 enlisted women (9.1 percent of its enlisted strength) and 7,609 female officers. Some support units were as much as 40 percent female.

By now, only 4 percent of enlisted specialties were closed to women by the new combat exclusion policy, with no limits on the number of women who could enlist. Potential female recruits were encouraged to select nontraditional career fields, and many were steered into a nontraditional MOS when they were told that their first choice was not available. The deactivation of the Women's Army Corps (WAC) in 1978 and the administrative integration of women into the regular Army brought Army women as close as they have ever come toward absolute equality with Army men. Even basic training was integrated at the squad level.

The Army would have added even more women if it had been able to recruit them. It was the only service that failed to meet the Carter administration's recruitment quotas for women. Since high-quality women were not as easy to attract as Binkin and Bach had predicted, the Army twice lowered its standards for female recruits. In 1979, after Army General Counsel Jill Wine Volner settled out of court a suit brought by the American Civil Liberties Union (ACLU), the Army equalized entrance standards for men and women, dropping the requirement for women to have a high-school diploma. It also made available to women special enlistment options like the buddy plan, which allowed three or four recruits to enlist together for the same training and assignment.

Recruiting barely improved. The Army fell short of its quotas for women in three consecutive years, from 1978 to 1980. It achieved 91.5 percent of its 1979 goal and 95 percent of its 1980 goal, once it began accepting women without high school diplomas. Later, the Army realized that its attempts to channel women into nontraditional jobs had turned many women away. Women of both high and low quality preferred jobs with no heavy lifting, no dirty fingernails, no days in the motor pool, no rainy nights in the field. Of all the services except the Marine Corps, the Army had more to offer of just such discomforts, and the recruiter's pitch could hide only so much.

Nevertheless, the ease with which the Army, unhindered by Title 10, was able to make room for women was an inspiration to women's rights activists in the Pentagon. As early as February 1978 the Defense Department formulated a proposal to repeal the statutory combat exclusions. In May 1979 Deanne Siemer, the Defense Department's general counsel, sent a letter to Thomas "Tip" O'Neill, Speaker of the House of Representatives, offering to submit legislation to amend Title 10 and repeal the combat exclusions. The offer was later backed by Defense Secretary Harold Brown.

Much had changed since 1967, when Congress and the Department of Defense had assured each other that having women in the services would not mean sending them into combat. And even in 1979 the ultimate goal of feminists in the Pentagon—putting women in the infantry—was too much for Congress and the general public. The request for repeal was draped with assurances that women would not be placed in direct combat roles; it would only grant the secretaries of the Navy and the Air Force the same authority already vested in the secretary of the Army.

During hearings held in November 1979 Defense Department representatives testified that the need to provide greater "flexibility and efficiency" in the use of military manpower was the primary reason for requesting repeal, although repeal was also a matter of fairness and equality.

> The Army's women-in-combat policy is so liberal that, if it had been in effect in WWII, women would have parachuted into Normandy.

The weight of testimony, and the persons giving it, suggest that things were actually the other way around. Anytime the Defense Department is allied with the ACLU, something is likely to be wrong. The Defense Department's Kathleen Carpenter, deputy assistant secretary of defense for equal opportunity, had earned a reputation as "the unguided missile" of the Defense Department. Carpenter once told author George Gilder in an interview that "while men have greater upper-body strength, women have greater midsection strength," so the services were restructuring jobs to make better use of the female midsection, thereby "enriching the work experience for all."[6]

Flexibility and efficiency received only brief mention before being abandoned in favor of an endless refrain of careerism and equality. "There must be policy changes to assure women that they can satisfy personal career goals and ambitions by moving up the ladder to senior management," argued Antonia Handler Chayes, undersecretary of the Air Force. "What we achieve by barring women from combat roles is an obstacle to career advancement."[7]

On the other side of the issue was a hastily organized battery of witnesses, called to arms in just four days by Phyllis Schlafly's Eagle Forum, the organization that had led the STOP ERA movement. Besides Schlafly herself and retired Army Brigadier General Andrew J. Gatsis, Eagle Forum's military advisor, witnesses against repeal of the combat exclusions included General William C. Westmoreland, former Army Chief of Staff; Admiral Jeremiah A. Denton, Jr., a former prisoner of war in Vietnam and future senator from Alabama; Dr. Harold M. Voth, a psychiatrist with the Menniger Foundation and an admiral in the Naval Reserve; and Brigadier General Elizabeth P. Hoisington, a former director of the WAC.

Dismissing the supposed need for flexible and efficient use of manpower as a fig leaf for the feminist agenda, Schlafly's witnesses concentrated their fire on the issue of women in combat. They repeatedly referred in their testimony to James Webb's article "Women Can't Fight," which had just appeared in the November issue of *The Washingtonian* magazine. Of the Carter administration's efforts to prove that women could fight, Hoisington said, "Studies cannot duplicate the realism of battle in a Vietnam jungle, in the cold Korean hills, the trauma from killing or witnessing death and terrible wounds."[8] Mrs. Schlafly targeted the politics behind the Defense Department's campaign for sexual equality. "What a way to run the armed forces!" she said. "We must be the laughing stock of the world."[9]

The subcommittee closed the book on the request for repeal. The antirepeal side had won, but they would not know how important their victory was until two years later.

Undaunted, the Carter administration tried again in January 1980. Two events—the takeover of the American embassy in Teheran and the Soviet invasion of Afghanistan—caused the Carter administration its first serious concern for the nation's security. In his 1980 State of the Union address, President Carter called for registering young men for selective service. When the request went forward to Congress one week later, the legislation included young women on an equal basis with young men. In defense of the request, Carter stated, "There is no distinction possible, on the basis of ability or performance, that would allow me to exclude women from an obligation to register.... My decision to register women is a recognition of the reality that both men and women are working members of our society."

Having just heard numerous witnesses denounce the Carter administration's understanding of women and war, the House Armed Services Committee defeated by voice vote a motion to include women in the bill.

In the Senate, however, feminist activists pressured Senator Nancy Kassebaum of Kansas to sponsor an amendment to include women in the Senate version of the bill, but before the Senate could hold hearings on the bill, Schlafly's Eagle Forum had formed the Coalition Against Drafting Women, consisting of prominent military, religious, and civic leaders, and had collected 200,000 signatures on "Don't Draft Women" petitions.[10]

The inclusion of women found more friends in the Senate but not enough. After hearings and debate, the Kassebaum amendment was defeated fifty-one to forty in June 1980.[11]

Both the ACLU and NOW had testified in favor of requiring women to register. Although both opposed registration and the draft on principle, they regarded a men-only draft as a greater evil. The difference, they said, was between a law that was evenly unjust and one that was unevenly unjust. When a men-only registration law was enacted, the ACLU assembled sixteen draft-age males to file a class-action suit in federal court challenging the constitutionality of the law on the grounds that it discriminated on the basis of sex. Not to be outflanked, Eagle Forum assembled sixteen draft-age women, who opposed a genderless draft and petitioned the same court for the opportunity to present opposing arguments.

Then, to everyone's surprise, a federal district court in Philadelphia exhumed a ten-year-old unresolved suit involving two men who had challenged the constitutionality of the draft law in 1971, using the same argument of sex discrimination.

The suit had been tabled by the court when the draft was discontinued in 1973 and had remained inactive until 1980, when draft registration resumed. In July the three-judge panel in Philadelphia ruled in favor of the plaintiffs, and the case of *Rostker v. Goldberg* was brought to the U.S. Supreme Court on appeal.

The defense of the men-only registration law before the Supreme Court was officially the responsibility of the Justice Department, which, under the Carter administration, was less than enthusiastic about the task. *U.S. News & World Report* noted that "some Justice Department officials hope the Supreme Court strikes down the draft-registration law that their agency is formally defending." Defense of the law fell upon the brief of Eagle Forum's sixteen young women, filed by eminent constitutional lawyer Nathan Lewin as an *amicus curiae*.

NOW filed its own *amicus* brief calling the men-only draft law "blatant and harmful discrimination" against women. The NOW brief held nothing back, however implausible. Excluding women from the draft, NOW argued, deprives women of "politically maturing experiences," consigns women to a second-class status, increases "the incidence of rape and domestic violence," and "causes harm to women by increasing the prospect of violence in their daily lives."

With the fate of all future generations of American women in the balance, the nation's media were conspicuously silent. Only the *Washington Post* seemed interested. Members of Congress showed greater concern. While the Court deliberated, they moved to fix the case by proposing legislation to withdraw jurisdiction from all federal courts over laws and regulations treating men and women differently with regard to military service. A finding against the government might have inspired the first serious check of judicial power in the history of the Constitution.

In June 1981 the Supreme Court reversed the lower court's decision and ruled that the men-only registration law was constitutional. The majority opinion written by Justice William Rehnquist reasoned that men and women were "not similarly situated" because women were barred from combat by Title 10 of the U.S. Code. A dissenting opinion filed by Justice Byron White, joined by Justice William Brennan, argued that men and women were similarly situated with regard to noncombat positions that would also have been filled by a draft.[12]

To feminists, the ruling was "tragic" and "outrageous." The ACLU called it "a devastating loss for women's rights and civil rights generally." Eleanor Smeal, then president of NOW, said the Court had "taken away our voice of protest. We can't even say, 'Hell no, we won't go.'"

To Phyllis Schlafly and the unbeatable Eagle Forum, it was another brilliant victory, but one which, to their surprise, hinged upon their earlier victory against repeal of the combat exclusion laws. No one had guessed that the desire of a tiny minority of female officers to fill combat slots in peacetime would have made all women subject to compulsory military service and possibly combat duty in time of war.

Chapter 6

DACOWITS 1, ARMY 0

> *Our Army is not a "corporation." Defending this*
> *nation is not an "occupation." And being a soldier*
> *is not a "job." There is no other business firm any-*
> *where that has, as its foremost objective, the*
> *requirement to fight and win the land battle.*

—COLONEL DANDRIDGE MALONE,
AN ARMY OF EXCELLENCE

IN EARLY NOVEMBER 1980, Ranger Class 2-81 bid good-bye to the world and disappeared into the woods of Fort Benning, Georgia. The class was composed of a few junior enlisted men assigned to the Army's two Ranger battalions and many more brand-new second lieutenants, mostly infantrymen and West Point graduates of the Class of 1980. For the next three months, they would have no rank, no names, no rest, and nearly no news from the outside.

At ten o'clock in the evening of the first long day, the class was struggling to stay alert after hours of classroom instruction in patrolling when a bull-faced Ranger instructor stepped forward and announced that Ronald Reagan had just defeated Jimmy Carter in the presidential election. The class erupted into a riot of fist-pounding, boot-stomping, hat-throwing, war-whooping joy. While their instructors stood by grinning, the would-be Ranger lieutenants and privates abandoned military courtesy and classroom decorum to join each other in cheering the defeat of their commander-in-chief.

No president before him earned less respect from the uniformed men than Jimmy Carter. From the top down, the American military disliked Carter for his weak personal bearing, timid foreign policy, opposition to defense improvements, and putting politics before military preparedness. At last, the chiefs of staff could candidly address the problems that confronted them, not the least of which was the hasty expansion of the role of women.

The United States entered the 1980s leading the world in the use of women in the military. In ten years the number of women in the military had increased sixfold. In 1981 women accounted for 14 percent of all new recruits and 9 percent of the total force. Numbers aside, American military women were more widely employed than military women anywhere else: 95 percent of all military jobs were open to them, and 28.5 percent of all women were employed in nontraditional jobs. In every possible way, the Defense Department had attempted to equalize the treatment of men and women, so that by 1981 all of the services except the Marine Corps had integrated basic training. No other country had gone so far.

While Jimmy Carter was in office, the nation's top military leaders were under great pressure to portray integration and expansion as completely successful and to support repeal of the combat exclusions. Dissent was not tolerated. Carter had chastised General Donn A. Starry for speaking too plainly about the Soviet threat in Europe and fired Major General John K. Singlaub for criticizing the president's proposed troop withdrawal from Korea. But though the services were officially muzzled, the civilian press turned up story after story exposing problems with integration. Letters to the editor from female service members complained of being "defeminized to the point of depression." Junior officers complained that fraternization and pregnancy were increasingly common. One article reported that nearly half the women assigned to a military police company in Germany had become pregnant within nine months, although only two of the nine women were married. Publicly, the Army advised commanders to treat pregnancy as a temporary disability and to work around it as they would work around casualties or desertions in wartime. Privately, Army commanders complained to the chief of staff, General Edward C. "Shy" Meyer, that something had to be done.

Meyer himself was well aware of the problems with integration. As commanding general of the 3rd Infantry Division in 1975, he had witnessed the dismay and confusion of officers and NCOs when the first batches of women were dumped into unprepared combat support units. Soon after taking over as chief of staff in 1979, Meyer had asked a trusted personal friend, retired Lieutenant General Arthur S. Collins, Jr., to take a firsthand look at the Army in the field and assess its condition. Author of the book *Common Sense Training*, Collins was widely respected for his insight and judgment. His informal report added other problems to those raised during the 1980 Commanders' Conference and strengthened suspicions that the presence of women was sapping the Army's strength.

Meyer did not wait for Jimmy Carter to leave office before advising Defense Secretary Harold Brown and Army Secretary Clifford Alexander that a thorough review of women in the Army was needed before proceeding toward the Carter administration's goal of 87,000 enlisted women in the Army by 1986. Brown and Alexander acquiesced unenthusiastically in the fall of 1980 to Meyer's proposal to freeze the strength of Army women at 65,000 until a review had been completed. One month after Reagan's inauguration, formal notice of the Army's freeze, or "pause" as it was called, was delivered to the new defense secretary, Caspar W. Weinberger. In May 1981 Meyer established the Women in the Army (WITA) Policy Review Group, a four-man, one-woman team of handpicked Army experts. Their initial report would take a full eighteen months to prepare.

Shortly thereafter, the Defense Department initiated its own study of women in the services, adding to the public impression that the Reagan administration was out to roll back Carter plans for women. In March 1981 Deputy Secretary of Defense Frank C. Carlucci directed the services to conduct a joint background review on the impact of present and projected numbers of women on readiness and on the ability of the services to accomplish their missions. Completed in October, the review confirmed the existence of a number of problems that commanders in the field already knew too much about. Women suffered higher rates of attrition, medical "noneffectiveness," and out-of-wedlock pregnancies. There was a rapidly growing number of couples with both partners in the service, about a third with children. Women were not suited for physically demanding duties and were more prone to injury than men. They joined the services for different reasons than men and were not attracted to nontraditional jobs. Both their morale and their opinion of the services were lower than the men's.

Yet the background review tried hard to minimize the seriousness of these problems. Not enough was known about their impact on the military, said the review, echoing Binkin and Bach's *Women and the Military*. There was "no concrete evidence" that single parenthood adversely affected readiness. The testimony of officers in the field did not count unless it was backed by some study, and most of the available studies were the work of the Carter administration: MAX WAC, REF WAC, and a number of other ideologically tainted works were all given the benefit of the doubt in the absence of anything else. Data collected by the Carter administration were accepted at face value, though they had sometimes been manipulated to support established policy. The background review used the Army's tally to conclude that single parenthood was not "a female issue" because men accounted for three-quarters of all single parents. It did not point out that the Army under Carter had included servicemen paying child support in its tally of single parents and that Navy statistics showed that women were seven times more likely than men to be single parents *with custody* of their children.[1]

The background review did make several original contributions to the study of women in the military, though these were not noted in the review's executive summary: as the services concentrated on recruiting more and more women, the proportion of male high school graduates dropped. In 1972 the services attracted 17 percent of all eligible men with high school diplomas; by 1980 they were attracting only 13 percent. Only the Marine Corps had concentrated on recruiting "a few good men," and only the Marine Corps had increased its share of the market.

Also not noted in the executive summary was the discovery that, for the second time in the history of the AVF, the experts had been fundamentally wrong in their assumptions and predictions. Just as the Gates Commission had wrongly assumed that the supply of eligible males would increase through the 1970s, the experts at the Brookings Institution had wrongly expected that the advantages of recruiting women would endure regardless of how many women were recruited.

Women on average were still older than men, but, said the review, "all other selected characteristics have either narrowed or been reversed." Binkin and Bach had figured that women were cheaper to enlist because they were less likely to be married and therefore have dependents, but the review found that by 1980 female recruits were more likely than males to be married. Commander Hunter had argued that women were higher quality recruits. But as entrance standards were lowered, test scores among female recruits plummeted until there was "no appreciable difference" between the scores of men and women. Women were still more likely to have graduated from high school, but the percentages of men and women in the lowest mental category were very nearly the same.

The only remaining advantage was that women were better behaved and missed fewer duty days for medical reasons than men missed for disciplinary reasons. Even this was not true for the service that made the greatest use of women. Air Force women had slightly higher rates of absenteeism, courts-martial, and desertion than Air Force men. Comparing the number of duty days lost by both men and women for all reasons, the Air Force figured, "If the FY 1980 force were all male, end-strength could be reduced over 600 spaces. FY 1986, end-strength cost of female nonavailability will be more than 1000 spaces."[2] All told, the Air Force expected to incur additional costs of $20 million to $30 million a year to meet the Carter administration's 1986 objective for female strength. The background review's executive summary did not mention this additional cost.

Though the background review did recommend that the services be given greater latitude to establish their own policies regarding women, that latitude was not meant for anything other than minor adjustments to accommodate further expansion. Clearly there were still those in the Defense Department who were more concerned about integration's political sensitivity than about the services. The review was, in fact, prepared by the office of Dr. Lawrence J. Korb, who, after leaving the Defense Department, joined the liberal Brookings Institution and became an outspoken proponent of expanded use of women in the military.

Unlike the background review, the Army's WITA Policy Review Group was charged with the dual task of reviewing the issues and formulating policy. General Meyer's dictum was that the Army should be prepared to go to war tomorrow with what it had today. Sometimes members of the review group doubted whether their recommendations would be politically acceptable, but they never doubted Meyer's desire that they confine themselves to considering what was for the good of the service.

To narrow its focus, the review group began by categorizing issues related to women into those which were institutional and those which were "soldier specific." Institutional issues were those that involved all soldiers. They included problems with attrition, clothing, hygiene, medical care, child care, being a single parent, physical ability, lost time, career development, and sexual harassment, though many of these were never considered problems until integration. Soldier specific issues were those that resulted directly from integration. They were further categorized as those specific to women only and those relating to men and women together. Initially only pregnancy was considered "female specific," but later the review group added combat exclusion policies. Male and female issues included fraternization and intra-Army and interservice marriages.

The WITA Policy Review Group referred all of the institutional and male-female issues to other Army staff activities, except the issue of physical requirements for the Army's many Military Occupational Specialties (MOS). A brief examination of the problem of pregnancy revealed that 16 percent (10,577) of Army women were pregnant in 1980. Defense

No president before him earned less respect from the uniformed men than Jimmy Carter.

Department policy prohibited pregnant women from entering service, but if a woman became pregnant after entering, the option to stay in or get out was hers. Of the Army women who became pregnant in 1980, one-third aborted their babies at their own expense and remained in the Army, a third chose to have their babies and remain in the Army, and a third chose to leave the Army. The review group noted that the commanders believed that pregnancy weakened the Army's mission and that the peacetime Army was unprepared for war, but because the policy on pregnancy had been established by the Defense Department, the issue was out of Army hands. The review group therefore confined its work to the issues of physical abilities and combat exclusions.

The problem with the Army's combat exclusion policy was that it did not exclude anyone from combat. The definition of combat upon which the exclusion policies were based did exactly the opposite of what was intended: it limited job opportunities for women in the Army without providing women much protection from danger. The authors of the Army's 1978 combat exclusion policy had ignored the realities of war, in which many soldiers assigned to so-called "noncombat" jobs work shoulder-to-shoulder with others assigned to "combat" jobs. Intelligence personnel operate ground surveillance radars collocated with front-line grunts, engineers are responsible for blowing bridges after combat units have withdrawn to the rear, and military police are often the last to leave an evacuated area. At the same time, many dangerous Army jobs have safe-sounding civilian job titles. An Army plumber, for instance, is responsible for laying and clearing minefields and priming and emplacing explosives. Supply and communications personnel work with combat troops near the frontlines. The realities of the battlefield made the Army's MOS-based combat exclusion policy nonsensical. Women could not serve in specialties primarily responsible for killing the enemy, but they could serve in specialties that exposed them to an equal opportunity of being killed.

In July 1981 an Army survey of women in the United States V Corps in West Germany found 175 women assigned to units operating forward of friendly lines, in constant contact with the enemy; 727 women were assigned to units operating in the Main Battle Area. A total of 3,799 women were assigned to units operating in the "combat zone," a pre-1978 Army designation.

To restore some integrity to its policy, the Army had two choices: it could drop the combat exclusions and admit that women were already filling combat roles; or it could make the combat exclusions meaningful by removing women from all combat-related jobs. The first option was politically impossible. Congress could not admit to the American people that it was allowing the Army to commit young women to mortal combat. And even if the Army were allowed to drop the combat exclusions, it would still have wanted to exclude women from certain vital units for reasons of efficiency and effectiveness—reasons the courts were unlikely to recognize over the demands of "equality."

The second option presented the problem of arbitrariness. If the Army appeared arbitrary in reducing opportunities for women, it left itself open to second-guessing by the courts. The Army's problem was to devise a method of arbitrarily drawing a line between combat and noncombat that did not appear arbitrary. In response, the WITA Policy Review Group created Direct Combat Probability Coding (DCPC), a seemingly scientific way of determining which jobs should be closed to women and which should not.

DCPC involved assessing each and every position in the Army for the probability of its being involved in "direct combat," an ambiguous designation that in practice meant "too dangerous for women." The WITA Policy Review Group made the term official and gave it essentially the same meaning as the term *close combat*:

> ...*engaging an enemy with individual or crew-served weapons while being exposed to direct enemy fire, a high probability of direct physical contact with the enemy's personnel, and a substantial risk of capture.*[2]

To ascertain the probability of direct combat for each position, the WITA Policy Review Group asked the Army's authorities to respond to questions concerning the position's assigned duties, the parent unit's mission, its place on the battlefield, and tactical doctrine. The results would give each position a numerical probability code of 1 to 7. Positions with the highest probability of involving a soldier in direct combat were coded P1, and those with the lowest, a P7.

General Meyer decided that women would be excluded only from positions coded P1, which included 53 percent of Army enlisted positions. Based upon the recommendation of the WITA Policy Review Group, Meyer closed twenty-three specialties, in addition to the thirty-eight already closed to women. Many Army leaders favored a more complete exclusion, but politics made the P1 exclusion, in Meyer's view, the best the Army could do.

The next great accomplishment of the WITA review group was to establish physical strength requirements for each MOS. Army commanders had long complained that women were unable to perform many routine physical tasks associated with their assigned specialties. Their complaints were substantiated by a 1976 study of the utilization of women in the military by the General Accounting Office (GAO). The GAO found that women trained as ammunition storage specialists had trouble handling rounds of ammunition that weighed between 58 and 120 pounds. Female medical specialists assigned as ambulance drivers had trouble loading and unloading patients, braking and steering ambulances, and changing tires on ambulances. Women trained as wheeled-vehicle mechanics faced similar difficulties. When women were unable to perform their routine duties, they were often assigned clerical or administrative duties instead, while male soldiers picked up the slack.

The GAO's recommended solution was simple: gender-free strength testing of potential recruits to enable recruiters to match the man or woman to the MOS. The solution was so simple that the 1978 Evaluation of Women in the Army (EWITA) made the same recommendation, saying, "The Army cannot be assured of accomplishing the ground combat mission if women are randomly accessed into positions with physically demanding tasks exceeding their capabilities."[3] The Defense Department's 1981 background review repeated the recommendation, praising similar tests in use by the Air Force.

In 1981 members of the WITA Policy Review Group verified the GAO's findings with their own eyes. At Aberdeen Proving Grounds, Maryland, they were amazed that women being tested and certified as ammunition handlers appeared to have no trouble moving and sorting large crates of ammunition, until they discovered that the women were moving empty crates because full crates were too heavy for them. At Fort Hood, Texas, they found that more than half of the female track vehicle mechanics assigned to some units were working outside their MOS because they were dissatisfied with the job and frustrated with their inability to perform routine tasks, such as separating the links in a vehicle's track with a sixty-eight–pound track wrench.

The review group then began the task of constructing a means of matching the physical abilities of each recruit, regardless of sex, to the physical requirements of each MOS. It started with the Department of Labor Occupational Classification System, devised in 1939, that divided jobs into five categories according to physical demand: sedentary, light, medium, heavy, and very heavy. Each category was defined as requiring the following:

	Maximum Lifting	Frequent Lifting
Sedentary	10 pounds	—
Light	20	10 pounds
Medium	50	25
Heavy	100	50
Very Heavy	in excess of 100	50

(In time, the sedentary category was deleted, and "moderately heavy"—lifting of eighty pounds and frequent lifting of forty pounds—was added.)

Next, the review group set about categorizing each MOS using four simple physical tasks: lift, carry, push, and pull. After extensive observations and many interviews, the review group assigned 64 percent of the Army's positions to the very heavy category, 12 percent to the heavy, and the remainder were distributed evenly among the moderately heavy, medium, and light categories.

The next step was to develop a test to be administered to potential recruits to determine their ability to meet the physical demands of their preferred MOS. The Military Enlistment Physical Strength Capacity Test (MEPSCAT) consisted of four components: a skinfold measurement to determine body fat content, a hand-strength test using a dynamometer, a dynamic lifting test, and a stress test for cardiovascular fitness.[4]

If valid, the MEPSCAT system offered several advantages to the present practice of randomly assigning recruits to an MOS. Obviously it would provide the Army with soldiers better able to perform their assigned jobs, but the Army also expected the system to reduce attrition, job migration, and "malutilization," especially among women. Forty-nine percent of women in jobs rated heavy and very heavy did not complete their three-year enlistments. Supervisors often assigned them duties unrelated to their MOS, and the women were more likely to change specialties to find less demanding work.

The disadvantage of the MEPSCAT system was that it would concentrate the great majority of women in a fraction of the positions. No job or position would be closed to all women on the basis of physical demands, but tests at Fort Jackson, South Carolina, had shown that very few Army women were likely to be able to perform work rated heavy (8 percent) or very heavy (3 percent). This meant that over 90 percent of Army women would be concentrated in less than a quarter of the Army's positions.

Before the results of WITA were ever announced, the study had found strong enemies. The Army's Recruiting Command was greatly opposed to standards that would make its recruiting goals any more difficult. Besides making it harder for recruiters to please potential recruits with their choice of jobs, the MEPSCAT test would completely disqualify many women who were physically weak. The review group had considered this a plus because it would turn away such women before the Army became liable for injuries they were likely to suffer during training, but the Recruiting Command doubted its ability to achieve recruiting objectives if recruits were required to meet the MEPSCAT standards. Meetings between the Recruiting Command and the WITA Policy Review Group, championed by the deputy chief of staff for personnel, General Maxwell Thurman, were tense contests between the best of both camps. Resident experts from the Recruiting Command picked and poked at any angle of the review they thought vulnerable, while the chief of staff and the vice chief of staff looked on. In the end, the review group prevailed. General Meyer was thoroughly satisfied that the recommendations of the WITA Policy Review Group were for the good of the service.

Implementing the recommendations wouldn't be easy. Hundreds of women held specialties recommended for closing, thousands were assigned to P1 positions, and more than half of all Army women were working in jobs rated heavy or very heavy. But the strongest opposition came from women not in the least affected by the changes, women outside the Army whose concerns were strictly ideological. Leading the fight was DACOWITS.

Excluding women from the theater of operations would expose that they were unnecessary to the military's essential function.

There was no special reason why the Army should have feared the opposition of DACOWITS. The committee's thirty-year career was an unremarkable one, beginning with its failed attempt to draw women into the Korean War. After the war, DACOWITS attracted little attention with modest recommendations for improving the standard of living among servicewomen and for enhancing career incentives for nurses and medical specialists. The military in those days was no longer interested in expanding the ranks of military women, and the directors of the women's components disliked the kibitzing of fifty civilian women with no military experience. DACOWITS survived for many years as little more than an opportunity for the wives of prominent Washington men to hobnob with famous women. Early members included anthropologist Margaret Meade, actress Helen Hayes, Vassar's president Sarah Blanding, and Dr. Lillian Gilbreth, the mother portrayed in the book and movie *Cheaper by the Dozen*.

DACOWITS's one triumph in its early years was the passage of PL 90-130 in 1967, after which the committee's enthusiasm waned rapidly. As the Vietnam War's unpopularity grew, members of DACOWITS lost interest. The year the first women were made generals, only thirty-one of DACOWITS's fifty members bothered to attend its fall meeting. By 1972 DACOWITS had earned a reputation as "a nice little group that doesn't do very much."[5] As a result of its inactivity, its authorized strength shrank from fifty to twenty-five, with only twenty-three actually appointed in 1976.

Another reason for the committee's shrinking membership was the shifting emphasis among DACOWITS members. Radical members wanted revolutionary change within the military and began pushing DACOWITS to become more politically active. "This group has got to become an action group," argued Sarah McClendon, a Washington correspondent and columnist appointed to the committee by the Nixon administration. Complaining that many committee members knew little about the military, McClendon, who had served as a WAC officer in World War II before being discharged for pregnancy, worked to bring in retired female officers who shared her revolutionary dreams. McClendon also agitated to open DACOWITS meetings to the press and public, a move opposed by many of the more conservative committee members who feared becoming a "focal point of the women's rights movement." DACOWITS did open its meetings to the public in late 1973, but only after the radically feminist Center for Women Policy Studies filed suit in federal court to force the issue.

Opened to outside influences, DACOWITS meetings became semi-annual *schutzenfesten*, providing feminist organizations the opportunity to hurl abuse both at the military for oppressing women and at DACOWITS for not doing enough about it. The committee began to make regular headlines in military newspapers not for what committee members said or did, but for what its audience complained about. In 1974 outsiders were already calling for the repeal of the combat exclusion laws and the integration of the service academies. That year, the committee passed on the issue of combat but did recommend that the services begin planning for the "inevitable" integration of the academies. The committee also recom-

mended that the Defense Department submit legislative proposals to Congress to "equalize [promotion] opportunities for
women… regardless of available billets." DACOWITS wanted
more female generals and admirals, whether the services
needed them or not.[6]

Thereafter, the committee's recommendations to the
Defense Department were merely modulated renditions of the
demands of professional feminists. When the Center for
Women Policy Studies complained that the absence of women
at the academies "seriously compromises their military career
opportunities," DACOWITS strengthened its call for the services to integrate the academies without waiting for legislative
authorization. And when NOW complained that enlisted Army
women were handicapped by their inability to win decorations
for battlefield bravery and combat service, DACOWITS asked
the Army to "clarify" its definition of "combat duty" and "combat assignment," with an eye to opening more jobs to women.[7]

The committee's less radical members faded away, and by
1976 the takeover was complete. The feminist minority had
become the majority. In a classic demonstration of the dynamics of revolutionary politics, the former military advisory committee was reborn as an active antimilitary lobby with legislative
and "civic action" subcommittees.

DACOWITS stepped off the deep end in 1976, calling the
combat exclusion laws "arbitrary and unnecessary." Barely two
years after exposing itself to organized feminism, the committee recommended

> [t]hat laws now preventing women from serving their coun-
> try in combat and combat related or support positions be
> repealed. Rationale: Self-explanatory.[8]

In the same meeting, DACOWITS condemned the Veterans of
Foreign Wars for discriminating against women and asked the
Defense Department to sever ties with the organization. It also
asked the services to review their physical standards

*to ascertain if height and physical standards are valid
requirements and necessary for job performance... or
should they be replaced with other job related
qualifications.*[9]

The qualifications the committee had in mind were high-school
diplomas and entrance exam scores, often used as easily measurable proof that women made better soldiers and sailors. The
committee's rationale for this recommendation included the
following:

*In keeping with current changes in the military as well as in
the civilian work world, it has been proven that an individual, regardless of sex, can fulfill the requirements of jobs on
the basis of their capabilities. According to medical science
it is commonly known that women are shorter in height and
have other physical differences but have proven they have
the capabilities to do a given task.*

What has been proved? That, regardless of sex, *all* individuals
can fulfill *all* requirements? Or that *some* individuals can fulfill
the requirements of *some* jobs? And why do thirty prominent
women need "medical science" to tell them what is "commonly
known"? What the committee seemed to be saying was that
women were just as capable as men of doing anything in the
military, their physical limitations notwithstanding. Certainly,
that was what was what was implied in what they said to the edi-
tors of *Air Force Times*, whose report on the event was head-
lined: "Women Can Do Anything Men Can Do."[10]

Ironically, the Carter administration posed a greater threat
to DACOWITS than any other presidential administration. In
its enthusiasm for advancing the cause of women in the military,
the Carter Pentagon hardly seemed to need the advice of
DACOWITS, and DACOWITS feared it would be disbanded
as unnecessary. But as it happened, the Carter administration
bolstered DACOWITS with increased membership appoint-

ments and additional full-time administrative support. Among those appointed in 1977 was retired Air Force Major General Jeanne Holm, a trusted advocate of the advancement of women. As director of the Women's Air Force in 1972, Holm testified before Congress in favor of integrating the service academies, though the directors of the Army, Navy, and Marine Corps women's components testified against it.

During the Carter years, DACOWITS knew no restraint. It called for the assignment of a general officer to head the predominantly female Army Medical Specialist Corps, for no better reason than that without one "the implication is that the corps mission is not as important as other medical corps." It wanted women appointed to the Court of Military Appeals and assigned to Minuteman missile silos. It demanded the elimination of sex bias in recruiting literature, which it faulted for being "predominantly male-oriented." It denounced open bay barracks, cushion-sole boot socks, and the ban on abortion in military hospitals. It endorsed tube socks, private entrances to officer quarters, and the ERA. DACOWITS attacked and tried to suppress the Air Force study upon which it based its decision to close the security specialist field to women. It blamed all of the medical problems that women experienced on poorly designed clothing and equipment and continued to recommend repeal of the combat exclusion laws.

The defeat of Jimmy Carter inspired fears that the Reagan administration would silence DACOWITS by packing the committee with antifeminists. But the committee maintained its ideological continuity partly because members were appointed by the secretary of defense for three-year terms, partly because new members were often selected upon the recommendation of old members, but mostly because the Reagan administration never opposed feminists in any significant way, except on the issue of abortion. Many of the women the Reagan administration appointed were establishment Republicans who, if not self-described feminists, nevertheless supported most feminist aims. Under pressure from senior members of the committee, the audience at DACOWITS meetings, and especially the committee's profeminist military advisors, the new members were quickly caught up in the committee's enthusiasm for radical reform.

Nevertheless, in the early Reagan years, DACOWITS's paranoia manifested itself in new complaints. In 1981 it blamed the services for too successfully promoting the view that women were needed to make the AVF work:

> *The services' focus on the expected shortage of available males in the next 10 years fosters the perception that women are merely "fillers" and not professionals contributing to the defense effort.*[11]

Never mind that DACOWITS had itself done much to foster the same view. It also reported sinking morale among military women, particularly Army women, as a result of "gender specific actions." The Army's "womanpause," as the press rendered it, and the WITA review were of special concern. General Meyer had tried to allay the committee's apprehensions by enlisting several present and former DACOWITS members as advisors to the WITA review group, but the review group had neglected to keep them informed of the review's progress. DACOWITS had no idea where the review was headed. One year after the review was begun, the Army was still keeping DACOWITS in the dark about the physical demands analysis and the combat probability coding. In April 1982 spokesmen for the WITA review group talked instead about problems related to pregnancy, which the review group decided was the responsibility of the Defense Department.

While the Army plotted major policy changes affecting women, the civilian leadership in the Pentagon hastened to assure military women that the Reagan administration was not a threat to their careers and firmly supported equal opportunity for military women. In February 1982 Assistant Secretary of Defense Korb told a group of Navy women that the Defense

Department was working "to break down any institutional barriers that still exist" within the services. In August 1982 the Army's new assistant secretary for manpower and reserve affairs, Harry N. Walters, told DACOWITS that the WITA review would be a "positive thing" for women. Assuring the committee that the Army was still committed to providing women "the same career advancement opportunities" available to men, Walters explained that the Army had "jammed an extra 55,000 women into the system without any thought being given to where they should be assigned." WITA was just trying to "unravel all the problems" caused by the hasty increases. Secretary of Defense Caspar Weinberger, who had been briefed on the results of the review by General Meyer and Army Secretary John O. Marsh, promised DACOWITS chairwoman Maria Elena Torralva that present Army policy would not change until the WITA review was approved by the Defense Department. Torralva was reassured. "I feel much better about what is happening," she told the committee. The study would be "a positive one for women."

> Approximately 90 percent of Army women would be concentrated in less than a quarter of the positions.

No doubt owing to these assurances, the reaction to the release of the WITA Policy Review Group's draft report in late August 1982 was mixed and relatively mild. Carolyn Becraft of the Women's Equity Action League (WEAL) said that the report was better than she expected, that the review needed to be done, and that the Army had responded properly to "political pressure by women, DACOWITS, women's organizations, and press reports." Sarah McClendon was "upbeat" about the report: "The report said women can do the job." Representative Patricia Schroeder of Colorado, a member of the House Armed Services Committee, was more cautious. "Every time there is a new study, it never helps morale," she said. Kathleen Carpenter, deputy secretary of defense for equal opportunity under Carter, called the report's unexplained recommendation that the Army add 5,000 enlisted women and 4,000 female officers a "public relations" move to divert attention from the review's impact.

Three months later, the mood had changed. "DACOWITS Rips Army Women Study," read the headlines in *Army Times*, after a "stormy, confrontational" meeting in November, during which members and spectators railed against Army representatives with charges that the study represented "poor Army management" and was "nothing but a snow job." Sarah McClendon, one of the unused advisors, suddenly wondered "why the hell they wanted us to help." Jeanne Holm told committee members that the study had created morale problems for women who felt the Army was blaming its mistakes on them. An Army enlisted woman said, "I'm not to be blamed for the problems. These are management problems."

Management's attempts to solve its problems were defended by William D. Clark, deputy assistant secretary of the Army for manpower and reserve affairs, and Lieutenant General Maxwell R. Thurman. They argued that WITA suffered from poor public relations, that the methodology employed was reliable, and that, in any case, the study still needed to be validated. If the validation process revealed problems with the study's findings, then changes would be made. Meanwhile the Army would make every effort to smooth the implementation of the recommended changes.

Specific criticisms of the review were fielded by the members of the WITA Policy Review Group themselves. DACOWITS questioned everything, and for everything the review group had an answer. Many of the committee members' criticisms were made out of ignorance of the Army in combat. Margaret M. Scheffelin, an educational researcher charged with spearheading DACOWITS's attacks, could not understand why women were to be excluded from the job of air traffic controller (ATC) when civilian women supposedly made especially good ATCs. Reading from an Army manual describing the duties of an ATC, a member of the review group pointed out that Army ATCs are required to do much more than sit in front of a radar screen. Other duties include clearing airfields and landing zones and erecting runway lighting systems, sometimes behind enemy lines.

By the third day of the meeting, the Army's defense of WITA had been so successful that one member of the committee admitted privately that the Army had managed to "take the wind right out of our sails." But the final report admitted only, "We are extremely concerned about the impact of this study on women in the military and on morale."

In the months following the meeting, members and friends of DACOWITS groped for ways to attack the study. The Labor Department's categorization of jobs according to physical demand was too old to be valid, they said. The sampling of female recruits at Fort Jackson was too small to predict the abilities of Army women accurately, they said. Even if both objections had been true, the Army's determination of strength requirements for specific jobs still stood on its own. The objections continued. One critic complained that the creation of the "moderately heavy" strength category amounted to "statistical sorcery" and that long-range weapons made close, physical contact with the enemy part of the Army's "historical memory, not its current operational concepts."[12] A 1985 study by the Air Force dismissed WITA's findings on physical strength because, it said, the WITA study group had assumed but not proved that soldiers who lacked the strength to perform their assigned tasks actually degraded unit effectiveness.

In April 1983 DACOWITS rallied its disheartened troops at another meeting, from which came recommendations that the Army establish an "objective panel," chaired by a retired female general officer and staffed with active and retired officers and senior noncommissioned officers, "with a predominance of women members." The proposed panel would review the WITA study and report its evaluation directly to the secretary of the Army. Concerned again for the morale of military women, DACOWITS requested that all of the services disseminate articles and reports to the field "showing the positive performance of women in the military." And the executive board would draft a letter to send to the secretary of defense explaining the concern of DACOWITS for WITA's impact on morale and career progression.

Signed by DACOWITS Chairwoman Mary Evelyn Blagg Huey, president of Texas Woman's University, and dated June 6, 1983, DACOWITS's rambling letter abandoned most of the criticism already leveled at the study. Instead, it fell back on the very arguments the committee had accused the services of overusing. WITA's probability-based combat exclusion "deprives our Army of many skilled soldiers" and "reduces available manpower." The effect of the combat exclusions on career development and promotion "poses concerns for morale, enlistments, and the continued success of the all-volunteer Army." And so on.

The only specific criticism was the charge that the Army's definition of "combat" was out of date. Modern combat, said the letter, is "of a fluid—and frequently remote—character." No mention was made of WITA's physical demands analysis, and no fault was found with the review's methodology. Nevertheless, the letter questioned the integrity of the review group and its motives:

> We have serious questions regarding the merit of the continual studying women's military participation. [sic] As a study reaffirms the positive performance and contribution by those of our gender, a new one seems to be ordered. This finally raises the question of whether objectivity or the "right answers" is the purpose.[13]

The letter also requested that a Marine Corps study of women marines be postponed indefinitely.

Secretary Weinberger's reply to Dr. Huey, dated July 27, 1983, was sympathetic and conciliatory. He assured Huey that the Defense Department was committed to ensuring that "women will be provided maximum opportunities to realize their individual potential" and that restrictions on women in the services were based solely on the intent of the combat exclusion laws. Regarding the Army's definition of combat, Weinberger agreed that the nature of combat was fluid, noting that "if hostilities break out, men and women in uniform are at risk no matter where they may be located." Though the Marine Corps study would proceed, Weinberger promised that implementation of any policy affecting women would be closely monitored by Assistant Secretary of Defense Korb to ensure that "artificial or institutional barriers to career progression are systematically broken down."[14]

Weinberger's July 19 memorandum to the service secretaries, enclosed with his letter to Huey, put things more bluntly. Recent press reports, said the memo, had given the impression that the Defense Department had changed its policy toward women. That impression was wrong. Women would be provided full and equal opportunity with men to pursue military careers:

> *This means that military women can and should be utilized in all roles except those explicitly prohibited by combat exclusion statutes and related policy.... The combat exclusion should be interpreted to allow as many as possible career opportunities for women to be kept open.*[15]

The Army might have successfully defended WITA had it not been for two important changes of personnel that occurred before the summer of 1983. "Shy" Meyer retired and was succeeded by General John A. Wickham, Jr.; Delbert L. Spurlock, Jr., replaced Harry Walters as assistant secretary of the Army for manpower and reserve affairs. Spurlock was a civil-rights lawyer with no military experience before becoming Army general counsel in 1981, no previous involvement with the WITA review, and no interest in defending it. After Weinberger talked to Korb, and Korb talked to Spurlock, Spurlock's recommendation to Wickham favored the emasculation of WITA. Wickham, who was not prepared to fall on his sword and end his stint as chief of staff so soon, dutifully presided over the greatest peacetime defeat in the history of the United States Army.

In the fall of 1983 Spurlock informed Korb that WITA had been "revalidated" after certain unnamed errors of methodology had been corrected. In fact, validation by an independent civilian agency, Advanced Research Resources Organization of Bethesda, Maryland, found no fault with the review.[16] In October 1983 the Army briefed DACOWITS on the changed WITA. Thirteen of the twenty-three specialties closed to women by WITA were reopened. The Direct Combat Probability Coding of many units was adjusted to keep as many positions as possible open to women. The physical capabilities test, long the answer to the problem of recruits who were physically incapable of performing their required tasks, was reduced to a recruiter's "counseling tool." An Army representative suggested that it took courage to reassess the study, but a DACOWITS member replied, "I don't think it is an act of considerable courage to do what they should have done in the first place."

Chapter 7

CONFIDENCE IS HIGH

My policy? Sir, I am a soldier.
I do not have a policy.

—FRENCH GENERAL HENRI GIRAUD

NOT SINCE THE PASSAGE of PL 90-130 a decade and a half earlier had DACOWITS achieved a greater victory. In suppressing WITA, the committee had done more than merely overcome the apathy of lawmakers; it had overcome the Army. It had bullied and embarrassed an organized opposition through loud, persistent, and sometimes irrational protest. In the end, the arguments of neither side mattered. The lesson learned was that the side that clamors loudest carries the day.

DACOWITS was exultant and emboldened. It emerged from the conflict full of fight, vowing to direct its appeals directly to the secretary of defense on other matters. Less than a year after questioning the objectivity and worth of repeatedly studying women in the military, DACOWITS was recommending that the utilization of women be "continually re-examined [but only] with a view to improving force readiness by making maximum use of this valuable human resource."[1]

New fears that the Reagan administration would silence the successful committee by appointing more conservative members quickly faded. By 1984 all of the members of DACOWITS had been appointed under Reagan with no discernible shift in the committee's ideological bent. The only woman who regularly deviated from the committee's radical consensus was Elaine Donnelly, an Eagle Forum member who had led the fight against the ERA in her home state of Michigan. Donnelly fought hard against the push for repeal of the combat exclusion laws and often raised embarrassing questions about pregnancy, dual-service couples, and the lesser physical strength of women, but all too often she found herself alone.

In the year of the "gender gap," the Reagan Pentagon was interested only in deflecting criticism by pleasing the feminist lobby. The Defense Department spent $70,000 to dress the Pentagon's Military Women's Corridor with exhibits and propaganda. (The hall was soon dubbed "Broadway" by the sexist denizens of the Pentagon's shabbier corridors.) DACOWITS was treated to repeated pronouncements that women were an "integral part" of the nation's defenses and the committee itself was "an integral part of the Defense team." Such flattery was intended to dissuade members from seeking to make DACOWITS a statutory committee, responsible directly to Congress or to both Congress and the Defense Department. Assistant Secretary of Defense Lawrence J. Korb told the committee that a statutory committee would create "an investigative or adversarial relationship" between the committee and the military. "The effect would be polarization of women from the military community," said Korb.[2] Of course, both situations already existed. The Pentagon nevertheless had good reason to fear closer ties between DACOWITS and Congress.

Both Korb and Weinberger strove to develop a more amicable relationship between the committee and the Pentagon. Korb, himself a true-believer in greater utilization of women, assured DACOWITS that "no issue has taken more of my time than women in the military."[3] Weinberger was described by a former DACOWITS chairwoman as "fatherly" and "almost sweet" in his desire to please the committee. He assured them of his personal commitment to the continued expansion of opportunities against the seemingly elastic combat exclusion laws, praised the achievements of women whenever the occasion required him to do so, created the Department of Defense Task Force on Equity for Women, and loudly called upon the services to accept more women into their ranks and open more jobs to them. Yet for all his efforts he never quite escaped the suspicion of insincerity. Some proponents of women in the military sensed that his policy was secretly one of appeasement: he was willing to give women an inch whenever they demanded one, but he showed no initiative to act without prodding and dodged the issue of combat at every turn.

The debate over women in combat was one battle Caspar Weinberger would not fight. His entire tenure in office was spent temporizing on the issue, trying both to please and protect his commander-in-chief, who was known to oppose women in combat, and to avoid angering the feminist lobby. He assured President Reagan that women could become "grease monkeys if they want to and things like that" but not combat soldiers.[4] He secretly advised the service chiefs not to worry about women in the combat zone because the president would order them withdrawn when the shooting started, an unsettling prospect for the chiefs because of the number of women in critical positions. And he suggested in an interview on NBC's *Nightly News* that evacuation of women from a combat zone was a possibility but qualified it by adding that the "value of having women in those positions [in combat], the value of leaving all career avenues open, is greater than the problems of dealing with [the] comparable small disruption." In fact, DACOWITS had already been told by Korb that evacuation was not a possibility: "We cannot afford to pull women back or protect them from the hazards of their duties. No one should expect otherwise."[5]

Weinberger would admit to being personally opposed to women in combat, but he always left his position conspicuously undefended. When pressed on the issue by DACOWITS, he proffered only flattery and a patronizing apology for his recalcitrant chauvinism:

Either I'm too old-fashioned or something else is wrong with me, but I simply feel that that is not the proper utilization [of women]. And I think, again to be perfectly frank about it and spread all of my old-fashioned views before you, I think women are too valuable to be in combat.[6]

Whatever his real reasons, he did not dare reveal them, not even to argue against repeal of the combat exclusion laws. Instead, he washed his hands of the issue and shoved it back at Congress, but only after surrendering all grounds for defending the exclusion laws as they existed. The greatest favor Weinberger granted feminists was to establish the Defense Department's current position—that there were no military reasons why women should be excluded from combat, that present limitations on the role of women were based solely on present law, and that the law was based solely on the preference of the American public. As far as the Pentagon was concerned, the law's repeal was a matter properly decided by the public's elected representatives—strictly without benefit of military counsel.

Despite its boasts, the Defense Department under Weinberger did not lead the way toward greater use of women by the military, but it did allow itself to be goaded steadily in that direction by complaints from Congress and the feminist lobby. After its humiliating defeat, the Army buried WITA unceremoniously. Army leaders were so intimidated that they made no attempt to explain the study to the troops in the field, who knew nothing about WITA except what they read in *Army Times*, where criticism of the report grabbed all the headlines, and charges of bias and faulty methodology were reported but never examined for their validity. Before retiring, General Meyer, who later said he would have resigned as chief of staff before allowing WITA to be emasculated as it was, had wanted to make a videotaped explanation of WITA for dissemination to the field, but he was persuaded to let General Thurman make the videotape instead. Thurman's videotape was never released.

A member of the WITA Policy Review Group prepared a painstaking explanation of the study for publication in Army journals, but that too was spiked. To explain why WITA made sense would have placed Army leaders in the difficult position of having to explain why so many of its recommendations had not been implemented. The two-year study, they decided, was best forgotten.

By 1988 the Army had added more than 10,000 officers and enlisted women, raising the number of women to almost 11 percent of its total strength. As a counseling tool, the MEPSCAT physical test had no appreciable effect on the placement of personnel in specialties, as recruiters were not about to discourage potential recruits from entering the MOS of their choice. Direct Combat Probability Coding suffered gradual erosion as exceptions overrode the rule whenever P1 vacancies went unfilled. By 1986, 4,000 Army women in Europe were assigned to P1 positions. The following year, the coding system was "fine-tuned" to provide greater flexibility in personnel assignments and more command opportunities for female officers. Nearly 12,000 active duty positions were opened to women in forward support battalions, which provide direct support to combat units forward of the brigade rear boundary. More than 2,000 women were assigned to such units.

The Pentagon wanted no part in deciding whether to employ women in combat—that was up to the elected representatives.

The Air Force also continued to move toward greater and greater use of women. In five years under Reagan the Air Force opened more than 30,000 new positions to women. Only 3 percent of jobs remained closed to them. With the reopening of the security specialist field in 1984, Air Force enlisted women could serve in all but four career fields, and all officer career fields were open to them. In 1984 women were assigned aboard Airborne Warning and Control System (AWACS) aircraft. In 1986, RC-135 reconnaissance aircraft and EC-130 electronic countermeasures aircraft were both opened to women, and the Air Force began assigning women to Minuteman missile crews, with plans to make 20 percent of Minuteman crews all-female. Since 1980 the female share of total Air Force personnel strength had risen from 11 percent to 13 percent, and it continued to rise.

But not everyone was satisfied with the Air Force's rate of progress. In 1984 members of Congress sought to force the Air Force to increase its number of female recruits faster. The 1985 Defense Authorization Act required the Air Force to raise its recruitment quota for women from 14.7 percent of all recruits to 19 percent in 1987 and 22 percent in 1988.

The act also ordered the Air Force to study the effect of recruiting more women and deliver its report to Congress. Written so as not to offend feminist supporters in Congress, the Air Force's report nevertheless concluded that the congressionally mandated quota would lower mission effectiveness, increase manpower costs, and aggravate attrition. The report said that women were less available for daily duty, less available to travel for temporary duty because of personal reasons, and less likely to deploy quickly. Because of the quota, the number of dual-service couples and single Air Force parents would double. Recruiting costs would increase because young civilian women showed less interest than men in military service, as would training costs because female recruits showed less aptitude for critical electronic and mechanical jobs and therefore required more training.[7]

The report rejected the theory that forcing the Air Force to recruit fewer men would significantly increase the number of men available for recruitment by the other services. Citing behavioral and motivational differences between Air Force and Army recruits, the report estimated that only one out of twelve men turned away by the Air Force would join the Army as a second choice. The report also predicted an increase in the number of quality male recruits for the Air Force by 1993.

But Congress refused to back off on its mandated quotas. The following year, the House committee recommended repeal of the 19 percent quota for 1987 but left in place the 22 percent quota for 1988. Later, Congress delayed the 22 percent quota until 1989. The Air Force finally succeeded in having a repeal amendment added to the fiscal year 1989 National Defense Authorization Bill. Nevertheless, it expected women to make up 19.6 percent of total Air Force accessions in 1989.

Like the Air Force, the Navy sailed ahead under Reagan with expanded opportunities for women, opening more jobs, more sea billets, and more command slots, and increasing the total number of women in service. The number of Navy officers and enlisted women increased 52 percent from 1980 to 1986. In the fifth year of the Reagan administration, 10 percent of Navy officers and 9 percent of its enlisted personnel were women. Plans called for adding another 4,000 enlisted women to reach the goal set by the Defense Department of 51,300 by 1989.

But, as with the Air Force, not everyone was pleased with the Navy's achievements. Female surface warfare officers found their opportunities for sea duty limited by their exclusion from ships of the Mobile Logistics Support Force (MLSF). When their complaints reached the ears of DACOWITS, the committee began calling on the Navy to open these clearly labeled "support" ships to women. The Navy argued that MLSF ships fit the definition of combat vessels accepted by Congress when it amended Title 10 to allow women on noncombat vessels in 1978. That definition excluded women from permanent assignment aboard any "unit, ship, aircraft, or task organization" whose primary mission was to "seek out, reconnoiter, or engage the enemy." MLSF ships regularly moved as part of a battle group and therefore were classed as combat vessels. DACOWITS was unconvinced. "The Navy has to develop a more definitive determination of what constitutes a combat ship and what constitutes a support ship so that women will stay with that service and be fully utilized," said Constance B. Newman, DACOWITS chairwoman, in January 1986.[8]

Some women blamed the secretary of the Navy, John F. Lehman, Jr., for the MLSF restriction. A female naval officer at a DACOWITS meeting said, "There are two words that explain why women aren't serving on MLSF ships: John Lehman."[9] Lehman himself told DACOWITS in November 1986 that opening MLSF ships to women was a "possibility, but we would need to adjust the legislation." Lehman belittled the problems of putting women aboard ship but said the move might provoke opposition from the wives of MLSF sailors. The Navy was "antifamily" enough without putting men and women together on ships, said Lehman. "That is the same excuse we heard about Air Force wives when women were being sent into silos," Carolyn Becraft of WEAL retorted. An aide to Senator William Proxmire of Wisconsin, a stalwart supporter of women in combat, observed that the National Military Family Association had endorsed the idea of women on ships, "so I think Mr. Lehman doesn't have to worry about Navy wives."[10]

Not long afterward, the Navy reaffirmed its exclusion of women from the MLSF and renamed it the Combat Logistics Force. In March 1987 Vice Admiral Dudley L. Carlson, the Navy's chief of personnel, defended the name change before the Senate Armed Services Committee's subcommittee on personnel by showing pictures of World War II ships burning and sinking after enemy attacks. "This is a picture of a combat logistics ship burning," said Carlson. "The people on that ship thought they were in combat." Not known for tact, Carlson tossed the grenade back into the lap of Congress, challenging it to do what it seemed to want the Navy to do. Said Carlson, "Our position is, if you want to change the combat exclusion law, fine. But, please don't mandate which ships are combat and which are not."[11] Congress backed off.

Other problems plagued the Navy during the years of expansion. The rush of women into the nation's sea service was not a rush to sea, because most female recruits preferred traditional jobs comfortably ashore to dirty work on the rolling waves. In 1983 three-fourths of Navy enlisted women were concentrated in one-fourth of Navy ratings, leaving very few sea billets in those ratings for women to fill. The Navy had opened more than 6,200 sea billets to women but could fill only 5,000 because there were not enough women in other ratings.

Because of this problem, the Navy was not enthusiastic about increasing its total number of women. More women only aggravated the problem of sea/shore rotation. When Congress tried to increase the Navy's female strength from 46,000 women in 1986 to 55,000 in 1987, Admiral James D. Watkins, chief of naval operations, made it known that the Navy had all the women it needed. Watkins's successor, Admiral Carlisle A.H. Trost, came to the same conclusion after several months in the job. In February 1987 Trost ordered a five-year freeze on the number of Navy enlisted women. Instead of proceeding toward the Reagan administration's goal of 51,300, Trost intended to hold women to 46,796—9 percent of Navy enlisted personnel. Unfortunately for Trost, he had neglected to forewarn the secretary of defense or the secretary of the Navy before making his decision public. Two days after the decision was announced, Weinberger met with DACOWITS chairwoman Jacquelyn K. Davis to hear her complaint about the effects of the decision on the Navy women, then brusquely countermanded the order.

The Task Force on Women in the Military contributed nothing new and never left the confines of its Pentagon conference room.

Another defeat involved civilian women employed by the Navy as technicians to work on Navy vessels. One such technician, Pamela Doviak Celli, was barred from going aboard a Navy submarine for sea trials and filed suit with the Equal Employment Opportunity Commission (EEOC), charging the Navy with sex discrimination. Celli's suit argued that Title 10 applied only to Navy servicewomen, not to Navy civilians, and that excluding her from sea trials had harmed her career advancement. The EEOC ruled in Celli's favor. The Navy at first resisted the EEOC intervention on the grounds that it had no jurisdiction over the service, but on the last day of the EEOC's ultimatum, the new secretary of the Navy, James H. Webb, Jr.—

Naval Academy graduate, wounded Marine Corps veteran, best-selling author, and outspoken opponent of women at the service academies—ordered that Celli be allowed to participate in sea trials aboard submarines. Webb also ordered that decisions to allow anyone aboard ship should be left to ships' commanders, but that "the basic policy that female employees shall have full opportunity to participate in sea trials still applies." Soon after, female officers began complaining to DACOWITS that civilian women could serve aboard ships closed to naval officers.

Webb's first appointment as assistant secretary of defense for reserve affairs in 1984 was opposed by feminist groups and some Pentagon officials, but Weinberger wanted him anyway. To better Webb's chances for confirmation, Weinberger submitted a letter to the Senate committee announcing that Webb had "reversed" his views regarding women in the military and was fully in line with administration policy. To Webb, the announcement was a slap in the face. Though he admired and respected Weinberger greatly, he disliked being treated, in Webb's words, "like a reformed smoker." In fact, he did not recant his earlier views, though he did promise not to try to "turn back the clock."

Webb's appointment as secretary of the Navy was less controversial because of his apparent good behavior. Nevertheless, as if to test his sincerity, Jacquelyn Davis and DACOWITS toured Navy and Marine installations in the Far East in August 1987 and returned with a platterful of unappetizing issues that it served up to the Navy with great fanfare—sexual harassment; fraternization; pregnancy; lesbianism; the burden of dependent children; problems with uniforms; troublesome male attitudes; lack of decent housing; inadequate female medical care; insufficient promotion opportunity; poor communication between women and Navy leaders; and restrictions of women from the CLF, the P-3 Orion antisubmarine aircraft, and the Marine Corps embassy guard program. The report harped on the theme that the "institutional hierarchies" of both services "continue to project attitudes that are biased against women."[12]

Secretary Webb had already ordered a comprehensive review of the "progress" of women in the Navy. The review was completed in December 1987, and Webb announced his approval of several of the review's recommendations in January 1988. More women would be allowed to compete to enter Navy ratings, and more women would be assigned to aviation units, aboard P-3 aircraft, and to sea duty. Three kinds of CLF ships (oilers, ammunition ships, and store ships) would be opened to women, and the Navy's definition of *combatant* would be changed to include units, ships, aircraft, and task organizations which have as their primary missions "to seek out, reconnoiter, *and* engage the enemy." The 1978 definition required combatants to perform only one of the three tasks, instead of all three tasks. Webb himself was not keen on these changes, but the admiral responsible for the study insisted they were for the good of the Navy.

Webb also had directed the Marine Corps to review its policies regarding the growing number of women Marines. In some ways, the Marine Corps remained the most conservative of the services. It still had fewer women as a percentage of its total force than any of the other services, and women Marines did not begin weapons training until 1987. But in six years under Reagan, the Marine Corps' female strength increased almost 50 percent, exceeding the Carter administration's goal of 9,600 women Marines in service by 1987. The Women Marine Review of 1984 set the "ideal" strength at 10,500, with 3,800 women in the Fleet Marine Force. The study also approved the deployment of women with a Marine Amphibious Force and with headquarters units and air combat elements of a Marine Amphibious Brigade, but kept them out of battalion and smaller units.

The study ordered by Webb was not completed until after he had resigned over unrelated differences with the new secretary of defense, Frank Carlucci. The study produced 83 recommendations, of which 66 were approved for implementation by the commandant of the Marine Corps, General Al Gray.

Women would be assigned to many new jobs and units, including Hawk anti-aircraft missile battalions; barracks would be integrated to discourage lesbianism; the Marine Corps would seek expanded child care and recreational facilities for women; and the Corps would work with the Navy to make female medical care more convenient. Gray did not approve several of the more controversial recommendations. He refused to allow women to crew C-130 transport aircraft and several small passenger jets, to deploy aboard amphibious ships, to undergo the same combat training as men, and to be assigned to the Corps' new security force battalions, which recently had taken on a counterterrorism mission.

Gray also rejected a recommendation that women be assigned as embassy security guards on the grounds "that embassy guards are expected to be more than just fancy-dress doormen, but on that count he was overruled by Carlucci. Carlucci also later ordered women admitted to Marine security force battalions. While briefing DACOWITS on the results of the study, Gray made known his displeasure at being overruled as a result of the committee's meddling and disputed DACOWITS's claim that many women Marines wanted to be embassy guards. "I believe that was a carry-over from your agenda," he told DACOWITS. "I'm getting hustled along here. I'm having the opportunity to do what's best for my people taken away from me, and that gets my attention." At one point, he asserted that he was the only government official completely responsible for the good of the Marine Corps, saying, "I am the one who is totally responsible for their well-being.… I am the one who will make these kinds of decisions always," adding under his breath, "or you can get yourself another commandant."[13] The remark was played up by the press, but subsequent statements by Gray and Carlucci denied that the two were at odds. A spokesman for Gray explained, "What the commandant really meant was that DACOWITS made a recommendation directly to the secretary without passing through him."[14]

The appointment of Frank Carlucci to replace Caspar Weinberger as secretary of defense did not help the Pentagon to withstand the feminist lobby. As deputy secretary of defense in the early years of Weinberger's watch, Carlucci was largely responsible for shaping the Defense Department's official non-position on women in combat. Later, he confided in subordinates that he didn't share "Cap's hang-up about women in combat." Carlucci's wife, Marcia Carlucci, had been a member and supporter of DACOWITS from 1984 to 1986. Before that, she had helped Marybel Batjer, the youthful director of political affairs for the strongly feminist National Women's Political Caucus, get the job of special assistant to both the secretary and the deputy secretary of defense. Batjer saw to it that most offices were filled with people sympathetic to women in the military. The joke around the Pentagon was that a candidate had to be conservative enough to please the White House and liberal enough to please Marybel Batjer. James Webb made it past Batjer because of Weinberger's patronage, but some of Webb's associates were not so fortunate.

> The men in the field and fleet were prohibited from joining the debate.

As secretary of defense, Carlucci responded to DACOWITS's Far East visit by creating a new Task Force on Women in the Military headed by Dr. David J. Armor, a sociologist serving as principal deputy assistant secretary of defense for force management and personnel. Membership included, among others, Marybel Batjer, who had recently joined the staff of the National Security Council as deputy executive secretary, and Delbert Spurlock, the assistant secretary of the Army responsible for emasculating the WITA study. Jacquelyn Davis acted as an official observer. The task force was charged with examining three issues affecting women: career development, combat exclusions, and how women were regarded by their male counterparts. The task force contributed no new knowledge and never left the confines of its Pentagon conference room. It presented its brief report to the House Armed Services Committee's military personnel subcommittee in January 1988.

Most of the task force's recommendations were modest renditions of demands made by DACOWITS. To aid the career development of servicewomen, it recommended that the secretary of defense direct the services to develop plans to draw more women into nontraditional career fields, which they had been trying to do for years. To combat sexual harassment, the task force recommended that the services: improve sexual harassment training, establish a means outside the chain of command for reporting incidents of harassment, improve support facilities to "eliminate conditions that detract from servicewomen becoming full and equal members of their units," and enforce the policy of providing servicewomen priority over dependent women for obstetrical and gynecological care.

The task force's only original contribution concerned combat exclusions. It recommended that the secretary of defense instruct the services to adopt a new method of determining where women may or may not serve, based upon the principle of "equal risk." Noncombat units could be closed to women "provided that the type, degree, and duration of risk is equal to or greater than that experienced by associated combat units." To the Army, the principle of equal risk would mean "opening those [infantry or armored] brigade positions which, like forward support battalions, experience less risk than regular combat battalions." To the Navy, equal risk might mean opening more ships of the CLF, depending upon how the Navy decided to measure risk, said the task force. To the Air Force, any aircraft not incurring an equal risk with similar combat aircraft would be open to women. The task force expected that the Air Force's comparison of risk would keep some tactical reconnaissance aircraft, like the RF-4 Phantom, closed to women, but would open strategic reconnaissance aircraft like the SR-71 Blackbird, the U-2, and the TR-1. Some search and rescue aircraft might also be affected.

If applied to provide maximum opportunity to women, the doctrine of equal risk could have virtually the same effect as a bill sponsored in the 100th Congress by Senators William Proxmire of Wisconsin and William S. Cohen of Maine and by Congressman William L. Dickinson of Alabama. The Proxmire-Cohen bill would have permitted women to be assigned to all units, vessels, and aircraft that "have as their mission the direct support of combat units," no matter where they might be located or what threat they might face. The Air Force would have been forced to open all positions aboard tactical and strategic reconnaissance aircraft and transport aircraft, though they routinely operate over hostile territory. The Navy would have been forced to open all CLF ships, and the Army would have been asked to open an estimated 140,000 positions in the main battle area.

The bill's sponsors insisted that the bill was a "moderate, combat support measure," not intended to "undermine" the combat exclusion laws but to provide a more efficient use of manpower and allow women greater opportunity for advancement. Members of their staffs, however, admitted that the bill would be a big step toward repeal of the combat exclusions. Others on Capitol Hill said the bill was intended not to become law but to please the feminist lobby by goading the Defense Department into extending women's roles. After serving its purpose, the bill died in committee.

The Defense Department's policy of "equal risk"—bringing women closer to combat—increased the threat that the courts might one day rule the combat exclusions laws unconstitutional on the grounds that the distinction between combat and non-combat was purely arbitrary. In *Rostker* v. *Goldberg*, the Supreme Court upheld the exemption of women from the draft by reasoning that the draft existed to provide the military with combat troops, and because women were barred by law from combat, the draft exemption served a legitimate purpose. But by not then addressing the issue of the constitutionality of the combat exclusion laws, the high court missed an opportunity to

validate those laws when legal grounds for their constitutionality still existed.

Since *Rostker* v. *Goldberg*, the Reagan Defense Department
had pulled all of the pillars of legal support out from under the
combat exclusions by insisting that the exclusions rested solely
upon the will of the American people. In the late 1980s opinion
polls were already showing that a majority of Americans favored
women in combat, although most would have qualified the
proposition with "if they can do the job." They had not heard of
WITA and knew nothing of the political dangers facing anyone
who dared say that many women cannot do the job. They had
only the report of high-level Pentagon officials who were reliably
effusive in their public praise of women in uniform. The men in
the field and fleet were prohibited from joining the debate.

Chapter 8

FROM HERE TO MATERNITY

The whole of military activity must... relate directly or indirectly to the engagement. The end for which a soldier is recruited, clothed, armed, and trained, the whole object of his sleeping, eating, drinking, and marching is simply that he should fight at the right place and the right time.

—KARL VON CLAUSEWITZ

FOR MANY YEARS, the party line in Washington was that all was well with women in the military, that with the exception of a few minor annoyances to be dispelled by the magic wand of policy, sexual integration was proceeding smoothly without degrading military readiness. Women were "an integral part" of the nation's defense, and they can do the job "as well as if not better" than their male comrades, said responsible officials.

The proof, they said, was in the women's consistently faster rate of promotion. In the spring of 1987, the Army promoted 33 percent of eligible women to the rank of E-7 but only 16 percent of eligible men. Throughout the services, women are promoted with less time-in-service than men to every grade from E-2 to O-7. Female officers are promoted to rear admiral and brigadier general (O-7) fives years earlier than men, on average, and enlisted women to senior NCO or chief petty officer rank (E-7) two to four years earlier than enlisted men.

But there are several reasons for doubting the significance of promotion comparisons. Higher rates of attrition and lower rates of retention trim much of the dead wood from the women's ranks. In the past, those who survived until retirement were intensely dedicated women who forsook marriage and family for the sake of their careers. Today less dedicated women are favored by promotion systems that emphasize education, test scores, and personal appearance—areas where women tend to outdo men. Moreover, promotions are centrally controlled and therefore not immune from manipulation. The services not only exert considerable pressure to safeguard the advancement of women; they use rigid quotas to guarantee that women succeed. (See Chapter 11.)

The assertion that women in general are performing as well as or better than men has by no means been proven. No doubt some women outperform some men, but the many good servicewomen who excel at their jobs do not compensate the services for the problems that women overall have caused them, problems that have been known for many years, but which are religiously ignored for political reasons.

PHYSICAL LIMITATIONS

The general lack of physical strength among servicewomen bears directly upon their ability to perform assigned duties. Yet the notion that technology has alleviated the need for physical strength is almost universally accepted. Say the words "modern warfare" and the minds of many Americans fill with images of control consoles and video displays. "There's an awful lot of button-pushing going on out there," says a reporter for *Time* magazine who thinks the physical demands of the military have been exaggerated.

There is, however, no evidence that technology has in fact reduced the need for physical strength and endurance among military men and women. Endurance has only increased in importance; operations are now conducted around the clock and throughout the year, whereas they were once limited to the daytime in seasonable weather. Many modern military jobs still require more physical strength than most women possess. Technology has not provided the Air Force with automatic litter-loaders to move wounded soldiers onto MEDEVAC aircraft, a task women are unable to do, nor of sorting artillery rounds by hand. What technology has done is to make service members able to do more, thereby making more for them to do. Many of the buttons that need pushing are attached to large pieces of equipment that must be hauled in haste back and forth across the battlefield.

Women's physical advantages are that they are less susceptible to altitude sickness and, normally, have a greater tolerance of cold temperatures due to their extra body fat. But by all other measures, men have enormous advantages physically. The average female Army recruit is 4.8 inches shorter, 31.7 pounds lighter, has 37.4 fewer pounds of muscle, and 5.7 more pounds of fat than the average male recruit. She has only 55 percent of the upper-body strength and 72 percent of the lower-body strength of the average male. She is also at a significant disadvantage when performing aerobic activities such as marching with heavy loads and working in the heat, since fat mass is inversely related to aerobic capacity and heat tolerance. Her lighter frame, moreover, makes her more likely to suffer injuries due to physical exertion. An Army study of 124 men and 186 women done in 1988 found that women are more than twice as likely to suffer leg injuries and nearly five times as likely to suffer fractures as men. Women were, consequently, less available for duty.[1]

There is without doubt a significant gap between the physical abilities of men and women. Tests of men and women entering the West Point class of 1980 found that, on average, the upper-body strength of women was 56 percent the strength of men, their leg strength 80 percent, and their gripping strength 69 percent. Even when height was kept constant, women possessed only 80 percent of the overall strength of men. After eight weeks of intensive training, male plebes demonstrated 32 percent more power in the lower body and performed 48 percent more work at the leg press than female plebes. At the bench press, the men demonstrated 270 percent more power and performed an extraordinary 473 percent more work than the women.[2]

Little wonder that servicewomen should find so many workaday duties beyond their ability. Even in the modern Air Force, routine tasks are often too much for them. The GAO found that 62 of 97 female aircraft mechanics could not perform required tasks such as changing aircraft tires and brakes, removing batteries and crew seats, closing drag chute doors, breaking torque on bolts, and lifting heavy stands. Female missile mechanics often lacked the strength and physical confidence to harness and move warheads and to maneuver large pieces of machinery. Some had trouble carrying their own tool boxes.

In the late 1970s the Air Force began screening recruits using the "X-Factor" strength indicator, but Army researchers found that the screening had degenerated in practice into a meaningless question-and-answer drill. Had the X-Factor actually kept women out of jobs for which they were unfit, it would have gone the way of the Army's MEPSCAT. The very presence of women in the ranks was made possible only by lowering or eliminating physical standards. When the services found that weight standards for recruits excluded 22 percent of potential female recruits but only 3 percent of potential male recruits, the standards were revised to resemble the insurance industry's standards, excluding 7.3 percent of women and 5.8 percent of men. A five-foot-six-inch female may now enlist in the Army weighing a hefty 165 lbs. All of the services have double standards for men and women on all the events of their regular physical fitness tests. Young male marines must perform at least three pull-ups to pass the test, but women marines must only hang from the bar with arms flexed for sixteen seconds. In the Army, the youngest women are given an extra three minutes to complete a two-mile run. All of the services require men to perform more situps than women, though the Army just pledged to change this.

To justify the double standard, the American military abandoned the worldwide consensus of the purpose for physical training in the military—that soldiers should be tougher, faster, stronger, and more physically able than the rest of the populace. The U.S. military prefers weak but healthy people because they are cheaper in the long run. Physical training is meant to "ensure a minimum level of fitness, not to delineate any measure of job-related productivity," thus "the premise that men 'do more' because they must achieve higher physical fitness standards is not a valid one."[3]

Of course, on the job, men actually do more to make up for the limitations of their female coworkers. As long as there are enough men around, commanders can pretend that women have not degraded a unit's ability to accomplish its mission. But as their number increased, the concentration of women in some support units began to threaten mission accomplishment. Naval Air Station Adak in the Aleutian Islands of Alaska recently boasted a fire department that was 76 percent female. The women were issued special, lighter fire fighting equipment, and portions of the International Fire Service Association manuals were rewritten to cover how the women should cope with physically demanding tasks. But because the women were still unable to open and close fire hydrants, connect large diameter hoses, advance hose lines, and control nozzles, the department was forced to assign five women to engine companies that normally required only four men—a 25 percent increase in personnel to do the same job.

Aboard ship, the entire crew is charged with fire-fighting and rescue duties, and here the substitution of women for men can have deadly consequences. A 1981 Navy study found female recruits woefully unable to perform five common damage-control tasks: carrying stretchers up and down ladders and across level surfaces, moving and starting emergency pumps, turning engine bolts, and directing fire hoses. Test results are shown below:

Number of Recruits Not Capable of Performing Damage-Control Tasks[4]

Task	# of Women before training	# of Women after training	# of Men before training	# of Men after training
Stretcher carry level	63	38	0	0
Stretcher carry up/ down ladder	94	88	0	0
Fire hose	19	16	0	0
P250 pump, carry down	99	99	9	4
P250 pump, carry up	73	52	0	0
P250 pump, start pump	90	75	0	0
Remove SSTG pump	99	99	0	0
Torque engine bolt	78	47	0	0

The implications were ominous. "Unless the Navy has the luxury of customizing damage control assignments based upon the capabilities of individual sailors, the lack of physical strength among female soldiers can only decrease the survivability of Navy vessels," wrote Dr. Paul Davis, an exercise physiologist, in an article for *Navy Times*. "Seen in this light, the Navy's recent enthusiasm for putting more and more women aboard ship makes little sense, unless the Navy doesn't mind sacrificing survivability (and possibly the lives of its sailors) for the sake of enhancing opportunities for women."[5]

Army experts who were not personally involved in the WITA study have innocently compared a soldier's need for strength to an athlete's, without considering the implications for women. According to Major James Wright, chief of the Exercise Science Branch of the U.S. Army Fitness School:

Upper-body strength is an important component of virtually every Army task. There are still hundreds of manual-type tasks which require strength. There will always be a lot of setting up and tearing down of equipment when units go to the field. In fact, several studies show that the lack of upper-body strength is actually a limiting factor for our overall military readiness.[6]

Navy Lieutenant Ed Marcinik, an exercise physiologist working with the Naval Health and Physical Readiness Program, agrees:

There are general shipboard tasks that every sailor must perform, all requiring upper-body strength: extricating injured personnel, controlling fire hose nozzles, handling stores, and opening and securing watertight hatches, doors, and scuttles.[7]

Marcinik says that fully 84 percent of all shipboard duties involve heavy lifting, carrying, or pulling. Four ratings (boatswain's mate, gunner's mate, hull technician, and machinist's mate) are among the most physically demanding jobs in the military.

Before the Navy became so sensitive to the feelings of women, it developed a program of shipboard weight training called SPARTEN, or Scientific Program of Aerobic and Resistance Training Exercise in the Navy. One part of SPARTEN involved the installation of nautilus equipment on ships like the battleship *New Jersey*.

To military women, however, such emphasis on physical strength is anathema. When men in the military are encouraged to think that being strong and quick is good, the professional reputation of military women suffers. Because the services are committed to protect and advance women as equals, they devalue physical prowess as a professional virtue, which is why programs like SPARTEN are only marginally effective.

Apart from the lack of strength and speed, the smaller size and different shape of women has caused innumerable problems solved only by a boom in special clothing and equipment. The defense inventory has burgeoned with end-items specially designed for both sexes or women only, including smaller everything from snowshoes to flight suits: smaller wire-cutters, longer wrenches, lighter firefighters' helmets, specially cut boots; special helicopter seats because women complained of back pain; flak vests to accommodate female breasts; gas-masks to fit softer, smaller, less bony faces; and a disposable cardboard tube to enable female soldiers to urinate in the field without dropping their trousers (developed but not adopted). In the interest of uniformity and standardization, the Army has tried to develop clothing that will fit both men and women with minimum variation, but the unsightly compromises fit neither sex well.

A more serious result of the differences of shape and size is the relaxation of anthropometric standards devised to fit the operator to the equipment. The services have always been willing to relax standards for height, weight, and reach in order to admit women to special programs and training. None of the first women to undergo Navy flight training in 1975 satisfied the Navy's own stringent standards that excluded many men. In 1983, to enhance pilot safety and aircraft performance, the Navy tightened requirements for sitting height, leg length, buttock-to-knee length, and functional reach, but when female aviators complained that only a quarter of them would qualify, the Navy backed off.

Anthropometric differences also affect the design of new systems and equipment with potentially serious consequences. There is no such thing as a one-size-fits-all high-performance jet fighter. For the safety of the pilot and for the performance of the aircraft, cockpits are made to be tight fits. When designers introduce a 25 percent variable in the size of the pilot, something must give.

The need to accommodate smaller, weaker soldiers played a part in the Army's decision to replace the M1911 .45 caliber Colt pistol with the 9mm Beretta. The best buy the Army ever made, the .45 automatic was designed to stop a drug-crazed Moro warrior dead in his tracks. It served all of the services well in every war since World War I, but lately fell victim to complaints that it was difficult to use effectively because it was unwieldy and heavy—so heavy that female military policemen were issued .38 caliber revolvers instead.

The Army insists that the .45's ineffectiveness and the need for standardization within NATO, not the inability of women to use it, motivated the change, but this raises the question of why the Army is not also considering a replacement for the M16 rifle. Since its adoption, the M16 has been criticized by experienced soldiers as being mechanically unreliable, lacking in stopping power, ineffective at long ranges, and too fragile for combat use. The NATO standard rifle caliber is 7.65mm, but the M16 is a 5.56mm rifle and United States is the only country in NATO to use it. But any 7.65mm alternative weighs many pounds more than the M16, posing a significant problem for female soldiers. And in almost every instance the good of equal opportunity takes precedence over the good of the service.

Women's rates of attrition are consistently higher than those of men.

Ultimately, of course, the lack of physical strength among women will directly degrade the ability of units to fight and survive on the modern battlefield, inevitably resulting in a greater loss of life and a greater risk of defeat.

MEDICAL DIFFERENCES

Lack of physical strength contributes to another problem with women in the military: they need greater medical attention. Women in all of the services are hospitalized two to three times as often as men. In the 1970s the percentage of Navy women requiring hospitalization fluctuated between 25 percent and 30 percent, while hospitalization of Navy men declined from 13 percent in 1966 to 11 percent in 1975. When men and women are subjected to the same work requirements and living conditions, as during recruit and cadet training, women's hospitalization rates are significantly higher than men's rates for nearly all diagnoses: mental disorders; musculoskeletal afflictions; acute upper-respiratory infections; medical and surgical aftercare; rubella; infective and parasitic diseases; and digestive, diarrheal, and genitourinary disorders.[8]

A 1990 study of medical requirements aboard ship found that the monthly sick-call rate for women was nearly twice the rate for men. Women visited sick call more than men for most illness categories, including many common ailments such as strep infections, sunburn, poison ivy, acne, nose-bleeds, headaches, fainting, fever, fatigue, insomnia, conjunctivitis, diarrhea, and mental problems. Men visited sick call more than women for athlete's foot, jock itch, ingrown facial hair, ingrown toenails, skin infections, and obesity. About 25 percent of all illness-related (noninjury) sick-call visits by women were for female-specific problems, including pregnancy and related conditions, genitourinary disorders, and sexually transmitted diseases. The study found that 20 percent of female crew members became pregnant during the year-long study (5 percent per quarter), despite the ready availability aboard ship of virtually every form of birth control. As a result of all this, the study recommended assigning more Navy doctors to sea duty—bad news for the Navy, which has long had special problems recruiting doctors.[9]

Other studies have shown that, in the services at large, differences in military occupation and off-duty behavior mean different rates of hospitalization. Men are generally more prone to injury (fractures, lacerations, and dislocations) because of their poorer driving records and greater involvement in hazardous work and athletics, though Navy women in the lower grades assigned nontraditional jobs have shown "considerably higher" rates of injury than similarly assigned men, probably because of their lack of physical confidence, mechanical experience, and upper-body strength.[10] Women generally are still more prone to mental illness, genitourinary disorders, and disease, with pregnancy-related conditions accounting for one-third or more of all women hospitalized. Among mental disorders, men show higher rates of schizophrenia, alcoholism, and drug-related conditions, while women show higher rates of neuroses, eating disorders, and "transient situational disturbances."[11]

Though many military women deny or downplay the effects of premenstrual syndrome (PMS) on the behavior of women, medical experts estimate that 5 percent to 10 percent of all pre-menopausal women experience severe PMS-related symptoms, including incapacitating depression, suicidal thoughts, extreme mood swings, self-abuse, and violence. "These are women who suffer chronic, debilitating distress—women who are often unable to take care of themselves or their family," says Nancy Reame, associate professor of nursing at the University of Michigan at Ann Arbor.[12] Most women experience milder symptoms such as bloating, headaches, backaches, irritability, depression, breast tenderness, and food cravings. Roughly half of all women who suffer PMS characterize the condition as "mildly distressing." Only about 10 percent of premenopausal women experience no symptoms of PMS. The impact of PMS on unit effectiveness is compounded by the natural, involuntary tendency of women living in close quarters to synchronize their menstrual cycles.

Much of the debate about the medical cost-effectiveness of women versus men has focused on rates of "noneffectiveness" or "nonavailability," the amount of duty time service members miss while receiving medical attention. The medical nonavail-ability rate for women is consistently 2 to 2.5 times the rate for men. Much of the difference is attributable to pregnancy, but the women's rate exceeds the men's rate for all diagnoses. The women's nonavailability rate compared to the men's is 8.7 times for genitourinary disorders, 2.6 times for morbidity (disease), 1.4 times for mental illness, and 3.8 times for spurious com-plaints. Women lose five times as much time as men for attempted suicide but are successful at suicide only half as many times as men.[13]

But, proponents of women in the military argue, if women lose more time for medical reasons, men lose more time for dis-ciplinary reasons. These, however, are quite different problems.

The lack of discipline among men is itself the fault of a feminized force, a force that fails to instill discipline during basic training because of its be-nice-to-privates approach. Still, a commander has much more control over a unit's disciplinary problems than its medical problems, and indiscipline varies dramatically from unit to unit and from time to time. Since 1980—the last time the comparison of nonavailability for all reasons was made—better quality recruits have resulted in declining rates of indiscipline among men. The Defense Department no longer knows whether men or women lose more time overall.

In contrast, the medical demands of women in the peacetime force have been relatively steady. Modifications of clothing and equipment have reduced their need for medical attention only slightly. Sex education has done little to reduce pregnancy. If the medical nonavailability rates of women change at all, they will likely increase as more and more women are assigned nontraditional duties for which they have not the physical ability. Nonavailability will also increase if women are employed closer to wartime fighting. The services can expect an increase in mental illness and infectious disorders among women. And unsanitary conditions combined with inevitable shortages of such items as sanitary napkins will aggravate genitourinary infections. In Honduras, servicewomen were forced to use sponges and birth control pills when there was nothing else. In future wars, even those poor comforts may be luxuries.

That servicewomen place a considerable additional burden on the already overburdened military medical system is generally admitted, but the weight of the burden is unknown and not likely to become known for political reasons. In 1985 the Defense Department's Health Studies Task Force recommended that the department fund an independent study of the full impact of integration on the health care requirements of the services, at a cost of $780,000. The task force noted that a joint study by the Defense Department and the Veterans Administration would cost less but would be "suspect in the civilian community and among various women's groups" and might "provoke a political controversy."[14] No study, independent or in-house, has ever been done.

PREGNANCY AND ATTRITION

One problem with women in the military that does receive some attention is attrition—the failure to complete an enlistment contract. Attrition reduces service strength, increases personnel turbulence, and robs the service of its training investment. Women consistently attrit at higher rates than men. The difference is most dramatic between male and female high school graduates, the very people the services want most to keep. In 1981 nearly half of all Marine Corps female high school graduates failed to complete their enlistment contracts, more than double the male rate of high school graduates: 48 percent to 23.5 percent. In the Army, the attrition rate for female graduates was two-thirds higher than for male graduates: 40.3 percent to 24.8 percent. More recently, attrition among all servicewomen compared to males has been 36 percent higher: 34 percent to 25 percent.[15] The difference is least in the Navy, in which men see an unequal share of sea duty. As more women are required to go to sea involuntarily, their attrition rates will soar.

Defenders of women in the military once argued that the combat restrictions frustrated the ambitions of women and thus contributed to their higher rates of attrition, but this was not supported by the evidence. Attrition among women in nontraditional career fields is consistently higher than among women in traditional career fields, and studies indicate that women who attrit tend to hold more traditional views regarding the roles of men and women. A Marine Corps study identified "traditional family and career orientation" as the most important factor among women who attrited.[16] Thus, those inclined toward leaving service are not likely to be persuaded to stay if offered opportunities for nontraditional work, and those who complain about limited opportunities are not likely to leave service because their ambitions are not fully satisfied. As the services push more women into nontraditional jobs, including combat, attrition among women will increase.

By far the largest reason for attrition is pregnancy—25 percent to 50 percent of women who fail to complete enlistment contracts do so because of pregnancy. Pregnancy and parenthood accounted for 23 percent of all women discharged in 1980; an estimated 7 percent to 17 percent of servicewomen become pregnant each year. As mentioned earlier, the Army found that one-third of the women who became pregnant opted for voluntary discharges under the policy that leaves the decision to stay in or get out in the hands of the woman.

The services once handled pregnancy very differently. Executive Order No. 10240, signed by President Truman in 1951, authorized the services to involuntarily separate women, married or unmarried, who were pregnant, gave birth while in service, or had custody of dependent children under eighteen years of age. For twenty years, the heads of the women's components zealously defended this right for the good of all concerned: the service, the women's components, the mother, and the child. A few activists like Jeanne Holm thought the policy discriminated against women because men were not similarly treated for fatherhood. They adopted the argument that the "ultimate responsibility for the care and welfare of children rests with the parent, not, we submit, with the Air Force."[17] Most senior officers, however, took the view of Brigadier General Elizabeth P. Hoisington, director of the WAC, who held that different treatment was justified because mothers and fathers in service were, in legal terms, not *similarly situated*:

> ...no basis exists to consider equalizing Army policy for male and female members concerning parenthood through adoption or other means. A valid comparison cannot be made between the civilian wife of a male member and the military wife of a male member. The interests of the Army

*will best be served by women who are free to travel. The
interests of the children will best be served by women who
have no military obligation.*[18]

Hoisington's successor, Brigadier General Mildred C. Bailey,
repeated the argument in 1974:

*No matter what you say about equal opportunity you can-
not deal with the situation of an expectant father and an
expectant mother in the same way. Mothers have a role in
child rearing that is different from fathers and we have to
think about the effect this has on mission readiness and our
ability to be available for worldwide assignment.*[19]

In 1972, however, servicewomen were granted two new
options which might have defused the issue: requesting waivers
to stay in service or having an abortion. The first came because
the AVF needed to retain more women and the services wanted
to avoid negative publicity and court challenges. Waivers were
liberally granted by all services. While the Army granted
waivers to 60 percent of the women who applied, the Air Force,
Navy, and Marine Corps granted waivers to more than 90 percent. The second option came as a result of the Supreme
Court's decision in *Roe* v. *Wade* striking down laws in all fifty
states banning abortion and allowing servicewomen to have
abortions at government expense, until Congress banned feder-
ally funded abortions in 1978.

But court challenges still continued until the 1976 federal
circuit court case of *Crawford* v. *Cushman* ruled that the discharge of a pregnant marine was an unconstitutional violation
of the Fifth Amendment's guarantee of due process. Pregnancy
was a "temporary disability," the court noted, and no other temporary disability resulted in automatic involuntary discharge.
Rather than fight the ruling, the Defense Department ordered
the services to stop involuntarily separating pregnant women
and to allow voluntary separations.

The classification of pregnancy as a "temporary disability" had long been an objective of feminist litigation against civilian employers. The term secured job-related medical benefits for civilian women and prohibited civilian employers from penalizing pregnant employees for the inconvenience their condition caused.

In the military, however, the term protects women from involuntary discharge but serves no other purpose. The military already assumes full responsibility for the medical health of its members regardless of the cause or nature of their infirmity. The term "temporary disability" itself does not protect service-women from adverse personnel actions because, unlike civilian employees, service members can be court-martialed under Article 115 of the Uniform Code of Military Justice for any self-inflicted disability that interferes with their performance of duty—from shooting themselves in the foot to avoid combat, to lying on the beach long enough to become too sunburned to wear a uniform. If a soldier's own negligence or misconduct was the proximate cause of his injury, whether intentional or unintentional, the soldier can be made to reimburse the government for his medical expenses.

Pregnancy is the only temporary disability that service members can inflict upon themselves without fear of punishment. It is also the only temporary disability that earns a service member the right to decide whether to stay in the service or get out, no matter the desires of her commander or the needs of the service. The court's ruling that pregnancy is like any other temporary disability has been applied only to favor and protect women.

The service comes out ahead only if the woman elects to have an abortion. Otherwise, either the woman contributes to the problem of attrition or she becomes a burden to her unit. Restrictions vary from service to service, but typically, the pregnant service member must not be made to stand at attention or parade rest for more than fifteen minutes (no parades or ceremonies). She must not be exposed to harmful chemicals or vapors (no chemical warfare training, no painting, limited duties in the motor pool). She must not receive routine immunizations (no deployments overseas). She must not remain aboard ship in port past her twentieth week and must not go to sea (no sea duty). She must not be assigned to remote installations where there are limited medical facilities. She must not be assigned duties in which nausea, easy fatigue, sudden lightheadedness, or loss of consciousness would be hazardous to her or anyone else (no flying, driving, diving, or operating large machinery). The Navy bars pregnant sailors from participating in swim tests, drown-proofing, field training, and weapons training. The Army exempts pregnant women from over-night duty and limits their work week to forty hours or less, with frequent rest periods.

> Many of the most dedicated men and women see motherhood and military service as conflicting obligations.

Pregnant service members may choose to have their babies at the military hospital nearest their home and are allowed up to six weeks of paid leave not charged to their leave account. Difficult pregnancies may prompt a doctor to relieve a servicewoman of all duties for as long as necessary, sometimes six or seven months before birth, during which the woman is a complete loss to her unit, though her unit is not permitted to request a replacement because she is still on its roster.

Needless to say, pregnancy is not viewed by many as just another temporary disability, like a hernia or a broken leg. Most men and many women, particularly women officers, view it as a unique indulgence for no good reason. Many of the most dedicated men and women see motherhood and military service as conflicting obligations. Many military men still like to think that they endure the danger and hardships of service so that mothers and children can be safe at home. The sight of a pregnant woman at the head of a formation of troops does not increase their confidence or dedication. It is an absurdity. It is a combination of opposites that only proves how unmilitary the military has become, for mothers can be soldiers only when soldiers cease being warriors.

Pregnancy is perhaps the single greatest obstacle to the acceptance of women in the military among military men. Charles Moskos, professor of sociology at the Northwestern University, after interviewing Army women with their units in Honduras, concluded, "When there are no pregnant women, the incorporation of women into nontraditional roles is greatest." He added, "If there is an absolute precondition of the effective utilization of women in field duty, it must be exclusion of pregnant women."[20]

The policy of tolerating pregnant women in uniform, forced upon the military from above, has put the services in an impossible position. The services are duty bound to reduce pregnancies to improve readiness but legally and politically bound to honor pregnant women as fully accepted service members in good standing. Far from discouraging women from having sex, the services' nonjudgmental, safety-first approach tends to encourage promiscuity, even advising female soldiers on how properly to have sex in the field. Following the scout's motto, a pamphlet entitled "Feminine Hygiene in the Field Setting," published and distributed at Fort Meade, Maryland, tells women always to be prepared:

Sex does not just happen in the garrison setting. If you are on birth control pills, make sure that you bring enough packs along to last you for the exercise, and an extra pack in case something happens to the pack you're currently on.

MOTHERHOOD AND MARRIAGE

Problems for the service and the servicewoman do not end with delivery. Having elected to keep the child and remain in service, the woman must struggle to fulfill her duties as a mother and as a soldier, sailor, airman, or marine. She is required to certify in writing that provisions have been made for the care of her dependents during regular duty hours, extended duty hours, readiness exercises, unaccompanied tours, temporary duty, changes of station, and actual emergencies. If overseas, she must arrange for someone to escort her dependents during a possible evacuation of noncombatants. Should any of her arrangements fail, she is still required to report to duty. Failure to provide for the care of her children or to perform her military duty is grounds for receiving a bar to reenlistment or being involuntarily separated. But few women are separated for such failure, because commanders are reluctant to punish young mothers so severely and most have more important things to do than checking to see that everyone's child-care plan is working. The dependent care certificate is, in most cases, a bureaucratic formality. A recent Navy survey found that only half of all Navy mothers even had them.

All problems multiply if the mother is single, as an estimated 24,000 service mothers—or 12.5 percent of all servicewomen—are. And estimates indicate that more than a third of all pregnant servicewomen are unmarried.[21]

For years the Defense Department confused the issue of single parents by secretly including noncustodial single parents (e.g., a divorced serviceman paying child support) in its count of "sole parents." There is, of course, a vast difference between the obligation to pay a few hundred dollars a month to support a child in someone else's custody and the obligation to care for a child in one's own custody, but by lumping the two together the Defense Department could tell the world that "more than three-quarters of the military sole parents are males."[22]

The truth has been known since 1980, but it was ignored to exculpate women for the problem of single parenthood. In 1980 the services defined single parents differently. The Army and Marine Corps included those with custody and those paying child support. The Navy and Air Force counted only service members with actual custody, producing the embarrassing truth that Navy women were eight times as likely and Air Force women were five times as likely as Navy and Air Force men to be single parents.[23] These statistics, along with the inflated figures of the Army and Marine Corps, were reported in the Defense Department's 1981 background review, with footnotes explaining the inconsistency. Nonetheless, throughout the 1980s, the Defense Department included noncustodial single parents in its count to deceive the public.

The ratio of male single parents to female single parents shrinks as the number of women in service increases. In 1988 the Air Force, with women as not quite 14 percent of its personnel strength, estimated that half of its single parents were men and half were women, making Air Force women more than six times more likely to be single parents. The sex of single parents may vary considerably among the services. A 1988 survey of an 11,000-man (13 percent female) Marine headquarters battalion at Twenty-nine Palms, California, found that female Marines were fourteen times more likely to be single parents than male Marines.[24]

Single parenthood would not exist if there were no women in the services. Prior to the 1970s the services often separated service members who became single parents by any circumstance. But when the services were forced to protect servicewomen, the present policy was adopted, and today some 50,000 service members are single parents. The peculiar policy of tolerating service members who become single parents while not enlisting people who are already single parents has invited numerous lawsuits on the grounds that it illegally discriminates against women because the great majority of civilian single parents are female. So far, the ban has withstood all assaults, but because of the continuing cry of discrimination, Congress in 1986 amended Title 10 to permit single parents who had previously served in the regular armed forces to enlist in the reserves, so long as their single parenthood was not the cause of their discharge from service.

By and large, single parents in the military are a sorry lot. Duty calls at odd times, and single parents are often scrambling to arrange for somebody to take their children. All of the normal inconveniences of service life—overnight duty, field exercises, sudden deployments, early morning physical training, and late nights in the motor pool—cause problems. Some bring their children to their unit, some leave their children alone at home, sometimes all day.

The problems of many married service mothers are much the same. Two-thirds are married to servicemen and almost none have husbands who stay at home with the children. Deployments, emergencies, and evacuations are still a problem, but most married service mothers can at least afford to pay for child-care when it is available.

The military is rapidly expanding the number of child care facilities to accommodate the growing legions of dependent children. In 1988 there were 581 military child care centers on 412 installations, with another 100 centers planned for the next six years. Though current capacity is suitable for more than 20,000 children, the Defense Department estimates that 80,000 spaces are needed. The cost of caring for everyone's children has already eaten up funds for other projects. For 1987 Congress approved more than $20 million for nearly all child care construction projects requested by the services, but denied funding for nearly all other facilities related to morale, welfare, and recreation—chapels, libraries, theaters, exchanges, commissaries, and recreation centers. For fiscal year 1989 the Defense Department estimated needing $80 million for operation and construction of child care facilities. Fortunately for the services, the child care boom is one military buildup Congress still enthusiastically supports.

With or without children, marriages between service members are a problem. One-third of all servicewomen are married to servicemen. In 1981 there were some 45,000 "dual-service" or "in-service" couples (90,000 service members). By 1988 the number had grown to more than 56,000 dual-service couples. Some involve both officer and enlisted personnel, others involve members of different services, and more than half involve children. Dual-service couples are not simply "levied" to Korea or Turkey. Each assignment for a dual-service couple must be negotiated with special assignment managers who handle only "joint domicile" assignments. Elaborate computerized systems for making such assignments have not alleviated the need for sacrifice, either their time together or their careers. Usually the couple is asked to decide whose career will take precedence and who will simply tag along. Cost-cutting measures that keep military personnel in one place longer exacerbate the problem. Where the Army could once boast of providing joint domicile assignments (within fifty miles) to 90 percent of dual-service couples, it has lately warned that such assignments "may get increasingly difficult to approve."[25]

Not surprisingly, the demands of family take a heavy toll among female officers and enlisted personnel. Reenlistment rates are consistently lower for women than for men in all of the services, particularly in the middle grades. "We must find ways to retain [women]," the vice commandant of the Coast Guard told DACOWITS. "If family rearing is a major factor, we must explore alternatives."[26] Alternatives to what, he did not say. A Marine Corps study made a similar recommendation that the Corps "help women develop short-term alternatives to marriage and pregnancy for overcoming loneliness."[27] It gave no examples.

FRATERNIZATION

The problems of pregnancy, single parents, and dual-service couples were made possible largely by the erosion of the age-old ban on fraternization between the ranks. To be sure, the American military has been moving toward greater and greater egalitarianism for some time, but nothing has done more to cheapen rank and diminish respect for authority than cute little female lieutenants and privates. Military customs and regulations are no match for the forces that draw men and women together in pairs.

The services could hardly prevent nature from taking her course, but they might have had greater success if servicewomen had not been so opposed to their efforts. The call for liberalization of social restrictions has characterized the military service of American women from World War II and to the present day. Many women consider the customs of service quaint, silly, and boyish. Few understand the necessity for restrictions on social relationships.

Instead of making servicewomen conform to the service, the services have conformed to the women. Fraternization was traditionally understood to occur anytime persons of different rank dealt with each other as equals. Now the term "fraternization" is used only to describe certain officer-enlisted relationships forbidden by the Uniform Code of Military Justice (UCMJ). All other relationships between persons of different rank are permitted so long as one of the persons does not exercise supervisory authority over the other and the relationship does not result in favoritism or harm morale.

Pregnancy is perhaps the single greatest obstacle to the acceptance of women among military men.

The Navy, Marine Corps, and Air Force still prohibit romantic relationships between officers and enlisted personnel. The Army, however, liberalized officer and enlisted relations years ago. Announcing its new fraternization policy in 1984, it insisted that the old policy had simply been "clarified—not relaxed." But the practical effect of the clarification was to legitimize many relationships which were previously considered improper. Today, officers must avoid social involvement only with those directly under them. The finer points of propriety— such as whether a lieutenant should escort his enlisted girl-friend to an officers' dining-out—are left to the individual to decide. But the burden of proof rests with the accuser and the negative effect of the decision upon the service must be "demonstrated and documented."[28]

Instead of clarifying the issue, the new policy only caused confusion. Its authors had failed to consider the complexity of the problem. Commanders complained that the new policy was too permissive and set no clear rule for what was and was not proper, especially for less experienced soldiers. Commanders themselves were unsure what they should or should not condone. The Army's explanation of the policy included examples of inappropriate relationships that caused a "noticeable drop in morale," but what is noticeable to one commander might not be noticeable to another, and experienced commanders are likely to notice before the effect becomes documentable. "Clearly predictable" harm to morale was also highly subjective and sure to invite second-guessing by higher authorities in any contested case. Commanders therefore permitted more than they would have preferred to permit.

Increasingly, rank is seen as something one puts on before breakfast and takes off before dinner. Distinctions of class, culture, and calling, never well understood by Americans, are now not even acknowledged, and traditions that once seemed self-evidently sensible are surrendered without argument to an ideological imperative.

It does not speak well for American military professionals that the policymakers indulge in much devious rhetoric to argue that liberalization is actually good for the military and not simply an easy way to avoid a difficult problem, as evident in this letter from the adjutant general:

> *Personal relationships have always had a positive side.*
> *Close relationships are desired and required if we are to*
> *build cohesive units that can fight, survive, and win on the*
> *battlefield. Building this cohesion requires a professional*
> *sensitivity toward one another.*[29]

The ancient Spartans took a similar view of the connection between personal relationships and unit cohesion, believing that homosexuality increased the bond between comrades-in-arms. The modern American military also benefits from homosexuality in ways it will not admit.

HOMOSEXUALITY

Lesbianism has always been common in the military, but for many years, with so few women, the services preferred to ignore its existence. The truth, according to Helen Rogan, author of *Mixed Company*, was that after World War II, the women's components became havens for female homosexuals, who were naturally attracted to the opportunity for intimate association with other women and to the authoritarian structure of the services, in which personal relationships are based upon "dominance and submission."[30]

Despite the wholesome, feminine image of servicewomen presented to the public by the scandal-sensitive services, Rogan found that the style among lesbian members of the WAC was exaggeratedly masculine. The stereotypical image of the homosexual dyke was well founded in fact. "If you were going to be gay, you wanted to be like a guy, because they were the ones who could get things on," says one lesbian veteran in a documentary film quoted by Rogan. Women cut their hair in men's styles, donned men's clothing when off-duty, sat and walked the way men do, and even wore Old Spice aftershave. They partied together and sat around in the clubs drinking beer and were active in sports.

Within the women's components, lesbians created a secret society with their own informal chain of command that sometimes ignored traditional distinctions between ranks. Rogan quotes one woman whose homosexuality began when she was seduced by her company commander:

> As a baby troop, I noticed there was an in crowd, and all of them, all the important and nice-to-know people, were gay. It was desirable to be gay. The straight young enlisted person finds that out, and then she has to decide what to do. The assumption was that we didn't need men, not for our jobs.[31]

Senior WAC officers, most of whom had come up through the ranks, were more careful to avoid the appearance of lesbianism than enlisted personnel and junior officers. "Oh, sure, of course there were gays [among senior officers], but never publicly," one veteran told Rogan. Low-ranking lesbians respected the need of senior officers to be more discreet in their conduct, and senior officers, in turn, protected everyone's career and the reputation of the Corps by turning a blind eye toward homosexuality. The male heads of the Army left the women to themselves, and no place was safer than Fort McClellan, Alabama, the home of the WAC. There, women lived their lives as they pleased. "We had no need to conform to an artificial standard [of heterosexuality]," one woman told Rogan. "Women were entrenched at Ft. McClellan, with *real power.*"[32] (Emphasis in the original.)

Ironically, the expanded use of women by the services in the 1970s was unwelcome to many lesbians already in service. The influx of large numbers of heterosexual women eroded the power of gays over straights, and the integration of the women's components into the services stripped lesbians of their insulation against the heterosexual world. Once male commanders were relieved of their naïveté regarding lesbianism by complaints from heterosexual women, the nation's newspapers began to sizzle with sordid stories of secret homosexual rings among American servicewomen. In 1980 the USS *Norton Sound* earned an unhappy reputation as "the Ship of Queens" when twenty-four of sixty-one women aboard were accused of homosexual activity. In February 1984 the Army charged eleven women stationed at Fort Leavenworth, Kansas, with homosexuality. In October 1986 eight of thirty-five female military policemen assigned to the Military Academy at West Point were discharged for the same reason. In March 1988 the Defense Department revealed that women were three times more likely to be discharged for homosexuality than men. The disparity between the sexes in the number of investigations for homosexuality is even greater, with those involving women being four times the rate of investigations involving men.

Servicewomen accused of lesbianism have often denied the charge and argued that they were being persecuted for their masculine mannerism. Members of DACOWITS have opined that perhaps the services are not enforcing the ban on homosexuality with equal vigor among men and women—"perhaps the women are just more visible and get caught more readily" because "they don't have the places to go for homosexual bars like the men do," one member suggested.[33]

All indications are, however, that homosexuality is many times more common among female than male service members. Several female West Point graduates told Army researchers that they had been approached by lesbians, whereas no male graduates mentioned being approached by male homosexuals. Charles Moskos, professor of sociology at Northwestern University in Evanston, Illinois, found that lesbianism was a common cause of complaint among women deployed with U.S. forces in Honduras in 1985. "Accounts of lesbians would come up spontaneously in most extended interviews with female soldiers," he wrote.[34] Most recently, DACOWITS heard numerous complaints of lesbianism from Navy and Marine Corps women during a 1987 tour of installations in the Far East. Lesbianism was reportedly so rampant that one barracks was widely referred to as "Lessy Land." Naturally, DACOWITS blamed the Navy for allowing women to live in substandard quarters which contribute "to conditions in which extremist behavior [lesbianism] is fostered and, in some cases, supported by the chain of command."[35] (Men are often quartered in squalid barracks without any apparent increase in the same kind of "extremist behavior.") Yet when the Marine Corps moved promptly against eight female Marines accused of homosexuality, among other offenses, at Camp Lejeune, North Carolina, DACOWITS Chairwoman Jacquelyn Davis complained that the committee had not intended to spark a "witch hunt" for lesbians.[36]

For once, the boast of the homosexual community that gays comprise 10 percent of the population sounds modest. Some lesbians have estimated their strength among servicewomen to be closer to 20 percent. In some jobs and assignments, lesbians may even predominate. Drill sergeant duty has always been a favorite among lesbian NCOs because of the power it gives over young and impressionable female recruits, and lesbians are attracted to small, remote installations and to duty aboard ships, where they can exert greater influence over other women and receive greater protection and opportunity for license.

DACOWITS's charge that the chain of command some-times supports or encourages lesbianism is not entirely without merit. Few men view lesbianism with as much revulsion as they view male homosexuality. Many have been fooled into believing that the dyke stereotype has no foundation in fact and are wary of appearing, even to themselves, like crazed homophobes. All too many officers have adopted a relativist moral attitude which inclines them toward tolerance, despite law and policy. Then, too, lesbians are often their best female soldiers. Lesbians thrive in the military not only because it provides them the soci-ety of other lesbians, but also because it allows and encourages them to act like men. Lesbians are generally at home in the mil-itary. And they never become pregnant.

For these reasons, commanders are reluctant to investigate allegations of lesbianism thoroughly. Many commanders are especially averse to reporting such allegations to their service's security clearance custodian, as required by regulation. A com-mon procedure is to collect statements and evidence, confront the accused, and hope that she submits quietly to an adminis-trative discharge. Most accused homosexuals are discharged under officially honorable conditions. Very few are prosecuted for the criminal offense of sodomy. Of 4,316 men and women discharged for homosexuality from 1984 to 1987, only two were discharged following courts-martial.[37]

PSYCHOLOGICAL DIFFERENCES

Underlying all of the problems with women in the military are the significant psychological differences between men and women. At one time, all who were interested in the issue of women in the military were eager to analyze the ways in which men and women behaved differently. But this became politically dangerous in the early 1980s, and ever since the party line has been that there are no significant differences. Official research efforts seem intent upon proving that assumption. Sociologists studying academy graduates marvel at the psychological similarities between men and women, and when exceptions are granted, they are usually presented to show that women are in some way superior to men.

Significant differences do exist, however, and few are to the women's advantage. One obvious difference is that the military is still far more popular among young men than among young women. "Women do not grow up with the notion that they're going to be a soldier," explains the Army's chief of personnel. "They need a lot of convincing."[38] The expansion of the 1970s quickly exhausted the small pool of high-quality women who were eager to enter the military. Today, the supply barely meets the demand. Army recruiters must approach three times as many women as men for each enlistment, and the quality of female recruits is becoming increasingly difficult to maintain. Plans to recruit more women will only force recruiters to lower standards further.

Already, quality is no longer an advantage of recruiting women over men, as the quality of male recruits has improved dramatically in recent years. The number of men entering the Army with high school diplomas rose from 54.3 percent in 1980 to 90.8 percent in 1986. Today, more than 90 percent of active-duty enlisted males in all of the services have high school diplomas. Test scores for men have also improved, so that men now score higher than women on five out of eight tests of the Armed Services Vocational Aptitude Battery (ASVAB). And the ASVAB tests on which men score better than women are those most likely to indicate aptitude for the majority of jobs in the modern military: general science, arithmetic reasoning, auto/shop information, mathematical knowledge, and electronics. The tests on which women score better than men are those most closely related to traditionally female jobs: reading comprehension, numerical operations, and coding speed. Researchers have concluded that men are better suited for most military jobs and that women are best suited for those traditional jobs to which they are most attracted.[39] In view of these differences, the Defense Department's commitment to putting more women in nontraditional jobs makes little sense.

Men and women entering the services also differ in what they expect of their military careers. Charles Moskos found that few enlisted women saw themselves as future NCOs, certainly not in nontraditional jobs or assignments with extended field duty: "Most of the enlisted women, in contrast with the men, saw NCO status as inconsistent with their life goals and present or future family plans."[40]

The Defense Department's 1981 background review found that while men evaluate military jobs in the same manner as they do civilian jobs, being willing to accept less satisfying occupations to increase promotion opportunities, women tend to be less career-minded: "Findings indicate that women forgo promotion opportunities in favor of job settings less likely to interfere with commitments to husbands and children."[41]

Even when men and women in the military make the same choices, they often do so for different reasons. Their motivations for entering the military are widely separate. Women are much more likely to list practical, selfish reasons for joining the services, such as education, travel, and money. Women simply do not feel the same attraction and attachment to military service that men feel. They are much less interested in military history and world affairs. A 1986 poll by CBS News found that only 25 percent of American women knew which side the United States was supporting in Nicaragua, as opposed to 50 percent of the men. The same disparity exists among members of the military.

Men tend to give other reasons for joining the military, such as patriotism or love of country, but these lofty sentiments usually hide other, less currently respectable reasons. Most are too embarrassed to confess that they derive a profound sense of personal importance from their role as protector. Navy Lieutenant Niel L. Golightly, a fighter pilot and Olmsted Scholar, is not embarrassed. He writes:

> [C]onsider the young man under fire and neck deep in the mud of a jungle foxhole, sustained in that purgatory by the vision of home—a warm, feminine place that represents all the good things that his battlefield is not. Somewhere in that soldier's world view, though he may not be able to articulate it, is the notion that he is here... so that all the higher ideals of home embodied in mother, sister, and girlfriend do not have to be here.[42]

Not too long ago, this was conventional wisdom, admitted unabashedly by everyone from Harvard to Hollywood. In a scene from the movie *Operation Petticoat*, the crew of a submarine watches in awe as a group of nurses is brought aboard. The boat's executive officer says to a sailor, "If anybody asks you what you're fighting for, there's your answer." Today the line would evoke snickers at this caricature of sexism.

Many men are attracted to the military by its intensely masculine and deeply romantic character. The uniforms, the rank, the danger, the purposefulness, the opportunity to earn the respect of men and the admiration of women—all contribute to the military's enduring hold on the imagination of men and boys, and all are now threatened by the military's eagerness to present a female-friendly face. These things which have inspired many men to greatness are looked upon today as embarrassingly puerile. Progressive society prides itself with having evolved to a higher level where ancient impulses are deplored as childish *machismo* and where the most socially respectable motivations are, ironically, the most material and the most selfish. Young men today dare not confess their captivation with the romance of martial glory, even to themselves. Instead, when asked why they entered the military, they say "patriotism." The more thoughtful have better answers, but they are equally evasive. Ask a young man why he enters a service academy, and he is likely to answer "to get a good education" or "to pursue a military career."

Women, however, are not impressed with physical prowess, do not relish competition, are not intrigued by danger, do not need to prove their manhood, and see little reason to hide their weaknesses, psychological or physical. One researcher has suggested that women have higher rates of morbidity because they are not as reluctant as men to report feeling sick, perhaps because it is generally more acceptable for a woman to complain of sickness or injury and because the role of the patient is more compatible with the woman's passive, dependent role in society.[43]

But in war, physical prowess is important, and dangers must be faced. The military quite naturally encourages the suppression of personal hurts and stigmatizes those who hurt too easily or too often as "gimps" and "snivellers." Good soldiers pride themselves on ignoring illness and enduring pain, on never being found among the "sick, lame, and lazy."

Smart, ambitious female officers know this and do their best to assume masculine attitudes toward everything, as several studies have shown. Success depends upon becoming male as much as possible. They drive fast cars, compete fiercely at sports, disdain weakness, reject association with other women, devote themselves totally to their careers, and adopt male attitudes toward sex, marriage, and family. Women of the 1980 West Point class showed less interest in marriage and family than their male classmates. They also tended to describe themselves as psychologically more masculine than they were before entering the academy. Older female officers tend to view marriage and family as incompatible with military service for women. Despite assurances from feminist ideologues that they can have both, these women often choose to remain single for the good of their careers.

Unfortunately for the services, most women do not manage or even attempt to convert to masculinity. Even among the many dedicated military women it is too much to ask. They would be kicking against the goads of Nature by adopting mannish ways, since many fundamental behavioral differences between men and women are firmly rooted in biology.

Many feminists of course reject the possibility that sex differences are biologically based and therefore beyond the reach of social reform. Some cite the work of Howard A. Moss of the National Institutes of Health, whose experiments showed that men and women respond differently to newborn baby boys and girls and thus unwittingly influence their future sex differentiation. Moss made

> Nothing has done more to cheapen rank and diminish respect for authority than fraternization between men and women.

no overall claim, but his findings have been accepted as the last word on the subject by feminists. The reaction of a female Army colonel is typically dismissive: "Don't give me any of that hormones shit! I've had it up to here with hormones!"

The evidence is fairly conclusive, however, that hormones do play a significant role. A study by John Money and Anke A. Ehrhardt found that baby girls who had been exposed to androgen-like hormones in the early stages of growth in the womb developed "tomboy" characteristics such as an interest in vigorous outdoor activities and competitive sports. They were also slower to develop an interest in boys and dating, though still less aggressive than most boys of the same age.[44]

Similarities between boys and tomboys diminish as both sexes reach puberty. Tomboys develop into young women with the introduction of the female sex hormone estrogen, while boys receive an extra charge of masculinity in the form of the male sex hormone testosterone. As an artificial steroid, testosterone is sometimes used by athletes to improve their performance. It accelerates their metabolism, heightens their urge for exertion, and quickens their recovery. Before the use of steroids was outlawed in the Olympics, a U.S. Olympic athlete privately confessed, "I take one steroid that makes it possible for me to go through a brick wall. I take a second steroid that *demands* that I go through the brick wall." The "demand" steroid was testosterone.[45]

Testosterone's effects on behavior are plainly seen in the greater aggressiveness of men, "one of the best established, and most pervasive, of all psychological sex differences," say feminist scholars Eleanor Maccoby and Carol Jacklin of Stanford University. In *The Psychology of Sex Differences*, Maccoby and Jacklin write:

> *(1) Males are more aggressive than females in all human societies for which evidence is available. (2) The sex differences are found early in life, at a time when there is no evidence that differential socialization pressures have been brought to bear by adults to "shape" aggression differently in the two sexes. (3) Similar sex differences are found in man and subhuman primates. (4) Aggression is related to levels of sex hormones, and can be changed by experimental administration of these hormones.*[46]

Traditional socialization merely confirms what has been ordained already by biology. It ensures that a child's physical development and psychological development proceed in the same direction, and it teaches boys and girls to make sense of themselves, their bodies, and their relations with the opposite sex.

A favorite feminist theory holds that proper, nonsexist socialization can, over time, correct biology, producing women as psychologically aggressive and as physically capable as men. But there is no evidence that the biological contribution to sex differences can be completely overcome without modern drugs.

Some feminists argue that modern warriors need not be as aggressive as warriors of the past, or that the lack of aggressiveness offers definite advantages to the modern military. Women make better soldiers, they say, because they are well behaved, less dangerous to themselves and others, and better suited for many routine tasks that men find tedious. Two Army studies indicate that women are better at routine, repetitive tasks. One, during World War II, found that women performed much better than men when assigned the monotonous task of monitoring a radar screen for an anti-aircraft battery in Nova Scotia. The other, in 1984, found that female officers were quicker than men to decide on a course of action when presented with familiar situations, but slower in unfamiliar situations.

If war were always tedious and routine, women would be better suited for it. But war is not always tedious and routine. Even in peacetime, many military jobs require quickness and daring. Female intelligence personnel once assigned to shadow Soviet Military Liaison Mission (SMLM) vehicles proved too timid to keep up the chase through crowded German towns and on the open autobahn, where speeds in excess of 130 mph are common. The implications of this example for female fighter pilots are obvious, but Defense officials will not admit that women lack the killer instinct. Proof of their deficiency must await their first actual dogfights with real, all-male enemies.

A final problem with women in the military, one that has nothing to do with comparative abilities of men and women, is the impact of the presence of women on the behavior of men. It is not just a problem of morale, which has hardly been a concern during the integration process. When integration of the academies caused bitter resentment among males, integrators dismissed the low morale as sexist irrationality. But when Navy surveys showed junior enlisted men aboard integrated ships approving women, integrators attributed the higher morale to the presence of women.

The different responses among men to integration are an indication of the complexity of the problem. On the one hand, the best educated and most intellectual men with a keener appreciation of military ethics and tradition overwhelmingly opposed the presence of women. On the other hand, the less educated, less intellectual, and less career-minded men enjoyed their presence. At the same time, charges of sexual harassment are aimed most often at junior enlisted men, while senior enlisted men and officers are more prone to fraternization and are usually the most outspoken in defense of women. Clearly the integrators are mistaken in believing that opposition to women comes from older men simply because they are old-fashioned, and the lowest ranks simply because they are uneducated. Things are not that simple.

The roots of group behavior among men run deep into our being. All-male groups have existed in virtually every known society. Most anthropologists agree that all-male groups produce a peculiar kind of nonerotic psychological bond that men crave and cannot find elsewhere. In some societies, bonds between male friends are stronger and more sacred than bonds between husbands and wives. In his book *Men and Marriage*, best-selling author George Gilder writes:

> *The closest tie in virtually all societies, primate and human, is between women and children. But the next most common and strong connection may well be the all-male bond. The translation of the rudimentary impulse of love into intense ties between specific men and women appears to have been emphasized and sanctified later, in the course of creating civilized societies.*[47]

Typically, says Gilder, the all-male group is strongly hierarchical, placing heavy emphasis on leadership, loyalty, and excitement. Members are admitted and ranked according to their demonstrated ability to contribute to the group's common purpose. Competition is the key to entry and advancement. It is also a source of excitement. Leaders command the loyalty and respect of inferiors because they best personify the values of the group.

The military is also strongly hierarchical. It begs for leadership, demands loyalty, and lives for excitement. It is this way, first, because it was created by men, and, second, because such characteristics make it effective at making war. The military depends upon men acting as a team at the very moment when every man is under great temptation to seek his own safety. The personal bonds that men form with each other, as leaders, as followers, as comrades-in-arms, often enable ordinary men to perform acts of extreme self-sacrifice when ideals such as duty, country, or cause no longer compel.

The presence of women inhibits male bonding, corrupts allegiance to the hierarchy, and diminishes the desire of men to compete for anything but the attentions of women. Pushing women into the military academies made a mockery of the academies' essential nature and most honored values. Integration of Army basic training undercuts the motivation of male recruits. When this was first done under the Carter administration, drill sergeants noticed that the remaining all-male companies regularly exceeded training standards for tests of motivation and endurance, such as the twelve-mile road march, while integrated companies rarely exceeded standards for such events. When the difference, dubbed a "stretch factor," was brought to the attention of the Army's chief of staff, General Shy Meyer, in 1982, basic training was resegregated.[18]

The impact of the presence of women on all-male units was a major reason why military leaders for so long opposed integration of combat units. In the public debate over integration, however, politics has forced the military to concede all ground on the issue. Today, the services themselves are the first to assert that women have nothing but a positive effect on the behavior of men—assertions made possible by a social phenomenon that has received practically no attention from either side of the debate.

The services have not yet noticed the effect of *charm* on the daily relations of men and women. Men like women, and because they like women, they cannot treat women as they treat other men. They are rarely as firm, as harsh, or as critical with women as with other men.

Charm does not affect all men equally. Older men of senior rank tend to be most susceptible because their superior-subordinate relationship with women closely resembles traditional sex roles, and women find the maturity and authority of their male seniors attractive. Because of this affinity, the services have made special efforts to warn commanding officers of the dangers of fraternizing with women in their command.

Even if charm does not lead to fraternization, it does affect a woman's treatment and prestige. Charles Moskos reported that male supervisors of the women he interviewed in Honduras were "defensive" about their women and reluctant to criticize their performance.[49] ROTC cadets have complained that women "get babied too much by the drill sergeants."[50] Comely and confident women who perform well will almost always win exaggerated praise. Some are more successful at their jobs because they can easily elicit the cooperation of charmed men. It is not usually a matter of flirting to get their way, or of using sex as a bribe. This does happen, especially at the lower ranks, but most women benefit from the difference of sex in a more subtle way. All they have to do is let men act as men rather than as sexless bureaucrats. "Anyone who doesn't think he's a man first and a soldier second just isn't paying attention," says one old soldier, explaining his practice of sending his pleasant and attractive female sergeant to brief senior officers.

Unfortunately for the services, there are too many senior officers who aren't paying attention, too many who believe that our deepest thoughts can be easily manipulated, that the way men have always been is not the way they are now or will be soon. These men pretend that sex can be easily ignored. They insist that professionalism means putting aside one's manhood as a relic of prehistory and that the difficulties caused by having women in the military are merely "management problems."

Chapter 9

THE FOG OF PEACE

Marriage, to women as to men, must be a luxury,
not a necessity; an incident of life, not all of it.
And the only possible way to accomplish this
great change is to accord to women equal power
in the making, shaping, and controlling
of the circumstances of life.

—SUSAN B. ANTHONY
SPEECH ON SOCIAL PURITY, 1875

THERE IS CONFUSION in the camp and division in the ranks. Having won battle after battle, many feminists have begun to think they might have lost the war.

The source of their unsettledness is feminism itself. In her recent book *Women and War*, Jean Bethke Elshtain, feminist author and professor of political science at the University of Massachusetts at Amherst, writes:

> *From its inception, feminism has not quite known whether to fight men or to join them; whether to lament sex differences and deny their importance or to acknowledge and even valorize such differences; whether to condemn all wars outright or to extol women's contributions to war efforts. At*

times, feminists have done all of these things, with scant regard for consistency.[1]

Certainly some military feminists have been willing to argue anything in order to get what they wanted. DACOWITS claims alternately that women are needed to make the AVF work and that the view of women as "fillers" to make the AVF work harms women's morale. Antonia Handler Chayes, as undersecretary of the Air Force, told the House Armed Services Committee in November 1979, "The Air Force would be pleased to exceed its goal [for women]. Many of the most critical shortages—engineers, scientists, pilots—can be filled by qualified women." One month later, she told a conference on the AVF, "The fact is, we don't find large numbers of women to fill the technical areas, neither enlisted nor officers. It's very hard to find women engineers."[2]

Often feminists cannot agree among themselves on the way to achieve their goals. Since 1974 feminists have argued for an ever narrower definition of combat that would open as many jobs to women as possible within legal constraints, but in 1984 feminists at the Air Force Academy recommended expanding the definition of combat to cover jobs in which women are already serving, so that male cadets could not complain that women do not belong at the academy because they do not serve in combat. Sharon Lord, deputy assistant secretary of defense for equal opportunity under President Reagan, decried the resegregation of Army basic training in 1982, saying, "If soldiers are going to be asked to support and trust one another, it is important to believe that they have completed strenuous training."[3] Two years later, Air Force Academy feminists recommended resegregating cadet intramural sports to keep male cadets from noticing the physical limitations of female cadets.

A further indication of serious trouble beneath the feminist flag is the deep division that exists between female officers and female enlisted personnel. While female officers clamor to get into jobs previously closed to them, enlisted women are quite satisfied with those traditional jobs they already hold. The services have expended considerable effort to channel women into nontraditional jobs with some success. A third are working in traditionally male jobs, compared to only 3 percent of women in the civilian work force.

Still, enlisted women in nontraditional jobs are more dissatisfied and have higher rates of attrition than officers. Many enter these jobs as a second choice and migrate to traditionally female jobs at their first opportunity.

"The plain fact," wrote Charles Moskos, after his visit to Honduras, "is that the two female groups [officer and enlisted] had different career agendas and therefore different attitudes toward their positions in the Army." He continued:

> *Female officers often expressed resentment, sometimes anger, at emerging career constraints within the military. Female enlisted saw their time in the Army as a stepping stone from an unsatisfactory pre-military existence to a more hopeful post-military life. Female officers tended to deemphasize physiological and emotional differences between men and women while female enlisted were much more likely to acknowledge distinctions between the sexes.*[4]

Enlisted women almost always referred to themselves as "girls" though female officers rarely did. Female officers were also much more concerned about presenting a good view of women in the military than were female enlisteds, who readily complained about conditions in the field, the lack of privacy, and approaches from lesbians. They also favored a special chain of communication for reporting female complaints, but female officers thought it an impediment to complete assimilation. The only complaints more often heard from female officers concerned sexual harassment. Enlisted women defined sexual harassment narrowly as unwanted sexual advances. Female officers defined it as anything that offended their feminist sensibilities, including sexist language, traditional sex roles, and combat restrictions. Enlisted women tended to think that individual women were responsible for defending themselves against sexual harassment without involving the chain of command, while female officers saw it as a command responsibility.

Female officers and enlisted women are most at odds on the issue of combat. Half of the enlisted women Moskos interviewed thought that women should not be allowed in combat, while the other half thought they should be, but only if they volunteered. Among officers, however, half said that women should be allowed to volunteer for combat, and half said that women should be ordered into combat involuntarily, just as men are. None of the enlisted women said they would volunteer for combat if it were possible, but several of the officers said they would.

Comparisons by other researchers confirm Moskos's findings and vividly show that the views of female officers and enlisteds are not just different but fundamentally antagonistic. Michael Rustad quotes enlisted women complaining about the harshness of Army life: "I don't feel we should have to work more than eight-hour days. I think the military should treat us as persons and not as instruments," says one. Another says, "I cannot understand why military persons have to be so tough and callous."[5] These women would be horrified by the coarse bravado of lunchtime conversation among female officers at West Point, reported by Helen Rogan. "Women can easily do Ranger school," says a female officer. "As for that business about men and women sharing foxholes, if you are next to a male in a foxhole in a combat situation and you need to urinate or change your Tampax, you'll just *go ahead and do it!*" says a second officer. (Emphasis in the original.) "Why, I'd just bleed right through!" says a third, to the laughter of the group.[6]

At times, it seems, feminists want all people to be more like women. At other times, they want themselves to be more like men. Today we find mention of two groups among feminists: "equity feminists," who stress equal opportunity and the sameness of the sexes, and "gender feminists," who stress the estrangement of the sexes and the superiority of women.

At first, feminists agitated for a limited equality, requiring only that men and women be treated the same for certain specific purposes. As early as 1869, when Susan Brownell Anthony first used the slogan "Equal Pay for Equal Work," feminists held that sex should not matter as long as individual women are capable of performing specific tasks of a given job. Considerations that might still have motivated different treatment for men and women, such as an employer's personal preference, religious beliefs, or broader sociological concerns, were deemed irrelevant and unjust and were finally outlawed a hundred years later with passage of the Equal Pay Act of 1963 and the Civil Rights Act of 1964.

Though neither act applied directly to the military, the reasoning behind both was used later to speed integration of the services. The argument moved away from the general nature of military service to specific requirements for individual jobs. This tactic was deftly exposed by William J. Gregor in an essay entitled "Women, Combat, and the Draft: Placing Details in Context." Gregor, an Army officer then on the faculty at the U.S. Military Academy, argued that feminists ignored the complex reality of both combat and most combat organizations in order to reduce military service to performing a limited number of job-related tasks. Their assumption was, in his words, "If you place in a position a person capable of performing the tasks assigned to a position and train the person in those critical tasks, those tasks will be performed and the unit will be effective."[7] Tests like REFWAC, MAXWAC, and the Female Artillery Study all focused on the completion of limited, easily measurable individual or unit tasks. Completion of the tasks led automatically to the conclusion that women did not adversely affect the ability of a unit to accomplish its mission.

This approach yields feminists two advantages. First, it permits them to eliminate many concerns of war-wise military men

Having won the battles, many feminists now think they might have lost the war.

without ever addressing them. Any old soldier who tries to express his gut feelings about the effects of integration on morale is dismissed as lacking empirical evidence to support his opinions. The second advantage is that it permits the integrationists to pick and choose among job requirements for those that favor women. Academics rose to supreme importance at the academies because the grade point averages of women compare favorably with those of men. High school diplomas are preferred as a qualification for enlistment because women are more likely than men to have them. But requirements that tend to favor men are attacked as unrelated to job performance. Boxing, observed Judith Stiehm, is "an activity in which [Air Force officers] would never participate in combat" and therefore should be eliminated from the Air Force Academy's curriculum. Likewise, the practice of shaving the heads of male recruits should be abandoned in favor of unspecified "new ways to encourage group bonding" that do not exclude women.

This tactic can go only so far, however. Feminists must still confront the reality that some differences between the sexes do matter much more in the military than in most other sectors of society. But rather than concede the point, many feminists argue that all sex differences, physical and mental, are due to environmental influences. In the controversy over Nature versus Nurture, they side solidly with the environmentalists, who argue that the way we are raised determines who and what we are, the assumption being that the nurturing process can be altered to minimize if not eliminate sex differences. These feminists theorize that the participation of women in activities previously closed to them will cause women to develop greater physical strength and aggressiveness. They reject all evidence that sex differences are rooted in biology and therefore beyond the reach of social reform.

Yet, for all their talk of equality, many feminists still evince a strong belief in the moral superiority of women over men. They did not originate the idea. No doubt long before Aristophanes' *Lysistrata*, peace-loving women have been a reproach to warlike men. Feminism received a boost in the nineteenth century from the belief, common in many Protestant Christian churches, that women were morally superior, though today feminists often denounce Christianity as a male religion.

In the view of these "sexist" feminists, freeing women to participate in the governing of society is not so that women might enjoy the thrill of killing, but so that society will be less violent and more peace-loving. Pacifism has been a constant characteristic of the feminist movement, as in, for example, the antiwar 1960s and women's peace and disarmament groups of the 1970s and 1980s. Mary Jo Salter wonders in *The Atlantic Monthly* whether "we might not have invented war" had the world been populated solely by women.[8] Betty Friedan in her book *The Second Stage*, presses for an ever greater role for women in politics and in the military not for equality's sake, but as a way of weakening the forces of aggression in the world. Ultimately the thinking of such feminists leads to a view that men and women are naturally not very much alike, for if society alone is responsible for making men and women what they are, then the nonviolence of women is the product of patriarchy.

Many feminists have actively opposed militarizing American women. Some have organized antirecruiting campaigns; others have openly attacked proponents of women in the military in print and in person. In 1976 at DACOWITS's twenty-fifth anniversary meeting, the only opposition to the call for repeal of the combat exclusion laws came from three women representing the ACLU who found DACOWITS's argument that women were needed to make the AVF work repellent:

> *Military studies refer to the utilization of women (one might ask by whom). And articles in both the civilian and military press refer to women as filling the gaps recruiters can't plug with men.*[9]

The trio equated utilization with exploitation and argued that women should not give up "feminist ideals of nurturing, caring, and life-giving concerns" so that they might be used by the military. Women should, instead, work "to have their fellow soldiers think of all humans as human beings first rather than animals to be casually slaughtered."

Nevertheless, environmental, egalitarian feminism tries hard to convince that women can be warriors, too. Neither pacifism nor the supposed moral superiority of women holds great appeal with the American public. Integration of the military would never have happened if its purpose had been to make the American military less military. Many prominent feminists seem quite willing to walk all over feminism's traditional pacifism to advance the cause of military women. Dr. Nora Scott Kinzer, employed by the Carter Pentagon, told Mary Jo Salter, "We are brought up with a myth that women are nicer than men, that they are the keepers of the hearth and the mothers...."[10] When asked by the House Armed Services Committee in 1979 about the aversion to violence and killing among women, Antonia Handler Chayes, Carter's undersecretary of the Air Force, replied:

> *I do not see that there is any sex or gender difference in the degree of pacifism or willingness to go to war.... I think that is a cultural concept that really does not necessarily accord with the truth now.... I think that women throughout history, even in mythology, have taken up arms, and very effectively. Look at the Amazons.*[11]

In the past decade, military feminists have looked frequently at the Amazons, often in hopes of finding some evidence that they actually existed. After ten years of research for her book *The War Against the Amazons*, Abby Weltan Kleinbaum, professor of social science at the City University of New York, concluded that they did not. To some, her book was an unwelcome revelation:

*At least one woman told me that when she read in my intro-
duction that the particular Amazon nation described in the
well-known stories told by Greek and Latin authors probably never existed, she felt like crying.*[12]

Many feminists seem unable to understand that the ancient
Greeks and Romans entertained themselves with stories of
Amazons for much the same reason that people today enjoy
stories about vicious aliens from outer space. It was the
very barbarity of a society ruled by women that excited their
imagination, not the actual or possible existence of such a
society.

Many myths—like the nonexistent Amazons—have served
to advance the cause of military women. The most popular is
Israeli women. The tough but womanly Israeli *sabra* who
bravely deals death to the enemies of her embattled nation is
almost entirely a creation of Hollywood. The truth is so much
less glamorous that informed feminists never mention the
Israelis in any debate. If Israel is discussed at all among feminists, it is as an example of failure—a country founded originally
by men and women with radically egalitarian ideals that was
forced by a hostile environment to adopt more traditional ways.
In her book *Israeli Women: The Reality Behind the Myth*, feminist author Lesley Hazelton dispelled three common fallacies
about Israeli women. First, the early Zionist settlers were no
more sexually liberated than anyone else at the time. Second,
the Israeli army during the War for Independence did not make
great use of women in combat. Third, Israeli women today are
far less feminist than most Western women.[13]

In 1948 a handful of women did see combat with the
Hagana's fighting arm, the *Polmach*, but their presence resulted
in both sides suffering higher casualties. Israeli men risked their
lives and missions to protect their women, and Arab troops
fought more fiercely to avoid the humiliation of being defeated
by women. The women were withdrawn after three weeks.
Hazelton quotes Yigal Allon, a leading *Polmach* commander:

The girls stormed at any proposed discrimination, arguing
that it ran counter to the spirit of the new society being
built in Palestine.... In the end, the wiser counsel prevailed:
the girls were still trained for combat, but placed in units of
their own. Whenever possible, they were trained for defen-
sive warfare only.[14]

For the rest of the war, the role of women was strictly subordinate and supportive. "When things got too hot the women
would clean and reload the rifles for the men, so they could
increase their rate of fire," wrote Hazelton. Most served as
radio operators, nurses, quartermasters, or couriers. They were
particularly useful for smuggling arms, ammunition explosives,
and other contraband past chivalrous British guards who would
not search women.

Today, the Israelis use women far more conservatively than
most NATO nations. Conscription is universal, but with exemptions for marriage, motherhood, religion, health, and unsuitability, barely half of all eligible eighteen-year-old women are
required to serve. (Female recruits joke that the Hebrew ini-
tials of the Israeli Defense Force [IDF], THL, stand for three
Hebrew words meaning "We should have gotten married.")

Only the IDF's training units use women in nontraditional
roles as instructors of weapons and tactics and temporary leaders of men. But their effectiveness is debatable. Using women
as instructors is supposed to spur men to excel on account of the
sexist belief, accepted among many Israelis, that if a woman can
do it, so can any man. But, according to Israeli military historian
Martin Van Creveld, the credibility of the women is limited by
their lack of real operational experience; they are used, nevertheless, to free more men to fight.

Elsewhere in the IDF, the jobs open to women are few.
Members of the women's component, the *Chen*, serve mostly as
secretaries, clerks, teletypists, nurses, teachers, and army social
workers. *Chen* women are barred from many jobs involving
physical strain, adverse environmental conditions, or combat.

They do not serve as pilots, nor on ships, nor where there are no shower facilities. They do not pump gas and they do not drive trucks. As a *Chen* colonel explained to Hazelton, "And even if a girl could drive a truck, where would she drive it in wartime? To the front. And we don't send girls to the front in wartime."[15] Israeli law requires that women be evacuated from the front in the event of hostilities. The experience of women captured in 1948 and of men captured by the Syrians more recently has confirmed fears that women would suffer unspeakable tortures if captured today.

Chen women do not have equal status with male soldiers. They are paid less and serve only two years instead of three for men. Training for both officers and enlisted personnel is segregated by sex. *Chen* training emphasizes traditionally feminine skills and touches lightly on basic soldiering skills for morale purposes. Weapons training is cursory and does not include

The views of female officers and enlisteds are not just different but fundamentally antagonistic.

their combat use. *Chen* women are taught to assemble and disassemble weapons, to clean and to operate them, but they do not practice marksmanship. After basic training, the only time most *Chen* women carry weapons is on parade, a photo opportunity for journalists interested in perpetuating a myth.

Only in the *Nahal*, a special corps charged with protecting frontier settlements, do women routinely carry weapons and train to use them, but according to Lionel Tiger and Joseph Shepler, authors of *Women in the Kibbutz*, "even in the *Nahal*, the attitude to female military activity is relatively unserious, and the military functions of women are sharply curtailed."[16] Standing orders are for women to take to the bunkers in the event of attack. *Nahal* women are armed with older, inferior weapons, and target practice is often the occasion of lighthearted ridicule of the women's marksmanship. No one, least of all the women, takes their participation in the military seriously, whereas a man's standing in the army greatly affects his status in the kibbutz. The duality of the sexes is everywhere apparent in Israeli military service, a fact much bemoaned by Israeli feminists, who, according to Hazelton, see military service as reinforcing traditional sex roles and the subordination of women. The fact that "*Chen*," an abbreviation of *Cheil Nashim* or "women's army," is also a Hebrew word meaning "grace" or "charm" is not entirely accidental. "We never disregard the fact that the girls here are going to be married and become mothers," a *Chen* commander told Tiger and Shepler, "We don't want to impair their feminine personality in any way."[17]

The Israeli military's respect for sexual duality reflects Israeli society as a whole. Israeli art quite often uses medieval imagery to romanticize Israeli women as damsels in distress and Israeli fighter pilots and paratroops as their knightly champions. One senior *Chen* officer told Hazelton:

> *A woman's just not built for fighting, physically or mentally. Her aspirations lie in another direction altogether—marrying and having children.... I don't think women should fight, not because they're soft, but because their purpose in life is to tend to the next generation.*[18]

To most Israelis, a woman's primary civic responsibility is to be a wife and mother. Her brief stint of military service is to free men to fight. As for the idea of women in combat, Hazelton reports that 90 percent of Israeli women oppose the idea. Those who favor it are not in the *Chen*.

In the desperate search for precedent, some feminists turn to the Lucy Brewers of revisionist history. Others admire the exploits of women pressed into military service by wartime totalitarian states, though our knowledge comes solely from state propaganda, and today none of these states employs many women in the military or any in combat. Still others see hope in the deadly daring of suicidal female terrorists and the rising rate of homicides committed by women.

The world nevertheless does not see angry bands of women rising up in arms against their male oppressors, and even feminists who would relish such a sight admit that women, whether feminist or not, are, in the words of Judith Stiehm, "de facto pacifists." Says Stiehm, "Women have almost no credibility with regard to the use of force; they are believed to have no capacity for forceful insistence or retaliation."[19] If women were to surprise the world by assuming fully the male role of warrior and protector, says Steihm, "it will be a change so radical that one must turn to fiction rather than history to find a parallel."[20]

And this is in the making. Feminists are rapidly writing the fiction they need to further their cause, creating the illusion that military women deal well with danger and privation in the field. Many women are overly impressed with their ability to endure what men consider minor inconveniences. Consider the following report filed by a feminist sociologist employed by the Air Force to speak professionally on the subject of women in the military at the Air University:

> *The living and working conditions for everyone during this entire period were very primitive and dangerous. At no time was this made clearer than on the day when an Army airborne unit just 20 miles south of us suffered 120 injuries and 4 fatalities. Hostile environment conditions, which played a large part in this incident, also plagued our unit, and even though we experienced no fatalities and only a limited number of injuries ourselves, the knowledge of what had happened to a unit so close by had a sobering effect upon our morale for days.[21]*

What caused the four deaths and hundred odd injuries? Frostbite? Wild boars? In fact, they were all caused by high winds and peculiar topography, a special danger only to paratroopers participating in a mass tactical parachute drop. The author of this fiction was assigned to a safe and stationary radar site with tents, showers, hot meals, and portable latrines, yet she leads the reader to believe that her unit faced the same dangers as the unfortunate paratroopers in the 82nd Airborne Division.

Other more objective researchers have contributed in their own way to the fiction that women perform well "in the field." The women in Honduras interviewed by Charles Moskos for his report entitled "Female GIs in the Field," enjoyed the comforts of televisions, stereos, hot showers twice a day, electrical lighting, a local post exchange, and frequent trips into town. To a dogfaced infantryman, these are all the comforts of home. None of the women in the military today has endured the discomforts that infantrymen bear regularly. Despite proud boasts that women can easily "do Ranger school," no woman presently in service has done anything like it. Not one of them has ever walked day and night through freezing rain, up and down the Tennessee Valley Divide with a seventy-pound ruck on her back and a twenty-three-pound machinegun in her arms. Not one of them has gone nine days without sleep, with a single cold meal a day and nothing over her head but a canvas cap.

Such are the discomforts not of combat but of training. Combat—the business of barbarians, Byron's "brain-spattering windpipe-slitting art"—is many times worse. Of his time as a Marine platoon commander in Vietnam, James Webb wrote:

> We would go months without bathing, except when we could stand naked among each other next to a village well or in a stream or in the muddy water of a bomb crater. It was nothing to begin walking at midnight, laden with packs and weapons and ammunition and supplies, seventy pounds or more of gear, and still be walking when the sun broke over mud-slick paddies that had sucked our boots all night. We carried our own gear and when we took casualties we carried the weapons of those who had been hit.
>
> When we stopped moving we started digging, furiously throwing out the heavy soil until we had made chest-deep fighting holes.... We slept in makeshift hooches made out of ponchos, or simply wrapped up in a poncho, sometimes so exhausted that we did not feel the rain fall on our own faces.

Most of us caught hookworm, dysentery, malaria, or yaws, and some of us had all of them.

We became vicious and aggressive and debased, and reveled in it, because combat is all of those things and we were surviving. I once woke up in the middle of the night to the sounds of one of my machinegunners stabbing an already-dead enemy soldier, emptying his fear and frustrations into the corpse's chest....[22]

Webb's experiences were not unique, for soldiers in all wars have known similar hardships, equally gruesome. A Korean War veteran recalls the battle for Pork Chop Hill:

As I called for my final protective line fires, I looked up from the trenches, the enemy seemed to blanket the whole hillside. Men were screaming and shouting.... The fight was mass confusion and exhausting. We were like vicious animals in the hand-to-hand fighting that followed....

As daylight broke that morning, we could see the hill was covered with bodies, some of which had been there several days from previous battles. Our first task was to clean out the trenches by throwing the dismembered hands and limbs, caused from grenade and artillery explosions, over the tops of the parapets....

Later that morning the hot summer sun, with no wind, began to bear down upon the bare hilltop and the deathly scent of ripened bodies, several days old, created such an unendurable nausea that aircraft had to be called upon to spray the area.[23]

Such experiences should hardly need retelling. In the late twentieth century, macabre depictions of war's horrors in art and literature have become so commonplace that they no longer shock. Yet everyday combat seems less and less horrible to many in Washington and elsewhere who think of military service as, in Webb's words, "something akin to a commute to the Pentagon." A reflexive opposition to war remains, but the horror of old-fashioned, hand-to-throat combat is hidden in a fog of forgetful peace, allowing the rhetoric of sexual equality to turn the brain-spattering art into a career opportunity.

This changing view of war once had feminism confused and divided. Thoughtful feminists did not miss the irony that a movement dedicated to womanly nonviolence and life-giving concerns had been largely, if not solely, responsible for trivializing war. Yet few feminists rose up to denounce the work of the integrationists, though many quietly lamented the changing face of feminism. The half-heartedness of their objection to the new feminism evinced a growing ambivalence toward "the militarization of women's lives." Many feminists were caught between an automatic revulsion at anything military and the recognition that, like it or not, the military was doing what pacifistic feminism was not. It was changing American society. "The armed forces have done as much, if not more, to advance the social and economic role of women in our society than practically any other factor or organization I can think of," said Sue Berryman, a researcher for the Rand Corporation, in 1986.[24] Her perspective, shared by many, was that "the country's verbal and legal war over whether women should be trained and used in combat can ultimately be seen as a war over women's rights and obligations not only in the military but also in the larger society."

It is the power of the military to direct society that united feminists in pursuing a greater role for military women. Power is a favorite word among all feminists, and they are not at all embarrassed to use it. Carolyn Becraft, who for years headed the Women's Equity Action League's Military Project, told a panel on the military at the Eighteenth Annual Conference on Women and the Law, "The issue of women in the military is really an issue of power—power, policy, and women in policy positions."[25] DACOWITS never ceases to demand that women be placed in policy-making positions. When the Marine Corps established two panels to investigate complaints from Marine women, a Marine spokeswoman boasted that the panels would include "enough women to have real influence." A study group at the Air Force Academy recommended that cadets receive classes on "power relationships" and on the transition of women from "powerless to the power broker" positions. Lois DeFleur, long the academy's adjunct feminist, once complained that "it is clear to everyone at the academy that the power is in the hands of males and the current positions of females confirm this."[26] She recommended putting women in the "power positions" of commandant and superintendent.

Power is what the military has to offer all feminists—not just power for individual women over others in the military, but power for all women over all of society. Writing for *Parameters*, the journal of the Army War College, Judith Stiehm explains:

> The rhetoric of sexual equality turns "brain-spattering" combat into a career opportunity.

> Women, who are rarely collectively violent, may not realize that their lack of violence represents a political limitation.... Women have been deliberately and often legally excluded from society's legitimate, organized, planned, rewarded, technological force—the force applicable by the police and the military.[27]

Stiehm presents a sound, practical argument against women in combat but nevertheless endorses their involvement in combat because "the implications of exempting women from combat thus seem to include the exclusion of women from full citizenship." Stiehm sees "full citizenship" as an end and power as a means to an end, but she is unclear as to the value of full citizenship, except insofar as it empowers women to wield more power in society's political arena.

Other women, those who benefit directly from the advancement of all women in the military, are clearer about their objectives. Helen Rogan witnessed a brash display of personal power by senior military women at the second biennial reunion of the WAC. She tells of General Elizabeth P. Hoisington telling the crowd, "On the program it says 'Mistress of Ceremonies.' I'm no mistress of ceremonies, I'm master of ceremonies." A former director of the WAC said, "I was sitting next to General Hoisington on the stand, and when it started to rain she told it to stop, and it did." Says Rogan, "It was the first time I had seen powerful women joke so openly about their power."[28]

Such boastfulness would have been considered extremely bad form coming from military men. Pretensions of personal power are incompatible with the ideal of selfless service. In any civilized military, the force exerted by superiors over subordinates is not power; it is authority. Men who exercise authority acknowledge that they themselves are subordinate to others. Men who wield *power* answer to no one. In the armed forces of a democratic republic, the only power that should matter is firepower.

Chapter 10

PATHS OF GLORY

If we can't win a war without our mothers,
what kind of a sorry fighting force are we?
Even the evil Saddam Hussein
doesn't send mothers to fight his war.

—SALLY QUINN
WASHINGTON POST

WHEN THE UNITED STATES invaded Panama in December 1989, some six hundred women deployed with their units for Operation Just Cause. One, Army Captain Linda Bray, commander of the 988th Military Police Company, became the first American woman to lead men into combat.

The initial press report of Bray's heroics was written by a reporter for the Scripps Howard News Service and appeared in the *Los Angeles Times*. It described a fierce three-hour firefight to secure a kennel of vicious attack dogs defended by the Panamanian Defense Forces. The battle climaxed with a daring assault by Captain Bray herself, crashing her jeep through the gates of the kennel, machine guns a-blazing. A female soldier "single-handedly captured an enemy prisoner." No less a source than Marlin Fitzwater, White House spokesman, confirmed many details. Fitzwater told the *New York Times*, "It was heavily defended.... Three PDF men were killed. Gunshots were fired on both sides. American troops could have been killed.... It was an important military operation.... A woman led it, and she did an outstanding job."[1]

A week later a very different story appeared in the *Los Angeles Times*. Unnamed Army officers were quoted saying the original report of Bray's heroics was "grossly exaggerated." The kennel was lightly held, the firefight lasted ten minutes, and no one was killed or injured. Bray was not present during the firefight but was half a mile away at her command post. Arriving late for the fight, she stood by while her driver used the jeep to force the gate open. By then, the kennel's defenders had fled. The lone Panamanian captured was a harmless civilian who showed up later to check on the dogs. The dogs really were vicious, so the MPs slaughtered them in their pens.

Bray herself appeared on national television to set the record straight. Looking tense and uncommunicative, she gave every indication of having been chastised by her superiors but took no responsibility for the exaggerations of her actions. Shortly thereafter, while covering an unrelated hearing on Capitol Hill, I ran into Peter Copeland, the reporter who broke the story for Scripps Howard. With the look of a man who knew that no one would believe him, Copeland insisted that he had written up the incident just as it was described to him by Bray and her MPs. In his view, he had made her a hero by reporting what she had told him, and she had turned around and disowned him to protect herself. (Bray was later medically discharged from the Army, after suffering stress fractures in both legs—injuries she blamed on the extra weight she carried on road marches to prove herself to her male colleagues.)

Of course, events could indeed have happened as initially reported, and it is not at all unusual for combatants to embroider their war stories. But the Army was clearly concerned that the incident would be used politically to challenge the service's ban on women in combat roles, as indeed it was.

This episode contrasted sharply with the slight stir caused by another incident involving women and combat in Panama. Two weeks after the truth about the captain came out, CBS News reported that two female truck drivers stood accused of cowardice in the face of the enemy for tearfully refusing to drive a company of Rangers to the site of the fiercest fighting. The accusation appeared in the after-action report of the infantry battalion the women were supporting. An early draft of this report had included the recommendation the use of female drivers in combat be reevaluated.[2] The commander of the infantry battalion complained to the commander of the support battalion, to which the women belonged. The drivers were "counseled" for their behavior, which means in Army parlance that they were chewed out by their supervisors, but no further action was taken until the story made the evening news. Only then did the Army in Panama conduct a hasty investigation, the purpose of which quickly became obvious.

Just two days after the investigation began, and several days before it was completed, the Army's public affairs office in the Pentagon publicly absolved the women of any fault. An Army colonel told *USA Today* that the women had been driving for nine hours and had asked to be relieved because they were tired and feared they might endanger the lives of their passengers. "Does that indicate cowardice? I don't think so," he was quoted as saying. An Army spokeswoman, Paige Eversole, told the *Washington Times,* "They were driving through fire all night long.... There's no indication we had anything other than two exhausted soldiers." The *Washington Post* quoted an unnamed Army official saying the women "performed superbly."[3]

None of the spokespersons denied the women had cried before being relieved of their duties, a point not lost on *The New Republic,* which called the Army's praise of the women "ludicrous and patronizing."[4] The media were overwhelmingly far less critical, however. If they had reported the initial accusation, which few had, they later reported the Army's excuses of the women and left it at that. CBS News itself followed up with only a terse statement of the Army's final official version. It was an isolated incident, "just two women out of how many others," said a reporter for *Army Times*, an independent newspaper, to explain why his paper had not pursued the matter even after receiving additional details from sources in Panama that contradicted the Army's official account.

But according to officers of the infantry battalion the women were supporting, the women had *not* been driving "under fire" for nine hours. They had come under fire briefly only in the first hour of the invasion and had spent the next eight hours peacefully awaiting their next mission. (At one point they had to be rousted out of their barracks rooms and made to stay with their trucks.) Only after they were told where they would be driving did one of the women object. When she began to cry, the second woman said she didn't want to go, either. The men at the scene had no doubt but that the women were afraid, not tired.[5]

The investigation did not in fact exonerate the women. Rather, it recommended against prosecution on the basis of dubious complicating legalities. The investigating officer, an Army lawyer, reasoned that the women could not be prosecuted for failing to obey orders which came from someone outside their chain of command and because the spirit of the so-called combat exclusion laws made it unlawful to order women on a combat mission. One thing was certain: the women did not flat-out refuse to obey orders. But when they broke down in tears, the NCO replaced them with male drivers.

This tale did nothing to quiet calls for repeal of the combat exclusions, all made in the name of Linda Bray. For the popular press, the case for repeal was finally proven. Shortly afterward, Representative Patricia Schroeder introduced a bill to repeal the Army's combat exclusions for a four-year trial period, but at House hearings in March most military witnesses politely opposed the proposal. "I don't feel that the test is necessary," said Lieutenant General Allen K. Ono, the Army's deputy chief of staff for personnel. "I think we can learn what is needed to be learned by other means."[6]

Several enlisted women were less circumspect, arguing that enlisted women, unlike female officers, by and large do not want combat: "I think we're setting ourselves up for failure," said Army Staff Sergeant Christine Brown, an intelligence analyst with the XVIII Airborne Corps. "I don't think women are emotionally or physically ready to do it," said Specialist Rose DeBerry, an administrative specialist with the 16th Military Police Battalion.[7]

Legislators were also lukewarm, praising women but admitting doubts and advising caution. The bill died quietly. It was born a year too early.

THE GULF WAR

The Gulf War against Iraq was a watershed in the history of women in the military. Shortly after the war, the military's timid arguments against expanding military women's roles were swept away in a gush of media admiration.

The war began in August 1990 with Operation Desert Shield. Hundreds of active and reserve units were mobilized and deployed to the war zone, in expectation of a momentous, highly lethal ground and air war. Six percent of the troops were women, 35,000 women in all: daughters, wives, girlfriends—and mothers.

It was a sight the world had never seen before: young mothers saying good-bye to their newborn babies before trooping off to fight a foreign war. Virtually every major newspaper in the country printed the Associate Press photo of a helmeted Hollie Vallance, Army specialist and brand-new mother, wearing big bug-eye glasses and battle dress uniform, cradling her seven-week-old infant daughter before leaving Fort Benning, Georgia. Vallance would not see her newborn again for more than six months.

The images and accounts of such heartbreaks provoked an outcry in unexpected quarters. Sally Quinn, sometime journalist and wife of *Washington Post* editor-in-chief Ben Bradlee, wrote an outraged article for the *Post* in which she asked, "If we

200 · WOMEN IN THE MILITARY

can't win a war without our mothers, what kind of a sorry fighting force are we? Even the evil Saddam Hussein doesn't send
mothers to fight his war."[8] Quinn's perspective was personal.
Growing up as an Army brat, she remembered when her father
shipped out to fight in Korea when she was nine. "I was trau-
matized by his leaving, couldn't retain any food, and was hospitalized.... I was fed by IV for nearly a year," she wrote.

Quinn quoted Harvard pediatrician Dr. T. Berry Brazelton,
who had stepped forward publicly to volunteer his opinion that
sending mothers to war was "terrible, reprehensible, and not
necessary.... A child whose parents leave has two resources.
Either to mourn and turn inward or to say, 'I'm bad. Why did
my mommy leave me?' Or, 'Is my mommy bad because she left
me?' I can't imagine a country doing that to its children." Quinn
also quoted military child psychologists warning of lasting
wounds that children can suffer from being separated from
their mothers. One told her:

> For the very young child, the absence of a parent is like the
> death of a parent. You create an orphan if you send the
> main caretaker away.... We are going to have to protect
> these children. Their mothers are conflicted and torn....
> They have to use denial in order to go. They can't face
> what's happening to their kids.

Dr. Jay Belsky, a psychologist at Pennsylvania State University,
told the Presidential Commission on the Assignment of Women
in the Armed Forces:

> [T]o voluntarily send off single parents or both parents, and
> psychologically, from the child's perspective, abandon them,
> I contend is immoral, and nobody has the right in a nation
> that's not being attacked to do that.... In fact, one of the
> things I'm struck by when we have the issues of children
> and the issues of careers (and typically female careers)
> posed against each other, we have this new emergent

language of child development. All we hear about is their
resilience. Lost is the language of vulnerability. And I con-
tend to you, every time you hear resilience spoken, you will
hear simultaneously, really, a driving motivation which is
an adult's career development.[9]

Psychologist Brenda Hunter warned the commission of the
injury done to children abandoned by their parents, but also of
the injury done to mothers who are forced to abandon their children. Hunter quoted Harvard pediatrician Brazelton saying,
"When mothers know they must leave
their babies for either full-time employment or war, they retreat and withdraw
emotionally. They withdraw not because
they don't care, but because it hurts to
care." Citing other authorities as well,
Hunter said that when "mothers are
separated from their young children
over a long period of time, their feelings of maternal love are apt
to cool." Thus, said Hunter, not only do abandoned children suffer while their mother is away, they also suffer after their emotionally detached mother has returned. Quinn quoted another
child psychologist for the military saying, "We're going to be
dealing with the effect of what we're doing for a long time.... It's
the children who are paying the price."

> Quite a few military
> women were willing to
> raise the white flag in the
> fight for equality.

Other voices questioned the nation's priorities. "It is not in
the public interest to gain a few thousand more hands for a military or any other public mission, at the expense of severely
undermining the basic personality development of several
thousand children," wrote Professor Amitai Etzioni of
Georgetown in *The Responsive Community*, a "communitarian"
publication with a liberal bent. Newspapers across the country
asked the editorial question, "Should Mothers Go to War?"—
generally answering in the negative.

Even familiar feminist bulldogs in Congress took up the
issue, although with their own agenda. "This is not a mommy

issue per se. This is a parent issue," Pat Schroeder told Quinn. Some 1,200 military couples (mother and father both serving) and 16,300 single parents deployed to the Persian Gulf, leaving more than 17,500 children, many quite young, without their usual "custodial parent" to care for them. At least to remedy this situation partially, Representative Barbara Boxer (now a U.S. senator) sponsored a bill called the "Military Orphan Prevention Act" designed to prevent the assignment of both parents of minor children from being sent to a combat zone. The bill would not have spared Spec. 4 Vallance and her daughter Cheyenne, or the 16,300 single parents, but it would have spared others—at the expense of military readiness. Representative Jill Long went even further with her own bill, called the "Military Family Preservation Act," which would have prevented the military from deploying single parents anywhere there were not "reasonably available" child-care facilities—things not usually found in war zones. Another bill, similar to Long's, was introduced by Representative Beverly Byron, chairwoman of the military personnel subcommittee of the House Armed Services Committee.

The Pentagon, however, opposed any attempt to complicate its assignments for men and women further. In hearings before Byron's subcommittee, Defense officials emphasized that members of the military have all "freely assumed the duty and obligation" of military service in full knowledge of its requirements. "Expecting the same sacrifices of all military members, married or single, with children or without, is the only understandable and fair policy and one which is consistent with the American tradition of equality," said Christopher Jehn, assistant secretary of defense for force management and personnel.[10]

Admitting that women are "more likely to be single parents," Jehn warned that if Congress forced the services to exempt single parents from deployment, the services would be forced to close many units to such service members, resulting in fewer job opportunities for women, "with deleterious effect on their promotability." In coolly impersonal terms, he outlined the various administrative "procedures" for dealing with "service members" who cannot provide "adequate dependent child care." He boasted of the military's "family support infrastructure," which had increased its counseling staff and "instituted special programs for children," with expert advice from National Association of School Psychologists and a special task force to monitor the family support effort through the war. The bureaucrats were convinced that providing child care for abandoned dependents was an easily absorbable military activity.

Military doctors in Saudi Arabia, however, were doling out valium to heartsick young mothers too distraught to do their duty. No number of counselors could ease the hurt of having left their little ones behind. When a reporter for the *Colorado Springs Gazette Telegraph* asked a female truckdriver about her two children, the woman suddenly broke down in tears. "It's like this: I'm a woman and a mother before I'm a soldier," she sobbed. "Out here I think more about my family than my job.... If this is a test, I'm gonna fail. A lot of other women are, too, and I guess we're just going to have to accept that."[11]

The *New York Times* profiled Lori Moore, a former Army sergeant and self-described "gung-ho careerist"—until the Army ordered her to the Persian Gulf and she was forced to send her three preschool children across country to live with relatives they had never known. Moore was so overcome by guilt and grief that she refused to deploy, so the Army mustered her out. "[W]hat I came up with is a mother should be left with her children," Moore told the *Times*. "I hate to say it because it doesn't fit with the whole scheme of the women's movement, but I think we have to reconsider what we're doing."[12]

Quite a few military women were willing to raise the white flag in the fight for equality. "I'd rather be home cooking and cleaning, all those things I've been complaining about for twenty-six years," one woman told a reporter. "I don't think females should be over here. They can't handle it," said another. "Those feminists back home who say we have a right to fight are not out here sitting in the heat, carrying an M16 and a gas mask, spending sixteen hours on the road every day and sleeping in fear you're gonna get gassed." Their male comrades were understandably resentful. "It took us this long to get used to the idea of women in the Army, and now they say they don't want to be here," said one. "What are we supposed to think?"[13]

In several instances, the services sent mobilization orders to female reservists who had left active duty specifically to care for their new babies. The *Times* found one Army reservist, Sergeant Twila Schamer, preparing to leave her ten-week-old son. Her husband had already deployed. Said Schamer, "I've tried to convince myself that it's going to be OK and displayed that attitude to other people. If I didn't, I'd be in a constant state of emotional breakdown. I'd be crying all the time."[14] Many such women simply refused to respond, hoping the services would back down, which they did.

Although motherhood did not automatically exempt from serving, pregnancy did. Many active and reserve units had a month or more to prepare for deployment. In that time, at least four of the twenty-two women assigned to the 360th Transportation Company from Fort Carson, Colorado, became pregnant. "I can't say whether they did it on purpose to get out of this, but they knew we were going for more than a month," said Captain Steve Fraunfelter, company commander.[15] Other units reported similar problems. "It was like an epidemic at Fort Riley," a female staff sergeant told a reporter for the *Washington Post*. "We knew in August we would probably go, but we didn't leave until the end of October. When these women saw the deployment start, they said, 'Come on, honey, let's go to bed and get working on this baby. I'm not going over there.'"[16]

During the Gulf War, women were more than three times less likely to deploy with their units than men, primarily due to pregnancy, which accounted for nearly half of all women who failed to deploy. This meant that even if the military routinely discharged women for pregnancy, as they had prior to 1972, women would *still* be less likely to deploy than men. Marine Corps women were nearly four times less likely to deploy, and fully one-fourth of Marine Corps women whose units were ordered to the Gulf did not go with them. Between August 1989 and August 1991, rates of voluntary and involuntary discharge "for the convenience of the government" were roughly twice as high among women as among men, and up significantly over previous years.[17]

Rates of nondeployability did not include women who deployed to Saudi Arabia only to be shipped home early for various reasons, including pregnancy. Doctors at some sites in Saudi Arabia were reported to have run out of pregnancy tests, with women coming in to be tested time and time again, "because a positive test would be a ticket home."[18] There were also rumors of pregnant women selling their urine to others to fake their pregnancy. Of course, servicewomen were under no obligation to continue their pregnancy after evacuation, and there was no attempt to redeploy women if their pregnancies were terminated, either by abortion or miscarriage.

> The military resigned itself to rampant sex within the ranks.

During the war, when the press and the public were most interested in the performance of women, Pentagon spokesman said the services were not keeping statistics on the number of women evacuated from the war zone because of pregnancy. The services *did* keep detailed statistics on all *medical* evacuations, but pregnancy was not classed as a medical condition. After the war, the services produced statistics showing that rates of early return were higher for women than for men by at least 25 percent, although precise statistics were still not available.[19]

In all likelihood, the problem of nondeployability and early returns was worse than the Pentagon was willing to admit. The Defense Department was not particularly interested in documenting potential problems with women during the war, and the services were under no mandate to keep careful statistics on such matters. After the war, they had no reason to expose the problem, so they downplayed it. Thus it fell to the GAO to reveal that the services screened reservists to avoid calling up those who could not deploy, thus masking the full magnitude of the problem.[20]

Not all women who deployed to the Gulf were eager to go home. Some were reported to be making out like bandits, selling black market condoms for forty or fifty dollars each. The condoms were actually provided to troops free of charge by Uncle Sam, prompting one female soldier to complain, "Who do they think those guys are going to use them with, the ladies in veils? That's like telling them it's OK to, you know, do it with us."[21]

For "R&R," troops in Saudi Arabia were rotated on and off a cruise ship dubbed "the Love Boat." The female troops on board were under intense pressure from men in all-male combat units who had been stationed in the desert for months. Many women found male patrons to protect and comfort them. Army Reserve Sergeant Lori Mertz, testifying later before the presidential commission, said, "The friendships helped us get by, and I don't think there's anything wrong with that." Asked if by "friendships" she meant sexual relationships, Mertz answered, "There were some that were sexual, there were some that were—you know, if you kissed him or whatever. And that happened, and there were friendships."[22] The testimony of Army Sergeant Mary Rader of the 213th Supply and Service Battalion brought her to the verge of tears:

> SGT. RADER: …*I served in Desert Storm, also, and it was a very bad situation…. We had very—quite a few males and quite a few females, and it was just an all around bad situation…. I feel there was a lot of very unprofessional behavior out of the lower enlisted personnel…. We had female—one female in particular that we could not keep out of one of the male bunks. She was caught sleeping in the male tent more than once. We had females and males that would go to guard duty together and be caught necking, and they're supposed to be out there protecting us and*

*pulling guard duty at 2:00, 3:00, 4:00 o'clock in the morn-
ing. And they had no idea what was going on out there.*

COMMISSIONER ELAINE DONNELLY: *Did this happen
to—was it—were a large number of people involved or was
it a small number, was it a few, half, most?*

SGT. RADER: *It was very heavy. Our company only has
69 people, and it was very heavy in our E-4s and below. It
didn't just stop there. We had a captain and an E-4 having
an affair, and he went to a sexual harassment board for it. I
had a female officer who had an affair with an E-5 male
that she worked with. It was very heavy.*

COMMISSIONER DONNELLY: *So when you say, "Very
heavy," would you say more than a majority, a heavy
majority?*

SGT. RADER: *Yes.*

COMMISSIONER DONNELLY: *When these things happened, what kind of discipline was there?*

SGT. RADER: *There wasn't any.*

COMMISSIONER DONNELLY: *There was none?*

SGT. RADER: *(Shaking head) No....*[23]

One might excuse the military for assuming that some soldiers would have sex with each other, but the military went well
beyond simply assuming as much. To prepare soldiers for
return to normal life, the Army distributed a "Guide to
Developing and Conducting Reunion Programs." Intended to
be used by Army chaplains, the guide reads as if it were written
by Dr. Ruth:

*If you choose to be sexually intimate with someone else
while on deployment, should you tell your wife or girl-
friend... well, we can't give you a "yes" or "no" answer?...
Who benefits from you telling and what are your reasons
for telling? Is it to relieve your guilt feelings or is it that
somehow in the telling, your relationship back home will be
strengthened? Also, what are the risks of not telling?...*

*Experimentation and new positions… give it time, she may
be suspicious of where you learned about these ideas!
(ha, ha).*[24]

The military not only assumed that soldiers would have sex,
it resigned itself to rampant sex within the ranks. Since the military could not control sex among its soldiers, it could only
approve the activity.

Physical conditions in the Army's make-shift camps only
contributed to moral laxity. For the first time since integration,
the Army actually spared women some of the special treatment
they were accustomed to receiving. In Saudi Arabia, men and
women slept under the same tents and shared the same showers
and latrines, separated only by crude partitions. One soldier,
back from the war, told of striking up a conversation in the
latrine, before he realized that the soldier on the hole next to his
was a woman. Lieutenant General Charles C. Krulak, later commandant of the Marine Corps, had his own war story to tell:

> *The restrooms were shared.… and the women waited for
> the men to complete, men waited for the women to com-
> plete, and it was very refreshing to see that. Men relieved
> themselves using what we called a piss tube.… I can remem-
> ber very vividly standing there using it myself, Lieutenant
> Colonel [Ruthanna] Poole and Major [Ginger] Jaecox walk-
> ing by and, as I was standing there, they whipped a very
> smart salute at me and had great grins on their face.*[25]

At first, the women themselves struggled to maintain some
sense of physical modesty under such conditions, changing
clothes in their sleeping bags or only when the lights were out,
and starving themselves of water (which made them susceptible
to dehydration) to avoid the unpleasant experience of using the
latrine.[26] But after months of inconvenience their sense of modesty gave way. No one expected modesty of them, or chastity for
that matter—least of all the military.

Sanitation was a special problem for women in the Gulf, who suffered higher rates of urinary tract and yeast infections, in part because of shortages of feminine supplies. As if beans and bullets and gasoline were not enough to worry about, quartermasters now had to make sure they stocked plenty of tampons and sanitary napkins. They were forever running out. Some units in the Gulf resorted to giving women hormone shots and bill-control pills to keep them from menstruating. Tambrands Inc., the makers of Tampax tampons, offered to send a free box of tampons to every woman in the Gulf whose friend or relative called their 800 number. One female sergeant wrote to tell Tambrands, "I read somewhere that an Army spokesperson assured your company that these items were routinely issued to female soldiers. Don't believe it. I've been in 10 years and it's never happened."[27] Women preparing for deployment were told to take a six-month supply.

A poll of Gulf War veterans conducted after the war by the Roper Organization confirmed the opinion of commanders who reported problems in the Persian Gulf. Overall, 98 percent of Gulf War veterans rated the performance of men as excellent or good, but only 61 percent rated the performance of women similarly. The greatest disparities between ratings for men and women were found in the Army and Marine Corps. In both, a majority of veterans rated the performance of women "fair/poor." Only in the Navy and Air Force did a majority rate the performance of women as "excellent/good":

Poll of Gulf War Veterans
On the Performance of Women[28]

	"fair/poor"	"excellent/good"
Army	52%	48%
Marine Corps	56	44
Navy	37	63
Air Force	17	83

Fifty-six percent of those who deployed to the Gulf with mixed gender units reported that women in their unit became pregnant just prior to or while deployed in the Gulf. Of that 56 percent, 46 percent said that such pregnancies had "very much" or "some" negative impact on unit readiness, and 59 percent said that it had "very much" or "some" negative impact on unit morale. Sixty-four percent of those who deployed to the Gulf with mixed gender units reported that there had been incidents of sexual activity between men and women in their unit. Of that 64 percent, 36 percent said that sexual activity had "very much" or "some" negative impact on unit readiness, and 55 percent said that it had "very much" or "some" negative impact on unit morale.[29] Clearly a large part of the U.S. military actually on the ground in Saudi Arabia did not share the Pentagon's high opinion of the performance of women, and whether the Pentagon admitted it or not, the troops in the field had a big morale problem because of sexual integration.

It seemed at first that the military's difficulties and embarrassments in the Gulf would certainly slow if not halt the trend toward greater integration of women, and it might have, if the war had lasted longer and cost more lives. As it happened, the ground war in February was so swift and so successful that it conquered not only the Iraqi defenses but all of America's accumulated fears about going to war—the fear of getting involved in distant foreign conflicts, the fear of escalating military actions, the fear of lost and shattered lives, public discord, and political recriminations—and the fear of sending women to war and losing them in combat.

The three women killed by an Iraqi Scud attack on an airbase barracks were used by proponents of women in the military as proof that there is no "front" in modern warfare and therefore the distinction between combat and noncombat made no sense. The *Washington Post* said as much in a single headline to a straight news story: "Scuds Put U.S. Women on Front Line: Law Shields Females from Combat But Not from Iraqi Missiles." At the same time, the absence of a public outcry over the first female fatalities (totaling six, including accidental deaths) allowed feminists to declare that the public was finally "ready" for women in combat. "I think after this war, the body bag issue can be put to rest," said Carolyn Becraft of the Women's Research and Education Institute.

The first American servicewoman to die in the Persian Gulf did so somewhat ignominiously. She was Army Staff Sergeant Tatiana Khaghani Dees of the 92nd Military Police Company from Baumholder, Germany. While training her weapon on a suspicious person, Sergeant Dees, a divorced mother of two young children, backed off the end of a pier and drowned under the weight of her equipment.

But, ultimately, we won, we won easily, and nothing else mattered. Everybody was a hero. The two female soldiers captured by the Iraqis (a flight surgeon and a truck driver) were apparently returned unharmed, laying to rest yet another fear that stood in the way of combat for women. The question every reporter asked was whether the women had been sexually molested by their captors. The Army said no. A year later it turned out the Army had lied. The flight surgeon, Major Rhonda Cornum, confessed that she had been "violated manually, vaginally, and rectally," a fact she treated later with manly indifference: "no big deal... a known hazard when you go to war."[30] (The twenty-four U.S. servicewomen who were violated by U.S. servicemen during the war were not so accepting.) Cornum received five decorations for her service, including the Distinguished Flying Cross, which is rarely given to nonaviators. She had been a passenger aboard an Army helicopter when it was shot down.[31]

The postwar push for repeal of the combat exclusions did not really begin until April, when Senator John McCain of Arizona, during a hearing of the Senate Armed Services Committee, commented that the sterling performance of

> Whether the Pentagon admitted it or not, the troops in the field had a big morale problem because of sexual integration.

women in the Gulf justified taking a new look at the ban on women in combat roles, particularly aviation roles. McCain's opinion carried weight because he was himself not only a veteran Navy pilot but also a former prisoner of war. Still, his comments were clearly self-serving. He had been badly tarnished by his involvement in the savings-and-loan scandals, and his praise of military women brought him the first good press he had seen in months. His sentiments were soon seconded by another Senate Republican eager to have good things said about him, John Warner of Virginia.

McCain's comments received a mixed response from the services. The Air Force, as usual, was out in front, ready to greet the new age. The Navy was cautious, with Vice Admiral Jeremy M. "Mike" Boorda, then chief of naval personnel, warning that if the exclusion laws were repealed "we would have to be willing to undertake the commitment to make it a truly equal opportunity for both males and females." The Army and Marine Corps opposed any change, but by the end of April, Defense Secretary Dick Cheney was hinting that more opportunity for women was in order. At its spring meeting, DACOWITS, which by then consisted solely of Cheney appointees, voted overwhelmingly to recommend repeal of the combat exclusions.[32] When asked about the recommendation, Cheney told the Associated Press, "Whether we want to adopt a recommendation to the Congress to change [the combat exclusions], I just can't give you an answer today." The headline in the *Washington Times* read, "Cheney would expand women's role."[33] Later, in June, Cheney signaled his willingness to go whichever way the wind blows, saying, "We basically follow whatever direction we're given by Congress in this regard."[34] Any hope that the Pentagon would take the time to learn from its experience in the Gulf was gone.

In the House, Representatives Pat Schroeder and Beverly Byron, both Democrats, were already in the lead, making the most of the opportunity created by McCain and Warner. In early May, the House Armed Services Committee had approved an amendment to the 1992 National Defense

Authorization Act to permit Navy and Air Force women to fly combat missions in combat aircraft. There was little debate, and the vote was forty-five to six.[35] Publicly, Cheney endorsed the amendment on the grounds that it merely eliminated statutory restrictions on the services without requiring changes in assignment policies, but his assistant secretary for personnel, Christopher Jehn, had already informed Senator McCain by letter that if the statutory restrictions were eliminated, the services "would be obligated to allow women to enter any career area for which they qualify."[36]

Leading Democrats on the Senate Armed Services Committee were clearly on the defensive. The committee's esteemed chairman, Sam Nunn of Georgia, and the chairman of its subcommittee on personnel matters, John Glenn of Ohio, had long opposed combat for women but had never been so politically alone in doing so. No one was speaking publicly against repeal except a lonely handful of old soldiers and conservative activists. It seemed certain that if Nunn and Glenn did not act to repeal the exclusions, the full Senate would act on its own without them.

In June, Glenn's subcommittee on personnel held hearings giving opponents of repeal a chance to speak. The service chiefs all stated their personal opposition to repeal, although with considerably less vigor as well as candor than guest witnesses such as retired General Robert H. Barrow, former commandant of the Marine Corps, and Elaine Donnelly, formerly a member of DACOWITS. The testimony of a panel of military men and women was divided, with female officers favoring repeal and enlisted women and military men generally opposing it. During and after the hearings, Glenn presented himself as a cautious skeptic, saying the Gulf War was far too limited an engagement to serve as the basis for drawing any conclusions about the military use of women, good or bad. Others on the committee gave the impression of being cautious and uncommitted, including McCain and Warner, who had taken some heat in conservative circles for their earlier remarks.

214 • WOMEN IN THE MILITARY

Behind the scenes, female military officers crisscrossed Capitol Hill lobbying in uniform for repeal, a violation of regulations that was overlooked by the Pentagon. Despite the pressure, the Senate's version of the 1992 Defense Authorization Act was reported out of committee later that summer without provisions for repealing the combat exclusions. As expected, Senators Edward Kennedy of Massachusetts and William Roth, a Republican from Delaware, quickly introduced a repeal amendment. As a counter move, both McCain and Warner joined Nunn and Glenn in offering an amendment to establish a presidential commission to study the issue. McCain himself advised that approving the Kennedy-Roth amendment would "rush ahead without proper study and a national consensus.... [By creating a commission,] we will be able to make the kind of judgment which will give the American people what they want. We will find the best way to both defend this nation's national security interests, and provide equality for women in all ranks and military specialties."[37]

Such timid double-talk came too late to stop the rush for repeal that McCain had started months earlier. When the final version of the authorization act became law on December 5, 1991, it included both amendments. Congress had passed the buck. The laws barring Navy and Air Force women from combat aviation were repealed, but the difficult issue of deciding just how women would be assigned was transferred from Congress to the White House, which was stuck with the responsibility for establishing the commission. Defense Secretary Cheney immediately announced that he would wait until the commission had finished its work before making any changes in service policy.

Chapter 11

THE WAR GAMES COMMISSION

To me, the very fact that this issue is being dis-cussed and this meeting is being held simply shows that you really don't take the military seriously. For you, the military is not a question of life and death.... So you can afford to make all kinds of social experiments, which we cannot.... The very fact that you have this debate may itself be construed as proof that it's not serious. It's a game. It's a joke.

—PROFESSOR MARTIN VAN CREVELD
ISRAELI MILITARY HISTORIAN

"PEOPLE ARE POLICY," as anyone in Washington knows, the point being that the formation and execution of political policy is entirely dependent upon the people appointed to do the job. Political appointees, even senior military officers, do not follow orders like good soldiers: they do as much of what they want to do, and as little of what they don't want to do, as they can get away with. Successful political executives will therefore make sure to pick just the right people for the particular policy they wish to see implemented.

In December 1991 the only policy the Bush White House wanted to see implemented was avoidance: they wanted to avoid offending as many potential voting blocks as possible, in preparation for Bush's bid for reelection in the coming year. The White House especially wanted to avoid offending both women voters, for fear of the gender gap, and conservative activists, for fear of Patrick Buchanan, who had already begun his 1992 presidential campaign.

The composition of the Presidential Commission on the Assignment of Women in the Armed Forces reflected these fears. Not announced until after Buchanan's stunning performance in the New Hampshire primary in February 1992, the commissioners included two known conservatives who had spoken out publicly against women in combat: Kate Walsh O'Beirne, vice president of government relations at the Heritage Foundation, a conservative think tank, an Army officer's wife, and a lawyer; and Elaine Donnelly, Republican activist from Michigan, former member of DACOWITS, and one of the most vocal critics of the military's use of women.

A third commissioner, Professor Charles C. Moskos of Northwestern University, had contributed to the public debate over women in combat, but without taking sides. Chairman of the Inter-University Seminar on the Military and Society and the most noted military sociologist in the country, Moskos had conducted some of the best research on the AVF and on the issues of race and gender in the military. His work revealed the sharp contrast between the attitudes and ambitions of female officers and enlisted women—as, for example, the desire of female officers for combat jobs and that of enlisted women to avoid such jobs. Always careful to maintain his academic objectivity, he had never publicly opposed women in combat, but he was clearly no pushover for procombat feminists.

Retired Army General Maxwell Thurman was another curious pick. Ten years earlier, while deputy chief of staff for personnel of the Army, he had overseen the Army's controversial WITA (Women in the Army) study and successfully defended the study's findings and recommendations before a hostile DACOWITS in 1983 (see Chapter 6). Since then, he had served as commander-in-chief of the U.S. Southern Command during the invasion of Panama. He was much praised and well respected in and out of the military, but there was no way of knowing how recent events might have affected his thinking on women in the military.

The biographies of four other members gave clear indications of being likely to support women in combat. They were: Meredith A. Neizer, a young former White House Fellow, 1978 graduate of the U.S. Merchant Marine Academy, and past chairwoman of DACOWITS; Captain Mary M. "Mimi" Finch, an Army helicopter pilot and West Point graduate; retired Army Major General Mary Elizabeth Clarke, known as "Mother Mary" to troops at Fort McClellan, Alabama, where she was once post commander and commandant of the Military Police Corps; and Brigadier General Thomas V. Draude, the Marine Corps's director of public affairs, whose daughter Loree was undergoing naval flight training at the time.

The rest of the commissioners had not been publicly associated with the issue. They included the commission chairman, recently retired Air Force General Robert T. Herres, formerly vice chairman of the Joint Chiefs of Staff and first commander-in-chief of the U.S. Space Command; retired Army Brigadier General Samuel G. Cockerham, a combat veteran and attack helicopter pilot; retired Army Colonel William Darryl Henderson, Ph.D., a recognized authority on unit cohesion, formerly commander of the U.S. Army Research Institute; retired Admiral James R. Hogg, former U.S. representative to NATO Military Committee and Seventh Fleet commander; Newton N. Minow, a Chicago lawyer, World War II veteran, and former Democratic political appointee; Marine Corps Reserve Colonel Ronald D. Ray, a lawyer, Vietnam combat veteran, former deputy assistant secretary of Defense, and past co-chair of the Bush campaign in Kentucky, whose wife had been appointed to DACOWITS the previous year; and Sarah F.

White, a master sergeant in the Air Force Reserve and the commission's only enlisted member.

The commission included voices from both sides of the debate without appearing publicly to lean in one direction or the other, although the commissioners themselves saw things differently. The five most conservative commissioners—Sam Cockerham, Elaine Donnelly, Kate O'Beirne, Ron Ray, and Sarah White (the "Gang of Five," as they came to call themselves), were convinced that pro-combat commissioners held the upper hand. All five had been picked by the White House to counterbalance the obvious feminist tilt of the original slate of nominees submitted by Defense Secretary Dick Cheney.[1] Of the commissioners nominated by Cheney, only two might vote against combat: Darryl Henderson and Charles Moskos.

Chairman Robert Herres was close to Democratic Congressman Les Aspin of Wisconsin, then the powerful chairman of the House Armed Services Committee. There was no doubt among the commissioners that Herres felt it his personal duty to steer the commission to appropriate, politically acceptable results. His only other interest was in making sure the commission's work was completed on time and with minimal bother. He was impatient with debate and ruled the committee and its staff with a heavy hand, moving the committee swiftly through the motions of hearing testimony and gathering information, without attempting a more conscientious examination of issues.

Officially, the commission was chartered by Congress to "assess the laws and policies restricting the assignment of female service members" and make recommendations to the president by November 15, 1992. Congress specifically directed the commission to recommend, (1) whether existing laws and policies restricting the assignment of women should be retained, modified, or repealed, (2) what roles servicewomen should have in combat, (3) what would be an appropriate transition process if women should be assigned to combat positions, and (4) whether special conditions and different standards should apply to servicewomen as opposed to servicemen.

Unofficially, for Robert Herres, the commission existed to justify opening as many combat roles to women as politically possible. Thus much of the work involved documenting the success of women in other military roles and certifying that their overall performance equaled men's.

Little attempt was made to argue that adding women to combat units would actually *improve* unit effectiveness. The recent draw-down in defense following the end of the Cold War eliminated the once powerful argument that women were needed to make the AVF work. The only appeal to military readiness left was that opening combat roles to women would expand the pool of qualified candidates, but this was weakened by the ready availability of qualified men, and it was vulnerable to arguments that women were not in fact qualified.

The only forceful argument was equal opportunity, "one of our most sacred cultural values," in Herres's words, a *sine qua non* of American justice. Said Herres, "One can argue, and I would argue, that an impact on military effectiveness or some other important public purpose must be shown in order to continue an exclusionary policy, as opposed to protecting such a policy."[2] In other words, the burden of proof was on those who argued against combat for women.

Still, Herres encouraged others to believe that military effectiveness and equal opportunity were not competing values:

> *I believe that military effectiveness is a vital criterion, as well. But I do not believe that all issues can be reduced to a simple choice between military effectiveness and equal opportunity, because they are not mutually exclusive concepts in all cases. The extent to which they are mutually exclusive is a judgment that each one of us must make for ourselves. I don't think anyone else can impose that assumption upon us, the assumption that they are mutually exclusive....*[3]

Others on the commission were less optimistic about their choices and clearer in their thinking. They did not assume the equality of men and women, as far as the military was concerned, and insisted on ranking military necessity above equal opportunity. As Moskos told Herres:

> You raise a question, Mr. Chair, where the burden of proof should lie. Other things being equal, you say, well, then let equal opportunity triumph. Well, most of the evidence that we've heard here—and there will be some debate about the degree—is that mixed-gender units, particularly as it gets closer to the combat area, have lower deployment rates, higher attrition, less physical strength, more sexual activity, higher costs, et cetera, et cetera. It would seem to me the burden of proof would be on the side of saying equal opportunity is of such significance that we're going to override some of these costs.[4]

Some of these costs came with dollar signs: $66,000 to $500,000 to refit a combatant vessel to accommodate women, $2 million to $4 million per aircraft carrier, and an average of more than $138,000 for amphibious ships. The Air Force testified to higher costs for feminine-specific equipment needed by pilots, and the Army estimated that it cost 50 percent more to recruit female candidates.[5]

Other costs were harder to put a price on—in particular the fact that women were less likely to be available to deploy with their units, a shortfall the units simply had to absorb without recourse to "overmanning." This was especially a problem in the Gulf War. A 1992 Navy study found that some ship commanders felt that pregnancy, single parenthood, and "dual military" parenthood did indeed "constitute a readiness problem."

On some matters, there was little doubt. The relative physical abilities of men and women were well documented, and the commission heard hours of testimony from the researchers themselves on the results. Colonel Dennis Kowal, who had been a part of the WITA study in the early 1980s, testified that the Army was still assigning women to jobs well beyond their physical ability, and that the cost of reassigning women to less physically demanding jobs could be as much as $16,000 per reassignment. The commission's report recommended gender-neutral strength tests for each of the services. It also noted that the Army had devised such tests a decade earlier, but they were finally eliminated in 1990 "for political reasons."

The testimony of Army Lieutenant Colonel William Gregor put the disparities in the physical abilities of men and women in sharper perspective. Gregor, a former faculty member at West Point, had compared the performance of male and female West Point cadets and Army ROTC cadets at summer camp. Using the standard Army Physical Readiness Test, Gregor found that the upper fifth of women achieved scores on the test equivalent to the bottom fifth of men, but even with equivalent scores, the men and the women were not physical equals:

> Unofficially, the commission existed to justify opening as many combat roles to women as possible.

> The women who achieved this level of fitness are unusual. They are confident, they are talented, but they are limited in their potential relative to men. The men, in contrast... have the potential to do much better.... However, criticizing the women who achieve a level of fitness such as this is only going to discourage them, because... you cannot reasonably expect more.[6]

The unbridgeable gap in potential physical ability of men and women presented unique problems for physical training in integrated units.

Gregor testified that the Army Physical Fitness Test (APFT) actually minimizes the gap between men and women by measuring only general cardiovascular fitness and not strength and job performance. The gap actually widens in tests for specific jobs which require strength and performance:

222 • WOMEN IN THE MILITARY

APFT scores do not measure relative strength or perfor-
mance [and are therefore] the kindest to the woman,
because she works only against her own weight. If we were
to add a load, the gap between males and females would
widen. If we were to reinstate the 40-yard man-carry that
was part of the readiness test 20 years ago, we would find
far fewer women achieving passing scores using the male
tables.

Of course, abandoning the double standard would have drastic consequences for women in commissioning programs: 80 percent would not qualify for an Army commission. Adopting a male standard of fitness at West Point would mean 70 percent of the women would fail at the end of their junior year, only 3 percent would be eligible for West Point's Recondo Badge, and not one would qualify for the Army Physical Fitness Badge.

Gregor also testified that a man is more likely to be able to meet minimum standards later in his career, whereas a woman has nowhere to go but down, and rapidly as she ages. According to Gregor, a woman in her twenties has about the same aerobic capacity as a fifty-year-old man. Women also begin losing bone mass at an earlier age and are therefore more susceptible to orthopedic injuries, which means that young women selected for physically demanding branches of service will not survive to finish their careers. (A case in point is Captain Linda Bray, mentioned in Chapter 10.) Gregor concluded that adopting the male standard of fitness for officers at midcareer would eliminate most women from the Army.

When Gregor had finished, Commissioner White wondered indignantly "why the Department of the Army has not provided the information that Dr. Gregor has just provided. I would like to know why *our staff* has not even provided a portion of this very valuable information that he has provided...."

An area of special concern, in view of Congress's repeal of the statute barring women from combat aviation, was the ability of women to fly high-performance aircraft. The most newsworthy testimony came from two daring young instructor pilots from the Navy's Top Gun air combat school, who boldly challenged the Navy's party line on integration. Delivering a statement signed by twenty-one out of twenty-three Top Gun instructors opposing women in combat aviation, Lieutenant John Clagett told the commission "that it mainly is the lieutenants out there, and the captains in the Marine Corps, that are screaming that, 'No, we don't want this to happen,' and our big reason for it is that we need to have those units act as units."[7]

Clagett revealed that in some areas female students were simply "not allowed to fail." The word from the top was that the Navy needed more female pilots, and everyone in the training command knew what that meant. In 1990, when the Navy decided to reduce its numbers at the end of the Cold War, Vice Admiral Boorda, then chief of naval personnel, ordered an arbitrary reduction of officers already in pilot training—excluding women, because the Navy still didn't have enough female pilots. Even before 1990 instructor pilots were under pressure to go easy on women. Clagett recalled his experience with a female student at Beeville, Texas:

> She didn't perform her mission what I considered up to standards. I chose at that time to try to give her an unsatisfactory for the flight and was told in private quarters that that wasn't what you did in this situation, that "she not only will pass the flight, but it will be an average grading."

Clagett challenged the commission to ask the Navy for statistics on women attrited from flight training involuntarily, "the ones that are told, 'You are not good enough to fly this airplane or any other airplane from this point on. Thank you. Your services are no longer required.'... quite frankly, they were zero when I was at Beeville. It was zero. And we attrited male candidates left and right." He added that "the point was that the male student aviators knew that the standards weren't the same, and that was a major point."

The Navy's statistics on attrition in aviation training for fiscal years 1990, 1991, and 1992 reveal an easily discernible pattern. Attrition of women was allowed only when there were many women in training and instructors felt safe in saying that not every woman performed up to standard.[8] In time, the Navy's failure-proof flight training would have deadly consequences for one of the women it was supposed to benefit.

Air Force instructor pilots were under the same pressure to make women succeed. As one Air Force captain told David Hackworth, writing for *Newsweek*, "We are told to evaluate women on a different scale than men. A woman who is adequate is rated as outstanding, or who is unacceptable is rated as acceptable.... We lie to the public, we lie to the Air Force, and most of all we lie to ourselves."[9]

The Army had a slightly different problem when it came to female flyers: it couldn't get enough women to volunteer to fill its ambitious aviation quotas. Colonel Gregor, head of the Army ROTC department at the University of Michigan, told the commission, "I got a message last year that said I had to push aviation because we had an insufficient number of women competing for aviation, and I couldn't understand that, because we have disappointed men every year."[10]

Quotas for Army women were disappointing in other ways as well. In the winter 1991 issue of *Military Law Review*, an Army lawyer, Captain Donovan Bigelow, blew the whistle on the Army's use of quotas in officer promotions to ensure that the percentage of women and minorities promoted matched the percentage of eligible women and minorities.

The Army didn't call them quotas; it called them "goals." According to the Army's affirmative action plan, "Goals are not ceilings, nor are they base figures that are to be reached at the expense of requisite qualifications and standards. In affirmative action efforts, goals are not quotas." The Army's goal for personnel promotions read: "Selection rates for all categories [of protected groups] should not be less than the overall selection rate for the total population considered." Of the thirty-four officer promotion boards convened in 1990, all but one met its affirmative action goals.[11]

Bigelow's step-by-step account of the promotion boards' business left no doubt how they achieved such success. When a board begins work, its first task is to review and evaluate the records of all eligible officers and rank them from best to worst, to produce what is called an Order of Merit List (OML). Next the board must identify those officers "best qualified" for promotion. If the needs of the Army require it to promote fifty officers, the board will count down from the top of the list and draw a line after the fiftieth officer. The process will end there if the percentage of women and minorities above this "best qualified line" equals or exceeds the percentage of women and minorities on the OML, but this almost never happens, so the board will begin moving officers above and below the line to achieve the desired result.

Bigelow's article began as a research paper for the Army's Judge Advocate General school in Charlottesville, Virginia, which would examine the legality of the Army's promotion system in light of the U.S. Supreme Court's 1989 decision in *City of Richmond* v. *J.A. Croson Co.* In that decision, the court struck down numerical quotas preferring minority contractors doing business with the City of Richmond, Virginia, on the grounds that such quotas were not a response to actual discrimination in the past awarding of contracts. According to the court, unless past discrimination was proven, the use of quotas was unconstitutional.

The Army cooperated fully with Bigelow's research. At the Total Army Personnel Command in Alexandria, Virginia, two colonels and a sergeant major explained to Bigelow the entire process, right through the practice of bumping qualified nonminority male candidates off the promotion list. In January 1992 Bigelow described for me the sergeant major's response when he asked what happened to the original OML, which evaluates the records of all eligible officers and ranks them from best to worst:

*He kinda laughed, and the colonels kinda giggled, and he
said, "We destroy it, sir." I said, "You destroy it?" He said,
"Oh yes sir! Could you imagine what would happen if that
got out?" I smiled and nodded [as if to say], "Yeah, boy, I'm
with you on that one." In the back of my mind, I'm thinking, "Yeah, I know, sergeant major, a whole lot better than
you do what would happen: There'd be lawsuits all over the
damn country."[12]*

Bigelow concluded that the Army's "goals" were really the
"rankest of rigid numerical quotas" and that the rigged promotion system was plainly illegal.

When Bigelow submitted his article for prepublication
review, the first response of the Army's judge advocate general
was denial. But a few months later the acting judge advocate
general, Brigadier General Donald W. Hansen, sent a memo to
the Army's deputy chief of staff for personnel saying that the
Supreme Court's ruling in *Croson* meant that "race and gender
may be considered by Army selection boards only when there
has been a specific finding that individual officers have been the
victims of discrimination." The memo, dated March 19, 1990,
recommended instructing boards that they could not move officers on the list solely to meet affirmative action goals.[13] But the
memo was "withdrawn in anticipation of litigation." In other
words, the Army had decided to continue knowingly breaking
the law until challenged in court.

To this day, the Army denies that it uses "quotas" but admits
using "goals." When asked how many recent officer boards met
their affirmative action goals, the Army provided only a brief
statement saying, "Historically, the select rate for minority officers
has been comparable to the select rate for non-minority officers."
This is not true. Not until May 1988 did the Army promotion
board selection rates become equal. Before then, boards were
given selection ranges as affirmative action goals. The Army
resorted to *requiring* equal selection rates because women and
minorities regularly fell at the bottom of the specified ranges.

In the spring of 1992 the Army's duplicitous use of quotas and double standards became a matter of public record when the Bush administration finally brought the state of Virginia and the Virginia Military Institute (VMI) to trial for refusing to admit women. In making their case against VMI, lawyers for the U.S. Justice Department called to the stand Colonel Patrick Toffler, head of the U.S. Military Academy's Office of Institutional Research. Led by federal lawyers, Toffler bore witness to the many achievements of female cadets and the overall success of integration. He was less forthcoming on the subject of how the integration of women had changed West Point. Remember, this is a senior Army officer representing the United States Military Academy testifying under oath in a federal court:

> Q: *Colonel Toffler, when West Point was required to admit women, were any changes made in the operation of the academy, in terms of adjustments or changes for women cadets?*
>
> TOFFLER: *The basic changes that were made involved accommodations, latrine facilities, locker facilities. But in terms of policies and programs and procedures, there were* no special changes *that were made.*[14] *[Emphasis added.]*

"No special changes" was apparently too much for even the Justice Department lawyer conducting the examination to believe, so to save Toffler from perjury, the lawyer asked again if there were any changes made to accommodate women that were not "policy changes." Toffler grudgingly admitted that "in the admissions process" the academy had substituted the flex-arm hang for the pull-up on a test of physical aptitude, and that "on admission to the Academy" women received instruction in self-defense while men were taught boxing and wrestling. "There may have been some other minor changes," he added, "but those are the ones that come to mind."

Under cross-examination by a lawyer for VMI, quite a few more changes came to Toffler's mind. Had not the academy eliminated peer ratings, rifle runs, Recondo awards, and obstacles on its obstacle course to make success easier for women? Answer: Yes. Had not the academy substituted other requirements for women in the name "equivalent training"? Answer: Yes. Had not the aforesaid accommodations failed to reduce the higher attrition rates for women? Answer: Yes. And had not West Point failed in its efforts to convince male cadets that integration was a success? Toffler resisted:

> Q: *There is turnover every year in the cadet corps, correct, Colonel Toffler?*
> TOFFLER: *Yes.*
> Q: *And because of that turnover, it's necessary to educate the incoming cadets about these physiological differences, and in your judgment the integration of women has been a success?*
> TOFFLER: *That's right.*
> Q: *It's fair to say so far the cadets have not bought your argument?*
> TOFFLER: *No, that's not fair to say.*
> Q: *It's not true that there are studies which show that the male and female cadets at West Point believe that integration has not been a success?*
> TOFFLER: *The current information we have comes from a survey that we do of first classmen just prior to graduation, and that survey indicates that there are substantial portions of the corps, both men and women, who do not view the integration of women as having been fully successful.*
> Q: *So, that's a yes answer?*
> TOFFLER: *That's my answer.*[15]

Toffler went to even greater lengths to avoid admitting that female cadets benefited from the use of quotas in branch assignments:

Q: *[I]t is a fact that women graduates of West Point do receive preferential treatment in their assignments due to the U.S. Army's quota system. Right?*

TOFFLER: *They receive preferential treatment compared with whom?*

Q: *Compared with other cadets who are eligible, that some units of the U.S. Army specifically ask for women even if they are not as well qualified as other men. Isn't that right?*

TOFFLER: *I am absolutely unaware of any requests by an Army unit for women that is in any way attached to their relative qualifications. I'm just not aware of what you are talking about.*

Q: *All right. Let me try to help you, colonel. We need to look at Defendant's Exhibit 152, volume 14. This is a memorandum about cadet perceptions on quotas. Correct?*

TOFFLER: *That's right.*

Q: *And one of the things it talks about down at the bottom under 2-B is the issue of proportional representation?*

TOFFLER: *Correct.*

Q: *And it states in there that in an effort to achieve proportional representation, we may well place a lesser but fully qualified cadet ahead of another fully qualified cadet. Correct?*

TOFFLER: *That's what it says.*

Q: *And this is a memorandum to the superintendent of West Point. Correct?*

TOFFLER: *It's by the current, by the then chief of staff, Colonel Derring.*

Q: *Over on page two it gives some examples. Some examples of some other impacts of the quota system, correct, specifically under paragraph two about engineer branching. Do you see that?*

TOFFLER: *Yes, but what quota system are you talking about?*

Q: *Well, let's look at the specific issue that he addresses. I think that will be clear. He indicates in the last sentence of subparagraph two that, "Five of six women who went engineers stood lower in the class than any of their 107 male counterparts." He says that probably contributes to the cadet perception of bias. Does that help you with respect to your statement you were unaware of any quota system?*

TOFFLER: *No, because the Army sent to the Military Academy a set of quotas for each branch that has a gender difference, so there is a set of quotas, if you will, for engineers that are for men and a set of quotas that are for women. And those quotas have got to be met, and so when the women are going for the engineer branch quotas, they are being compared with performance of women, and the men are going for the men. It has nothing to do with the Military Academy and it has nothing to do with any specific unit.*

Q: *But in the judgment of Colonel Derring, at least, or Deering, excuse me, that may contribute to the perception of cadets that there is some bias operating. Is that right?*

TOFFLER: *That's right.*

Q: *And the next paragraph about how female officers receive preferential assignments ahead of others with higher class standing. Correct?*

TOFFLER: *Again, this is a manifestation of the same type of situation where the Army has a requirement for a certain number of officers, and there is recognition of gender in that requirement, and so those women did not receive assignment preferences ahead of some men at all. They were not even competing for those positions against men.*

Q: *Well, I think you are answering yes to my question, is that right?*

TOFFLER: *I'm not answering that there is a quota system that gives women preferential treatment, no, I'm not.*[16]

There also appeared to be a "recognition of gender" in the selection of cadets for leadership positions at West Point. Many female cadets thought so, according to surveys, but Toffler denied it. He even flatly denied that the Army imposes a quota on the number of women admitted to the academy each year, although this had already been admitted by the Justice Department.

Embarrassments abounded for the services during the commission's nine months of fact finding, enough to worry feminist observers who continued to warn of a secret male conspiracy to deny them equality. "The Pentagon is apparently using the commission as an excuse to delay action," wrote a female Army captain in the *New York Times*.[17]
At every public hearing, uniformed military women were in the audience, registering their reactions to various witnesses with groans, snickers, and sometimes conspicuous silence.

> "War is not an equal opportunity endeavor."
>
> —Max Thurman

In early October 1992, preparing for the commission's final deliberations, Commissioner Darryl Henderson attempted to make sense of the mound of testimony by making a standard, scholarly "content analysis." He began by sorting the testimony into two groups, personal opinion and anecdotal testimony on one hand and factual testimony on the other. The former testimony, said Henderson, was of "limited usefulness."

Of much greater worth was the factual testimony heard by the commission, which could be expected to be valid, reliable, and accurate. Henderson identified some 133 facts established by the commission, only 2 of which supported the integration of women on the basis of military effectiveness. As he explained to his fellow commissioners:

> *The vast majority of facts presented were problematic for the integration of women and, as a result, problematic for readiness and combat effectiveness. It also should be noted that no case was made through factual testimony for the military necessity of integrating women into the combat forces or combat positions.*[18]

In other words, the weight of evidence was well on the side against women in combat, and so too were the majority of commissioners, at least at that time.

Before beginning their final review, the commissioners were allowed ten minutes each to present their own views of the issues at hand. In speaking for themselves, all three commissioners who had not so far firmly committed themselves to one side or the other gave clear indications of siding with the five commissioners against the use of women in combat. But when Henderson presented the results of his content analysis, Moskos, to everyone's surprise, became fearlessly combative. He took issue with Herres on where the burden of proof should lie, telling his colleagues that "women are not just little men. I want to underscore that. Women are not just little men. You're talking about a social chemistry variable, as well as [an] individual, physical strength attribute."

At times Charlie Moskos sounded like Brian Mitchell, challenging the advocates of women in combat to admit that they would sacrifice military readiness for equal opportunity:

> Now, we might say, on the other hand, "Listen, we've got a
> very powerful military. What is ever in second place is so
> far in second place, we can't see it. We have enough slack to
> experiment." If we want to say that, let's just say it outright,
> that we do have slack, we can take a slight degradation in
> effectiveness—or readiness, excuse me—a slight degradation
> in readiness for equal opportunity grounds. Let's not beat
> around the bush.

Dismissing all arguments based on culture, philosophy, or religion, Moskos insisted that only the military's interests mattered: "Readiness, readiness, readiness. And that's what the legislation says, and let's just pay attention to that only."

Moskos questioned the trustworthiness of testimony from commanders who said only good things about the integrated units under them. He also questioned the gender-neutral physical standards, which he said were not popular with enlisted women, "because they are realistic about those kinds of physical standards."

Max Thurman was also a surprise. In the preceding months, he had kept his thoughts to himself and dutifully supported the committee chairman as a fellow member of the "Four Star Club," with Admiral Hogg. When the time came to talk, however, he had quite a lot to say, and much of it ran counter to Herres's opinion. Thurman succinctly enumerated eight points he considered most important. Three of these points were neutral with regard to the issues; the other five supported arguments against a broader military role for women. Thurman told his colleagues that "war is not an equal opportunity endeavor" and that he saw no evidence that integration would do anything but exacerbate problems of sexual harassment or fraternization. Instead, he said, "Sexual activity, in my view, must not occur in direct combat units, because it will be dysfunctional to the accomplishment of the mission and the unit's effectiveness." Combat units should be spared the problem of nondeployability among women, and there was widespread opposition to sending mothers to war.

Of the predictable opponents of combat, Sally White was the briefest. Reminding the others of her experiences as an enlisted woman, she called the advocates of combat among military women a disruptive minority with no real knowledge of the object of their ambitions. Instead, she said, the commission should listen to the retired flag and general officers, who overwhelmingly opposed combat for women.

The other four against combat each delivered informed and impassioned appeals. Elaine Donnelly likened the many problems with integration and the military's equal opportunity ambitions to Jenga blocks pulled one by one from the original tower and added to its top, until the players have pulled away one block too many and the whole proud tower comes tumbling down.

Kate O'Beirne lamented the selfishness of many military women who were lobbying for combat:

I talked to a number of women Marines when we made a
trip to Camp LeJeune, and I said to one of them, "Do you
think women ought to serve in combat?" And she responded
by saying, "Not if it's not good for the Corps, ma'am." But,
boy, I haven't heard too many others express that opinion.
And I guess I'm at some level disillusioned to see people who
are putting their needs, their wants, their desires ahead of
that loyalty to the ethic, to the unit, to the group ethic....

O'Beirne ended by pointing out that equal opportunity wasn't
really the bone of contention, it was special treatment:

The consensus of opinion is for special treatment. The only
consensus is, it seems to me, that women ought to serve in
combat if they want to, but they shouldn't be made to. And
the majority of women don't feel they should have to meet
the same physical standards as men.... We're not talking
equality, here. We are talking about special treatment.

Sam Cockerham spoke from his thirty-plus years of military
service in three wars and contrasted the vastly different per-
spectives taken toward the issues: "the individual, be-all-you-
can-be approach" and "the military necessity/combat readiness
point of view." Ron Ray called the commissioners to a higher
plane of thinking with reference to history and philosophy, to
the legal doctrine of "military necessity," and the sacred principles that define and inspire a nation and a civilization:

We are at the level of high politics, and we have to ask our-
selves, "What are our beliefs? What are our assumptions?
What are these deeper societal processes that have been
going on in this country in the last thirty years? What are
our first principles? And by what standard shall we judge
the extremely important issues before us?"

The comments of those in favor of combat for women, with
the exception of General Herres, were short in length and lim-

ited in scope. Meredith Neizer said that her first concern was military readiness and, after that, "having the highest utilization of every individual that's in the military." Betty Clarke said barely more, mostly about herself, as did Tom Draude, who said he had once opposed women as Marine security guards and in other positions, but had since repented.

Admiral Hogg took up the standard and followed the party line at the Department of the Navy: Exempting mothers and single parents from deployments was bad; exempting women from involuntary sea-duty was bad; and the performance of Navy woman was "as good or better" than the performance of men. The Navy should not be restricted in its authority to assign women wherever it needs them. (The Navy has always guarded its prerogatives jealously, and Hogg was a very loyal Navy man.)

It was left to General Herres, the commission's chairman, to make the definitive procombat case. He began by trying to conciliate his opponents by asking the commissioners to agree that they were against quotas, against dual standards, and for gender-neutral tests of physical ability for all military jobs. He then argued that military effectiveness and equal opportunity were "not mutually exclusive." When the two goals are in conflict, Herres reasoned, the primacy of military effectiveness "is an argument that one can use for persuasive purposes, but not a criterion that should be imposed on one another," which is, apparently, an obscure way of saying that equal opportunity is more important.

"And, finally, what will influence my decisions when the time comes? First, the belief that an exclusion must be shown to be necessary to be preserved," he told his colleagues. Other factors were physical strength, physical endurance, pregnancy, and privacy, which he said "should not diverge drastically from the norms that our society can accept." He rejected the argument that women should be excluded from combat units to protect them from being killed, since they were already vulnerable in noncombat units. He also rejected the argument that women should not be trained to be killers:

We have long since crossed that threshold with the admission of women to the ranks of Minuteman nuclear missile combat crews. It is unrealistic to expect that we can turn the clock back, or even should, on that issue.

In nine months, a lot of bad blood had circulated among the more determined members of the commission. Elaine Donnelly's aggressive style infuriated Herres, who resented challenges to his chairmanship and hated having to deal with civilian women who to his mind did not belong on the commission. For their part, Donnelly, O'Beirne, and White had little use for Herres, whom they regarded as an unprincipled autocrat. And so it went.

In political committee work, two questions are key: who will run the show and who will write the report? Herres had run the show his own way from the start, much to the dismay of the conservative commissioners, who would have wanted the commission to dig deeper into the problems and complaints about the military's actual experience with integration. Now they feared that if Herres wrote the report, the evidence that supported combat exclusions would be ignored.

To avert this, three commissioners—Cockerham, O'Beirne, and Ray—submitted a letter to Herres outlining their desires for the report format and requesting that the commission discuss the issue. Herres put them off again and again. Finally, on the night before the last day of deliberations, the five conservatives agreed among themselves to force the issue.

The next morning, just after the meeting was called to order, Ron Ray asked once more about the letter, only to be put off by Herres once again. Sally White quickly moved to reschedule discussion of the report's format to the first item of business, before the Commission had voted on the issue of combat. Minow and Finch opposed the motion. Kate O'Beirne, speaking in favor of White's motion, said, "I think it's important, before we complete the commission business, with respect to voting on every single issue and option, that everybody, all commissioners, recognize that the final report will be a balanced, even-handed product. And I think the sooner people are assured of that fact, the better. There's no assurance of that at the moment."

As soon as she had finished speaking, Minow called for a vote on the motion. The vote was 8 to 7 in favor of ending discussion of the motion and voting on it immediately. Herres was reading the motion for the vote when O'Beirne interrupted him to offer a friendly amendment to limit discussion of the report format to fifteen minutes. The amendment was accepted, the vote was called, and the motion was defeated.

Without announcement, one by one, the five conspirators got up and walked out. Herres and the others continued working as if the commission had simply shrunk to only ten members. And the pretense of basing decisions on military effectiveness was discarded. In considering combat roles for women, Commissioner Draude read from President Harry Truman's executive order for racially integrating the military in 1948:

> It is essential that there be maintained in the Armed Services of the United States the highest standards of democracy, with equality of treatment and opportunity for all those who serve in our country's defense.

Notice, said Draude, "He used the words 'equality of treatment and opportunity,' not 'military necessity.'"[19]

Neizer, Hogg, Minow, and Herres all seconded Draude's sentiments. Minow said he was "very moved" by Draude's statement and offered to support it in writing for the commission's report. Herres put equal opportunity and military necessity on the same vague level, saying that "both are one of our most sacred cultural values" and both "could be protected" without sacrificing one to the other. Henderson was not persuaded:

> Everybody here almost said it, that military readiness is a primary concern. Now, when you start prejudging what

*might come up in later decisions, in later issues, early on
here, you're just biasing the whole process here. I think we
should take this opportunity to reaffirm that military readiness is a primary concern.*

To appease him, the others voted to say in its recommendation that "military readiness should be the *driving* concern,"
but "there are circumstances under which women *might* be
assigned to combat positions." The word *driving*, instead of *primary*, was meant to strengthen the first sentence, while the
word *might*, instead of *should*, was meant to weaken the second. Henderson still voted against the recommendation, the
only commissioner present who did so. Moskos abstained.

About 1 PM, just before the commission was to take up the
issues of women in combat aviation and aboard combat vessels,
the Gang of Five rejoined the others with the understanding
that they would be allowed fifteen minutes to make their case
on the report format. The discussion was contentious, with
Commissioner Draude accusing the gang of blackmail for walking out, prompting an objection from Commissioner Ray:

> *I respect General Draude enormously. I respect his
> integrity. I respect his combat record. But I will not be
> accused of blackmail in this room or anyplace else, nor will
> I be called a quitter....*
>
> *After my tour in Vietnam, I spent a year making the
> casualty calls, okay? I went to the families of the people who
> were going to die. I've heard it said by people in this room
> that America can stand a 20 percent degradation in readi-
> ness. In favor of fairness, I've heard that said. I disagree
> with that. We're smaller. We've got to be better. We're going
> to have to fight and win outnumbered. I've done that before,
> and it is not easy.*
>
> *Now listen: I take this as serious as a heart attack, and I
> think the rest of you here do. I will not let the reality of war,
> the demands and the physical demands of combat be other*

than fairly represented to the president of the United States, to the Congress, and, more importantly, to the American people.[20]

The commission voted in favor of a report format that would provide room for "alternative views."

After a short break, the commission took up the issue of women in combat aviation. Three commissioners—Thurman, Minow, and Clarke—chose not to speak on the issue. Moskos argued both sides. Henderson and the Gang of Five all spoke against integration of combat aviation, citing concerns for unit cohesion, aggressiveness, physical ability, medical problems, cultural factors, survivability as prisoners of war, and the consensus of the leadership of the services, retired flag officers, and aviators on active duty. (Integration of combat aviation was opposed by 71 percent of the retired flag officers and more than 80 percent of current aviators.)

Hogg, Finch, Neizer, and Herres spoke in favor of combat aviation for women on the basis of their appraisals of the past performance of women, the voluntary nature of aviation, public opinion, and projected improvements to "the quality of the talent pool."

Darryl Henderson motioned that the commission recommend a test period for female combat pilots, but Charlie Moskos questioned whether such testing could be done, free of political pressure. Sally White motioned that the commission recommend barring women from assignment aboard aircraft engaged in combat missions. Elaine Donnelly seconded White's motion. Eight commissioners voted in favor of White's motion—Thurman, Moskos, Henderson, and the Gang of Five. The other seven voted against it.

The key factor for Thurman was the matter of women as prisoners of war. Air Force Colonel John D. Graham, director of the Joint Services SERE Agency, which trains pilots from all services in survival, evasion, resistance, and escape (SERE), had told commissioners that having women among men as prisoners of war would make survival harder on the men:

*Females will have a harmful effect on the males. This was
not held by the students. In what was probably what they
thought was politically correct, neither males nor females
thought that females would have any impact on males in
captivity, but the instructors who observed the training,...
both male and female, noticed a marked difference in the
impact that the females had on men in this training.*[21]

SERE representatives attributed the male response to female abuse as a cultural need felt by men to protect women: "they feel the need to do something, feel a need to stop it, or they feel the need to protect."[22] One objective of SERE training was to make men less sensitive to suffering of women. Nevertheless, their lack of physical strength was expected to make them less able to survive as downed pilots. In the words of Marine Colonel John Ripley:

*When that airplane, with its female pilot, returns to earth or
collides with earth or she must bail out of it, she is no longer
a female pilot; she is now a victim, and made so by the
incredible stupidity of those who would permit her to
encounter with the enemy. She is no longer protected by our
own standards of decency, or the Geneva Convention,
which few of our enemies have paid the least bit of attention
to. She is no longer protected by the well-wishers and the
hand-wringing and the pleas and the prayers of the folks
here at home. She is a victim, and she will be treated
accordingly.*[23]

The commission now took up the issue of women aboard combat vessels. Fewer commissioners participated, but Admiral Hogg spoke at great length. His former reservations about women aboard ships was just his "macho-male baggage," he said.

*In summary, I can find no solid arguments or valid reasons
for excluding qualified women from serving in combatant*

ships. Taken a step further, to include them would improve all aspects of the ship's performance, as has been the case with our noncombatants.

The arguments against integration were based on privacy, pregnancy, deployability, sexual harassment, fraternization, unit morale, and detriment to the vessels' damage-control and war-fighting capabilities, especially in jobs where physical strength was important. Henderson accused the Navy of stonewalling requests for factual information on the performance of women aboard ship. He concluded his argument by saying that even the current policy of putting women aboard ships is "going to cost lives, and it probably will cost ships, given a real emergency at sea." Henderson attributed the Navy's enthusiasm for putting women aboard warships to panic over the Tailhook scandal.

For many, the key factor in the argument is the matter of women as prisoners of war.

Meredith motioned that the commission recommend repealing the restrictions on women aboard combatant vessels. Mimi Finch seconded the motion. Just before it went to a vote, Chairman Herres weighed in. The nation was expecting change, he said, and if the commission failed to recommend a change in the status quo, all of its other worthy recommendations would be ignored:

> *I submit that the words of caution that we have agreed upon, with regard to ground combat, with regard to quotas, and the potential for affirmative action, with regard to the establishment of gender-neutral physical standards where they are relevant to the occupations in which people will serve, all of those cautions will probably be lost in the smoke, because I submit to you that the great number—a great number of people who will be looking at this report and are likely to act on it—will not believe that we credibly considered these issues.*

If we had shown some flexibility that we realistically looked at this problem carefully and recognized that this is 1992, change is upon us, that there were things learned in the Gulf War, there are things that are different today, that women have proved that they can make significant contributions to the effectiveness of our military forces—if we demonstrate that we have recognized all of that, some of our other cautions may be listened to.

If we go status quo on this issue, this will be the last one, and I submit that what I think is very important, and that is codification of a combat exclusion for land combat, is never going to happen. Probably what will happen is our report will be ignored. The testimony that we have heard, the records that have been laid before us will be reviewed, and I suggest to you that others are going to come to different conclusions.

Robert Herres delivered this speech staring straight at Max Thurman, who had surprised him by voting against having women in combat aircraft.

As Herres spoke, Elaine Donnelly waited impatiently to offer a rebuttal, but Darryl Henderson dissuaded her. "Let it go," he whispered. "We have the votes."

But when the vote was finally taken, they didn't. Thurman voted in favor of the recommendation. Henderson hung in there with the Gang of Five voting against. Moskos, to everyone's surprise, abstained.

The commission voted on a very mixed bag of seventeen recommendations included in its final report: against quotas, for gender-*specific* physical training standards, for gender-*neutral* physical job standards, for gender-*normed* precommissioning standards, against women in ground combat, against women in combat aviation, for women on combat ships, against women in special operations, and detailed recommendations on how to deal with pregnancy, motherhood, single parents, and deployment. The "Alternative Views: The Case Against Women

in Combat," for which the Gang of Five had fought so courageously, was also included in the commission's report. Written
by Elaine Donnelly and signed by Cockerham, Donnelly,
O'Beirne, Ray, and White, it expanded on the issues of combat
aviation and combat ships, basing everything on combat effectiveness, while noting that the drive for change was motivated
not by a concern for the good of the military but by the demand
for equal rights.

"The Case Against Women in Combat" was followed by a
lengthy dissent on the recommendation against women in combat aviation, signed by all seven commissioners who voted
against that recommendation. Three commissioners (Clarke,
Finch, and Neizer) dissented from the commission's recommendation against ground combat for women, arguing that
women were already serving in ground combat and had thoroughly proved themselves in the Persian Gulf. Six commissioners dissented from the recommendation to retain the Defense
Department's "risk rule," which they called an "unrealistic,
inappropriate, and subjective" means to restrict women from
serving where they were needed. Seven commissioners dissented on the recommendation against women aboard submarines and amphibious vessels, on the grounds that the
secretary of the Navy should be given flexibility in such matters.

The report also included personal statements from twelve
commissioners, some of them pages long. Most of the statements stuck to the issues addressed by the commission, but the
statements of Clarke, Finch, and Neizer complained bitterly
about the influence of the conservative commissioners. Finch
wrote that "the work of this commission has been an insult to all
servicewomen." The three commissioners who did not submit
personal statements were Herres, O'Beirne, and the strenu-
ously nonpartisan Charles Moskos.

It all came to naught. The final votes on women in combat
were taken on Election Day 1992. By the end of the day, with
Bill Clinton as the projected winner of the presidential election,
it was clear that the commission's work was superfluous—a new

political order had arrived. The commission delivered its report to the White House on November 15, 1992. The White House forwarded the report to Congress without comment. Two months later, the raging issue was not women in combat—which was a done deal—but homosexuals in the military.

Still, the Gang of Five had accomplished many things. They had uncovered much evidence against gender integration of the military, evidence which might never have seen the light of day had there been no commission and no Gang of Five. The Gang of Five had spoiled the party, and sometimes, in politics, spoiling the party is all you can do—and just what is needed.

Chapter 12

THE MOTHER OF ALL HOOKS

*Tailhook should have been a three- or maybe a
five-day story. Those who were to blame for
outrageous conduct should have been disciplined,
and those who were not to blame should have been
vigorously defended, along with the culture and the
mores of the naval service. Instead, we are now at
four years and counting, and its casualty list reads
like a Who's Who of naval aviation.*

—FORMER NAVY SECRETARY JAMES WEBB

BEFORE TAILHOOK, there was Gwen Dreyer, a first-year midshipman who was "chained to a urinal" at the United States
Naval Academy in December 1989. The incident came on the
eve of the Army-Navy game, at the end of a long day of snowball fights and high-spirited high jinks, in which Ms. Dreyer had
willingly taken part. She was not actually chained but handcuffed to the urinal in her dormitory at the academy, in retaliation for her part of the snowball fights. Eyewitnesses reported
that she had laughed during the ordeal, and photographs
showed her smiling. Her torture lasted fifteen minutes. Dreyer
tearfully told her parents. Her father Gregory, a Naval Reserve

captain and Navy civilian employee, was incensed and complained in person to academy officials. The academy investigated and punished two midshipmen with demerits and the loss
of a month's leave, and six others with written reprimands.

Weeks before the incident, Dreyer told her faculty advisor
she was considering quitting the academy. Both her father and
her grandfather had graduated from Annapolis, and academy
officials believed that she had been pressured by her father to
go there. When she finally did quit the following May, her
father blamed the academy. He had not been satisfied with the
academy's response to the chaining incident and had continued
to badger the academy for months for sterner measures. When
his daughter quit, he went to a small local paper, the Annapolis
Capital, whose banner headline later read, "Tormented female
mid resigns," with the subhead, "Women handcuffed to toilet,
taunted." That got the attention of the *Baltimore Sun* and the
Washington Post, and before long, NOW was picketing outside
the academy's gates, and the school was facing no fewer than six
Navy and congressional investigations focusing not only on the
Dreyer incident but on the general climate between the sexes
in the Brigade of Midshipmen.

No one was alleging that Dreyer had been sexually
molested, and nothing indicated that Dreyer had been victimized because she was a woman. Not all of her tormenters were
male, and several female midshipmen were vocal in their support for the academy, telling the protesters from NOW that
"you don't know what the norm is… you are doing a lot of damage." Dreyer's humiliation was "not a matter of gender, it's part
of the life here." That same weekend, according to one female
mid, Dreyer herself had helped to "strip, tar and feather" a
male West Point cadet.

But this hardly mattered to the journalists who smelled a
good story or to the politicians looking for attention. For them,
the incident had cosmic meaning. The mythic Dreyer was a
hard-working, conscientious, capable woman beaten down by
mean and jealous men. "The trouble with Annapolis goes

deep," wrote syndicated columnist Mary McGrory, "—insecure men, feeling threatened by bright women excused from combat; a service-wide identity crisis caused by the fact that its ships have become little more than targets for Exocet missiles."[1]

Investigators found no evidence of a "service-wide identity crisis," to say nothing of Exocet missiles, but what they did find confirmed a feminist's worst fears. Fourteen years after the first women arrived at Annapolis, half the male midshipmen believed that women had no business being there. Eighty percent of males and 86 percent of females believed that women were not accepted as equals in the brigade. A "significant majority" of male and female mids said upperclassmen dating female plebes was a problem, although investigators noted that dating "both helped and hindered" the acceptance of women.

Gossip on who was seeing whom was broadcast by the academy's radio station as "Tales from the Dark Side," and a midshipmen magazine featured photos of attractive female mids as "Company Cuties." Through dirty jokes, derogatory language, and lewd e-mail, male mids let female mids know they were not welcomed. Former Navy secretary and best-selling novelist James Webb had become a cult hero among male midshipmen, who kept copies of his article "Women Can't Fight" in constant circulation at the academy, ten years after it appeared in the *Washingtonian* magazine.

A study group at the academy identified the causes of the "lack of assimilation" of women as a "misperception" of the academy's mission, "ignorance about the integral role of women in the Navy," and "perceived preferential treatment" of women. The "combat officer ideal pervades midshipmen's definition of [a] good leader," said the group's report. They would be more accepting of women if they understood that the academy's mission was to train not combat leaders but career naval officers. Midshipmen needed to be enlightened about the many things women do in the Navy. They actually believed that "equal treatment should mean identical treatment." Their complaints about unequal treatment—in admission standards, academic boards, leadership positions, and physical requirements—were only "perceptions." (Midshipmen merely *perceived* that male plebes had their heads shaved while female plebes didn't.) The study also blamed opposition to women at the academy on not enough female role models, not enough female mids, not enough jobs open to women upon graduation, and fraterniza-tion between upperclass males and female plebes.[2]

Politically, *l'affaire Dreyer* culminated in October 1990 with a press conference in the U.S. Capitol Building held by the academy's Board of Visitors to present the findings of its own investigation. The board was chaired by Arthur B. Culvahouse, Jr., but board member Barbara Mikulski, Democratic senator for Maryland, dominated the press conference. "What we found is that in order to achieve a fair and just society, a fair and just Navy, it is essential that the academy lead the fleet, not fol-low the fleet, in crushing racism and sexism," said Mikulski. "Sexism is wrong, and the U.S. Naval Academy cannot tolerate it. Attitudes must change." She was seconded by another board member, Maryland Republican Congresswoman Helen Bentley. The board's three male members hardly said a word, but the Naval Academy's superintendent, Rear Admiral Virgil L. Hill, Jr., did his best to appear fully understanding of the problem and eager to address it.

Mikulski's office distributed a statement castigating the academy for regarding Dreyer's handcuffing as an innocent prank and for tolerating openly sexist behavior among midship-men and faculty members. But in a closed-door meeting with Hill and Hill's superior, Vice Admiral Jeremy M. Boorda, just before the press conference, Mikulski was sufficiently mollified by the Navy's penitence and plan for reform that her initial written statement was withdrawn in favor of a more moderate statement.

During the press conference, Mikulski accepted the acad-emy's assurance that changes were under way, as per Rear Admiral Hill's plan. The plan included the creation of a stand-ing committee of female mids and faculty members to monitor the status of assimilation, six hours of sensitivity training for all midshipmen, zero tolerance for any expression by students or faculty inconsistent with official Navy policy, severe punishment for sexual harassment and discrimination, dismissal of midshipmen and faculty members who "question" the presence of women at the academy, and a strict hands-off policy that made touching a plebe grounds for dismissal. "Straightening someone's hat or tie or flicking dust off a uniform, that will not be done anymore," explained the academy's commandant earlier that summer. The plan did not include eliminating unequal treatment. To this day, the academy shaves the heads of its men but not its women.[3]

No one knew in 1990 that the shakedown of the Naval Academy was but a trial run for the legendary scandals that were to come. All of the conditions that made the Tailhook disaster possible were already in place: wild

Eighty percent of males and 86 percent of females believed that women were not accepted as equals in the brigade.

young men whose idea of equality was treating women as roughly as they treated each other; selfish, sensitive young women who could dish it out but not take it; self-righteous journalists who saw good copy in a "battle of the sexes"; feminist ideologues in need of another *cause célèbre*; shameless politicians eager for attention; and gutless Navy leaders who were unable or unwilling to defend their men, their service, or themselves.

At the Tailhook Symposium of 1991 two currents crossed path: the trend of increasingly licentious American sexuality and the countertrend of increasingly intolerant American feminism. Naval aviators had long been known as a wild bunch, but in recent years the annual meetings of the Tailhook Association had grown wilder than usual. A letter sent before the symposium by the president of the Tailhook Association, Navy Captain Frederick "Wigs" Ludwig, to all squadrons expected to attend admitted to problems in the past and asked attendees to be on the look-out for underage participants, to try to curtail "late night 'gang mentality,'" and to ensure that each squadron's "duty officer" remain sober. The letter ended with a final brief warning:

REMEMBER... THERE ARE TO BE NO "QUICK HIT" DRINKS served. LEWD AND LASCIVIOUS behavior is unacceptable. The behavior in your suite reflects on both your squadron and your commanding officer.

Even so, the letter was surprisingly tame, in view of the symposium's reputation. It did warn that an "accident" involving underage participants could cause the association, the Navy, and the hotel to be sued, "and Tailhook would come to an end," but it threatened no individual punishment. It even advised attendees to use "discretion" when sneaking prohibited supplies into the hotel: "Please cover your supplies by putting them in parachute bags or boxes. DO NOT BORROW LAUNDRY BASKETS FROM THE HILTON. THEIR SENSE OF HUMOR DOES NOT GO THAT FAR!!!"

The annual Tailhook symposiums were not without professional value. They regularly offered briefings from senior Navy officials on aviation safety, advances in aviation technology, air operations, personnel issues, and other professional topics. Of special interest at the 1991 symposium were briefings on combat operations, munitions effectiveness, and intelligence during the Persian Gulf War, which some of the attendees had seen first hand and others would learn about through the symposium. The capstone of the symposium's professional agenda was a flag officer panel bringing together half a dozen or more admirals to field questions from the audience. It was a rare opportunity—unique among the branches of service—for officers of any rank to question the most senior men in their profession, from the three-star head of "OP-05"[4] on down. Other official events included golf and tennis tournaments, a five-kilometer fun run, and two formal dinners, one to present awards to distinguished aviators.[5]

Nevertheless, the annual symposium had begun as a party and thrived as a party year after year. The first was held in Tijuana in 1956 as a reunion for aviators from the fleet. The symposiums were moved to Las Vegas in 1963, with the professional events added over the years, receiving official Navy support in the form of time off from regular duties, military transportation to and from the event, participation by Navy officials, and administrative support. An estimated five thousand people, mostly Navy and Marine aviators, attended the 1991 symposium, billed as the "Mother of all Hooks," but fewer than 2,000 were registered attendees, and, according to Navy investigators, even fewer were present at the best attended official event, the flag officer panel. Obviously, quite a few attendees were there for other reasons.

For years, the social side of the symposium was supported by the "hospitality suites" sponsored originally by Defense Department contractors, who laid out free food and drink for the attendees in rented hotel rooms concentrated on a single floor. In the late 1970s new rules governing relations between Defense Department employees and contractors meant that contractors could no longer sponsor the hospitality suites. That responsibility was taken over by individual squadrons, which funded their suites with money collected from squadron officers and from the sale of Tailhook souvenirs at previous symposiums. Before long, competition developed among participating squadrons to see who could throw the wildest party. After the 1985 symposium one Tailhook board member, Rear Admiral James Service, expressed concern for symposium misconduct that already included public drunkenness, damage to hotel property, and "lurid sexual acts on naval aviators." He proposed limiting the number of hospitality suites, black-listing ill-behaved squadrons, issuing warnings to squadron commanders, and even banning all suites for one year. Instead, the board decided to advise squadron commanders of ground rules and past problems and to require them to post duty officers to keep behavior in each suite under control.

252 • WOMEN IN THE MILITARY

Little changed, though, in the years following. By 1991 the annual gatherings had descended to degrees of excess and depravity far beyond the normal limits of even the rowdiest civilian professional or business convention, perhaps on par with the worst collegiate affairs. Competition among the twenty-two hospitality suites at the thirty-fifth annual Tailhook in September 1991 produced some innovative obscenities. In the "Rhino room," a recently deactivated Marine reconnaissance unit (the Rhino Squadron, VMFP-3), an eight-foot-long mural of a white rhino was rigged to dispense an alcoholic concoction through a dildo in the place of the rhino's phallus. The beverage, called "rhino spunk," consisted of rum, Kahlua, milk or cream, and ice. Women were encouraged to "please the rhino," and some made a show of simulated oral sex. For the favor of exposing their breasts, women received squadron T-shirts.

Outside the pool-side suite sponsored by VAW-110 (a carrier-based early warning squadron), a large banner advertised "FREE LEG SHAVES!" to female guests. Inside two aviators at a time shaved the legs of willing guests using hot towels and baby oil, and licking each customer's calves to ensure "quality control." Easily visible from the pool through the glass door of the suite, the shaves lasted between thirty and forty-five minutes and included a foot-and-leg massage. Some women wore only panties or bikini bottoms during the procedure, while a few exposed the edges of their pubic region for a "bikini shave." Some exposed their breasts during the operation. One woman who disrobed completely for a bikini shave was a stripper who did it for money. Investigators estimated that about fifty women allowed their legs to be shaved during the symposium, including at least three female officers, one while in uniform.

The suite hosted by Fighter Squadron 124 from the Naval Air Station in Miramar, California, boasted a disk jockey, pornographic movies, and two strippers performing sadomasochistic and lesbian acts, with occasional physical contact between performers and the audience. In this suite, several witnesses saw a

female officer serve "belly shots" of tequila to three male officers, who drank from her navel. The same female officer later
allowed two male officers to shave her legs in the suite hosted
by VAW-110. She told investigators that some women serving
belly shots (also known as "navel shots") wore short skirts with
no underwear and exposed themselves during the act. Some
men also served belly shots to both civilian women and female
officers.

There were several reports of men and women exposing
themselves in the pool area and sometimes from the windows
of rooms above the area. One woman was injured when hit by
glass from a window pushed out by someone mooning the
crowd below. The pool itself was the sight of "chicken fights," in
which women mounted on men's shoulders tried to rip the
bathing-suit top off other women. In the hospitality suites,
strippers were paid to perform fellatio, and at least one couple
copulated in the presence of others. There were also reports of
couples engaging in oral sex and sexual intercourse in the pool
area and near the tennis courts.

The various obnoxious behaviors exhibited by the partiers
also included pinching, groping, streaking, "sharking" (biting
women on the buttocks), "zapping" (slapping stickers of
squadron logos on people, especially women), and "ball-
walking" (exposing one's testicles in public). None of these
offenses originated with or was limited to Tailhook. Sharking
had been known among Marine aviators since the dark days of
Vietnam. Ball-walking began more recently as a sophomoric
show of virility and defiance.

Zapping originated among Navy and Marine aviators as a
territorial marking of aircraft from other squadrons visiting
their base. At the symposiums, it was practiced mostly on
women. Buttocks were a favorite target, but a few women
caught in the third-floor gauntlet were zapped on their breasts
and groin as well. Some women tried to collect as many zappers
as possible. One woman walked into the VA–128 suite, lifted
her shirt to reveal five or six zappers covering her bare breasts,

and asked the aviators to rearrange them. Another woman welcomed two men to zap her crotch. Aviators often requested permission to zap, and most of the recipients told investigators they were not offended and that zapping was mostly done with permission and among friends.

The infamous gauntlet was a relatively recent development in the history of Tailhook, arising in response to the changing nature of the gathering. For most of its history, the Tailhook symposium had been a stag affair. Informal rules prohibited aviators from bringing their wives or girlfriends. The few women present were usually prostitutes or "groupies" who knew the rules and went along. Only in the 1980s, after the squadrons had taken over the hospitality suites, did many more women begin attending the symposiums, not just wives and girlfriends but also female officers and many more single women attracted to naval aviators. These women did not always know the rules and so received a rough reception from the drunken aviators, who viewed them as outsiders and therefore free game.

The gauntlet evolved from a few men overflowing into the hall from the hospitality suites, to a coarse communal display of attention for arriving women. At first, the women were received with cheers, catcalls, and comments on their relative attractiveness. Then came the pinching, patting, and slapping, which later degenerated into grabbing, groping, and sharking. The later the hour, the worse the treatment. One civilian woman employed by the Navy told investigators of a conversation she had with another young woman whom she had met on a commercial flight to Las Vegas to attend Tailhook 1991. In describing the gauntlet, the young woman said that at about three o'clock in the morning, things get "real rough" and wild on the floor. Far from being put off by such behavior, the young woman said that it was the reason she was on her way to the convention.[6]

Much of the activity in the third-floor hall was spontaneous and unpredictable, sometimes crowded and rowdy, sometimes not. At times, though, the crowds functioned in an organized fashion. To lure women into the hall, the men would mill around casually, paying no apparent attention. At the first sign of an attractive woman, a self-appointed "master of ceremonies" would yell out "Clear deck!"—the signal for the men to line the hall in preparation for her passing. Once in the gauntlet men would close around her, slowing her progress but keeping her moving while plastering her with zappers or grabbing at her groin, breasts, and buttocks. Others would begin rhythmically pounding the walls while chanting, "Gauntlet! Gauntlet!" Unattractive women were greeted with "Wave off!" and "Abort! Abort!" or other carrier jargon, and were allowed to pass unmolested. Similar signals were given to announce the approach of senior officers and security personnel. Afterwards, the command was "Mill about!"—to return the assembly to its original, unthreatening appearance.

Many witnesses, male and female, told investigators that they viewed the gauntlet as just part of the party, and that most women seemed to enjoy or at least accept the attention and the contact, responding with smiles, giggles, playful retaliation against the men, and repeat passes. The attitude among many aviators was, "This is our party: if you come here, you play by our rules." Women who objected were told they should not be there. Women who resisted were often treated worse, although some managed to fend off men with well-placed punches or kicks. Two women reportedly showed up on the floor armed with electronic devices to ward off attackers.

Security guards and some officers warned quite a few women not to enter the third-floor hallway, but many did anyway and some regretted it later. Reluctant women were occasionally hoisted upon the shoulders of the "master of ceremonies" and carried down the hall against their will. One young college freshman, who was too drunk to resist, was passed hands-over-head all the way down the hall, having her slacks and her underwear removed along the way. At the end of the gauntlet, she was deposited on the floor, naked from the waist down, and left in the care of two security guards.[7]

For all the groping and grabbing, there were indications that the event was less threatening than some victims believed. One woman reported that after the "master of ceremonies" carried her down the hall against her will, he set her down gently and asked, "Are you okay?" Only when assured she was not injured did he rejoin the crowd. Two women told investigators that after being pushed and shoved through the groping gauntlet, one of the women noticed that she had lost her pager. A Navy lieutenant at the end of the gauntlet yelled to the men in the hall that the woman had lost her pager, and immediately, said one of the women later, "the whole crowd stopped and began to look for the pager." The pager was found and politely returned to its owner.[8]

Throughout the weekend, members of the Tailhook staff and some senior officers made individual attempts to rein in misbehaving junior officers. The president of the Tailhook Association, Captain Ludwig, chased five streakers into a bathroom and pounded on the door until they opened up, then chewed them out and sent them away in towels. A Navy commander chastised a junior officer for exposing himself in the pool. On occasion, officers broke up attacks on women in the hallway. There was, however, no concerted effort to bring the party under tighter control, although many of the activities described above were witnessed by several senior officers.

At the end of the three-day debauch, the third floor reeked of beer, vomit, and urine. Attendees had consumed (one way or another) more than $33,000 in alcoholic beverages (mostly beer) and caused $23,000 in damage to the Las Vegas Hilton ($18,000 to replace the third floor's carpet). In his epistolary debriefing to squadron commanders, Captain Ludwig declared the gathering

...the biggest and most successful Tailhook we have ever had. We said it would be the 'Mother of all Hooks,' and it was.... The professional symposium proceeded flawlessly and it appeared the information exchange was excellent. The

*flag panel was a resounding success with an estimated 2,500
in attendance. The questions were frank, on the mark, and
often quite animated. Our banquet and luncheon also
boasted of incredible attendance and were enjoyed by all.
Our very senior naval leadership, including the Secretary
and the CNO, were thoroughly impressed and immensely
enjoyed their times at Tailhook '91. Additionally, all of our
naval aviation leaders and many industry leaders had nothing but praise for the event. We can be proud of a tremen-
dous Tailhook '91 and a great deal of thanks goes to all the
young JOs in the various committees
that made Hook fly.*

**For the most part,
Tailhook, even at its
worst, was a consensual
encounter.**

But he also admitted that the 1991
gathering was the Mother of all Hooks
in one other respect, which Ludwig
could only call "unprofessionalism,"
stemming from a "blatant and total dis-
regard of individual rights and public/private property." Ludwig
mentioned the damaged carpet, the broken window, and five
reports he had heard of women abused by the gauntlet, including the young girl who was passed overhead without her pants.
Such things had put a "serious blemish on what was otherwise
a successful symposium" and a "black eye to the Tailhook
Association and all Naval Aviation." They had also strained
Tailhook's welcome at the Hilton, leaving Ludwig to do the
"damage control" while attempting to lock in Tailhook '92. He
ended with a warning: "If future Tailhooks are to take place,
attitudes and behavior must change." The challenge was "to figure out a way to have a great time responsibly or we will jeop-
ardize the very future of Tailhook altogether."

How could it have happened? How could it have happened
year after year? How could highly paid, greatly trusted, college-
educated professionals, dedicated, dutiful, upright, and obedi-
ent in the service of their country devolve into a wild, wanton
rabble with deliberate regularity?

Probing for answers, investigators saw evidence of a variety of contributing factors, including a lack of leadership, a tradition of excess, and an expected immaturity from junior officers. Some believed that unlike young platoon leaders in the Army and Marine Corps, young aviators were responsible for no one but themselves and their machine, and therefore their professional maturity was delayed. Even after ten years of service, they were still "the kids" to their superiors.

The stress of their jobs was another supposed factor. The "kids" were engaged in one of the most dangerous professions in modern times, regularly risking their lives in their routine duties. Flying was the easy part; what set them apart from even other aviators were the launches and landings on a busy carrier flight deck. Six naval aviators were killed in the Gulf War, and in the year of peace after the symposium, thirty officers were killed in military aviation accidents. Such stress had presumably produced a fatalistic hedonism—"Eat, drink, and be merry, for tomorrow we shall die." The convention was merely the appointed time to indulge.

Investigators also looked to the popular culture for possible explanations. The movies *An Officer and a Gentlemen* and *Top Gun* were thought to have contributed to the glamor and bravado of naval aviators, although these movies almost certainly had more effect on the women who flocked to Tailhook than on the aviators themselves, who considered the latter an exceedingly silly flick—"Top Bunk," they called it. Influences from popular American culture were more probably movies like *Animal House*, *Caddyshack*, and the movie and television series *M*A*S*H*, which encouraged an attitude of insouciant irreverence toward uptight, oppressive, hypocritical, old-fashioned norms of social propriety. A generation of American males had grown up without positive exemplars of dignified Christian gentlemen, an image that was more often insulted than honored by the quite un-Christian American media. No one seriously expected them to be "officers and gentlemen" anymore. The word *gentleman* had lost all meaning; the concept no longer existed. The same could be said for the word *lady* and the ideal it represented. Neither ideal was invoked by the modern moralists who condemned the aviators for their behavior. Instead, the event was judged by newer, feminist standards, which came down hard on the men but went easy on the women.

By these new standards, Tailhook was judged a general assault on women, a violent backlash against their presence in the military, a wild "harassacre" as one wit put it. The idea that the abuse of women, especially female officers, was motivated by antifeminist animosity dominated the thinking of a few female officers. The vast majority of male officers denied it, but there was some evidence to support the notion. When the subject of women in combat aviation was raised by a female officer before the flag panel, a male voice yelled out, "We don't want women!" The senior admiral present, Vice Admiral Richard Dunleavy, made a joke of pretending to duck under the table before giving an equivocating response that was not well received by either sex. A drunken argument over the issue between male and female junior officers that evening led to verbal and physical abuse. Several officers on the third floor sported T-shirts with "HE-MAN WOMAN-HATERS' CLUB" on one side and "WOMEN ARE PROPERTY" on the other. Still, the evidence is insufficient to establish sexism as a primary or even a secondary cause of events, for it does nothing to explain the general behavior of both men *and women* at the symposium, unless one interprets all sexual misbehavior as evidence of sexist misogyny.

For the most part, Tailhook, even at its worst, was a consensual encounter. Investigators identified 470 women who attended the symposium and interviewed 398. Less than one-quarter (83) were classed as "victims" for having experienced nonconsensual physical contact, mostly grabbing or fondling of the buttocks. Ten of those women, including five Navy officers, told investigators that they did not consider themselves victims. Some requested that they not be identified as such in the investigators' report. At least three women who did feel like victims blamed themselves for their experience, saying they "should have known better." Two alleged victims refused to cooperate with investigators. Ten women, mostly civilians, said they had experienced similar treatment at Tailhook symposiums in the past, but were not discouraged from coming back. Six men said they were assaulted by women pinching their buttocks, grabbing their crotches for a "package check," or pulling their shorts down in public. Only a handful of the female victims left the party after being assaulted; the great majority just changed places, moving from the hallway to the pool patio or from one suite to another. Only two women felt so violated that they called the police.

The investigators never attempted to explain the behavior of any women, although most of the women present had no professional reason for being there. Some single civilian women flew in from as far away as Massachusetts and Florida, just to join the party. Many more drove to Las Vegas from California and Arizona. Since Tailhook was an annual event in Las Vegas, most of the local women present knew exactly what to expect. The two who called the police were among the few women who just happened to be in Las Vegas that weekend and had no prior knowledge of Tailhook.

Ironically, it was Ludwig's second letter alerting squadron skippers to the "unprofessionalism" exhibited at the symposium that proved the Navy's undoing. The letter's specific mention of the gauntlet, the woman passed hand over head without her pants, the broken window, and $23,000 in damage was the smoking gun needed by Gregory Vistica, a reporter for the *San Diego Union-Tribune*. Vistica had been tipped off to the story by an unnamed source, a Navy captain, and had already identified a few of the victims, including the civilian women who called the police and an admiral's aide, Lieutenant Paula Coughlin, but it was Ludwig's letter, provided to Vistica by another Navy source, that made the story.[9]

The *Union-Tribune* ran the story on Tuesday, October 29, 1991. That very afternoon, Senator John McCain denounced the Navy on the floor of the Senate, demanding a "full and immediate convening of a high-ranking panel of civilian and military members" to investigate the "despicable behavior taking place as far as sexual harassment is concerned at this convention."[10]

McCain's denunciation was a resounding vote of no confidence in the Navy and its leadership, already badly beaten by a string of scandals: the Dreyer affair, a cheating scandal at the Naval Academy, the drowning death of a rescue swimmer, the persecution of a decorated enlisted man who blew the whistle on the inappropriate cannibalization of downed aircraft, and, most significant, the Navy's disastrous investigation into the explosion aboard the battleship *Iowa*. The Navy's political leaders were running scared, while its admirals were touchy and defensive.

The Navy's most senior leaders were caught flat-footed by McCain. With the exception of Vice Admiral Dunleavy, chief of aviation, they had not known of Ludwig's letter until Vistica called the office of the secretary for comment late in the afternoon the day before. Neither had they heard any complaints of impropriety. Several key leaders had, however, attended the symposium and were afraid of being implicated. They included the secretary of the Navy, H. Lawrence Garrett III, and the chief of naval operations, Admiral Frank Kelso.

Hours after McCain's attack, Garrett's office hastily drafted a letter to Captain Ludwig expressing the secretary's "absolute outrage" at the reported abuses at the convention and terminating all Navy support for the Tailhook Association, one of McCain's demands. Written with obvious exculpatory intent, the letter cited Navy-wide messages against sexual harassment sent by both Garrett and Kelso months earlier and mentioned the professional value of the symposium as justification for Garrett's and Kelso's presence.

That same day, Garrett announced two investigations of the symposium, one by the Naval Investigative Service (NIS) focusing on criminal allegations and another by the Navy's inspector general focusing on the gathering's noncriminal aspects. Garrett also announced the formation of a panel of senior executives who would monitor the investigations and the developing political situation. The panel was headed by Undersecretary of the Navy Dan Howard and included Rear Admiral George Davis, inspector general; Rear Admiral Ted Gordon, judge advocate general; Rear Admiral Duvall "Mac" Williams, NIS chief; Rear Admiral William Flanagan, congressional liaison; Commander Peter Fagan, Garrett's personal counsel; and, most auspiciously, Barbara Spyridon Pope, assistant secretary of the Navy for manpower and personnel.

The first head to roll was that of Rear Admiral John W. Snyder, commanding officer of Patuxent River Naval Air Station in Maryland, whose aide was Lieutenant Paula Coughlin. Snyder's crime was not responding quickly enough to Coughlin's allegations of assault. He was first briefed by Coughlin on the incident on September 19, but his letter notifying Admiral Dunleavy did not arrive until almost two weeks later.[11] Per Snyder's instructions, Coughlin wrote her own letter to Dunleavy and sent a copy to her friend in the office of Vice Admiral Boorda, chief of naval personnel. Less than a week after Tailhook went public, Boorda used the delay of Snyder's letter as proof that Snyder did not take the allegations seriously enough and recommended that Snyder's name be removed from the rear admiral promotion list, an action that would have demoted him to captain.[12] He also reassigned Coughlin to his own staff. On November 4 the Navy announced that Admiral Kelso had relieved Snyder of his command.

The aviation community met both investigations with a stone wall. Many officers refused to cooperate. Some denied that they had attended Tailhook, while others who admitted attending denied the existence of the gauntlet and refused to finger fellow officers. They did, however, report seeing Garrett, Kelso, and other senior officers on the third floor, although Garrett and Kelso insisted they had seen nothing improper. Nevertheless, some retired aviators began to complain that the top brass had known all along about the abuses at Tailhook and that it had unfairly sacrificed Snyder.

After six months investigators had identified twenty-six victims but only two likely suspects. One was an Australian exchange officer, easily identified by his accent, as the man responsible for several "shark attacks." The other was a Marine captain named Gregory J. Bonam, who was suspected of assaulting Paula Coughlin. Unfortunately for the Navy leadership, the Australian could not be prosecuted, and the case against Bonam appeared weak. He fit the general physical description of a man Coughlin accused of putting both hands down her shirt from behind and squeezing her breasts, and he had failed an NIS polygraph, but Coughlin had failed to pick him out of a photographic line-up, and a photograph taken the night in question showed Bonam in a green "Raging Rhino" shirt, not the burnt-orange shirt that Coughlin remembered. Bonam also showed no signs of having been bitten on the forearm, although Coughlin told investigators she thought she drew blood.

With no one to hang, the Navy leadership was in a pickle. Barbara Pope was the most upset. Pope had a reputation as an intellectual lightweight, whose only claim to an office on the E-ring of the Pentagon was her gender. Her resume hardly prepared her for her position. Like many in the Cheney Pentagon, including Cheney himself, she had never served in uniform. Before her nomination as Navy manpower secretary, she had been deputy assistant secretary of defense for family policy, a job of little significance. Before that she was an aide to Senator Barry Goldwater.[13] Pope lacked the political savvy of other female political appointees at the Pentagon like Marybel Batjer, then an advisor to Garrett who arrived during the early Reagan years as a protégé of Frank Carlucci and survived through the patronage of General Colin Powell, the new chairman of the Joint Chiefs. The pair was a study in contrast: Batjer dressed to kill in short skirts and high heels, and Pope in maternity clothes and dowdy business dresses. (She was nine months pregnant at her confirmation hearing and gave birth shortly after taking office.) They had one thing in common: they were both ardent feminists.

Pope saw Tailhook as the crime of the century. Frustrated that commissioned officers would not cooperate with the investigations, she wanted to come down hard on squadron commanders. She recommended grounding them, docking their flight pay, and relieving them of their commands as punishment for the alleged misbehavior of their men. She wanted the Navy to elevate the investigations to the level of a court of inquiry or blue ribbon panel, bringing in outsiders to really make a show of it. If nothing else, someone should apologize to the victims, preferably the secretary himself.[14]

The admirals involved in the investigations were aghast. They could not suspend constitutional rights to coerce testimony, and they were concerned that undue command influence would prejudice the process. They were also concerned with protecting the Navy leadership and the aviation officer corps from a hysterical witch-hunt run by people like Pope. They also doubted that the available evidence could stand up in court. In the words of Rear Admiral Williams, the NIS chief, the NIS investigation didn't stand "a fart's chance in a whirlwind" of producing convictions.[15] Embarrassing as the results were, when the investigation reports were released to the press and public on April 30, 1992, Navy leaders could do little more than express their indignation at the lack of cooperation.

The lurid details of the reports only stoked the fires of outrage and retribution. Publicly, Congresswomen Barbara Boxer and Patricia Schroeder called for congressional hearings, and Senators Sam Nunn and John Warner announced that they would hold up the promotions of some 5,000 officers until those who were involved in Tailhook were identified and removed from the promotion lists. Tailhook had become a threat to the republic. Who could expect the Navy to accomplish its mission if it didn't treat women with utmost respect?

Privately, Barbara Pope threatened to resign and even dictated terms to Secretary Garrett, including punishment for squadron commanders. She could afford to be bold. George Bush's reelection campaign was doing badly. The last thing he needed was the resignation of a female political appointee charging the administration with winking at Navy misconduct.

After Pope's threat, Cheney ordered Garrett to have the squadron commanders interrogated by the Navy's civilian general counsel, which the Navy's staff judge advocate opposed as a politicization of the judicial process. But Garrett went along with the order, and, to placate Pope, established a standing committee on women headed by her.

Larry Garrett was an aviator himself, a former enlisted man and naval flight officer, who retired with twenty years in the Navy. He was also a lawyer, and like most lawyers, he believed in handling things through a set process. One simply filed the right papers and spoke when it was time. It was the only way he knew, and it suited his personality. He functioned best among friends, and it was friends like former Navy Secretary James Webb who were responsible for his career in the Pentagon. Webb picked Garrett as his undersecretary and considered him "a good number-two man." Garrett kept his post after Webb left in 1987. When the secretary's office fell vacant again in 1989, Garrett was urged on Dick Cheney by Richard Armitage. Armitage could not have been more wrong in recommending Garrett as secretary of the Navy. The Navy needed someone who respected its headstrong admirals without being intimidated by them. Garrett was not that man.

> Now nothing separated the views of the Pentagon from those of the most feminist congresswoman.

By the summer of 1992 the press had learned that fifty-five pages were missing from the NIS report, including a statement by a Marine captain placing Garrett in the Rhino Room on the last night of the convention. Garrett had always denied visiting any suites and seeing anything inappropriate, but the missing pages cast doubt on his story and raised the question of a cover-up. Garrett was forced to request the Defense Department's inspector general, Derek Vander Schaaf, to investigate the missing pages.

On June 24, 1992, Paula Coughlin went public for the first time. She had been talking to Vistica at the *San Diego Union-Tribune* for months without allowing him to use her name. Vistica says she had once told him that if she went public she would do so in the *Union-Tribune*, but when the time came she chose the *Washington Post*, for obvious reasons.[16] The *Post* gave her a front-page feature with a photo, in which she looked pained but composed as she reflected on her ordeal. The story, by John Lancaster, was one of those pitiful victim profiles for which the *Post* is famous. (One is reminded of P.J. O'Rourke's joke about newspaper headlines at the end of the world: The *Post*'s will read, "End of the World: Women and Minorities to Suffer Most.") Under the headline "A Gantlet of Terror, Frustration," the story began:

> When Navy Lt. Paula Coughlin first spotted them—a youthful, clean-cut bunch of guys lounging in a third-floor hallway of the Las Vegas Hilton—it never crossed her mind that she should be afraid. After all, she recalls thinking, they were Navy and Marine pilots. Pilots just like her.
>
> But Coughlin, a helicopter pilot and admiral's aide, was quickly enveloped by terror. Grabbed from behind and propelled down the hallway to jeers of "admiral's aide, admiral's aide," Coughlin was repeatedly pawed and molested. One man grabbed her breasts, another tried to remove her panties....
>
> "It was the most frightened I've ever been in my life," Coughlin said. "I thought, 'I have no control over these guys. I'm going to be gang-raped.'"[17]

The story, in fact, was rather shy on details. Barely three hundred words described the incident in an article 1,450 words long. She said her reason for coming forward was frustration with the Navy's inability to punish her attackers, and she accused her former boss, Jack Snyder, of shrugging off the ordeal, telling her, "That's what you get when you go on the third floor of a hotel with a bunch of drunk aviators."

The rest of the story was self-defense. "People would come up and ask me, 'What were you doing in that hallway anyway? What's the big deal?'" says Coughlin. "I've heard, 'Didn't anybody warn her?' Warn me of what? That you'll go down that hallway and be assaulted by your fellow aviators?... I had no idea what was going to happen.... I'm not exactly the girl next door, but I'm the person in the office next door." She insisted she wasn't carrying out a vendetta against every man in the Navy, saying instead, "It's an education process.... I'm not a hero. I'm a victim who's speaking out."

Coughlin had reason to appear defensive. Many details of her experience did not reflect favorably upon her. Lancaster wrote that Coughlin "attended a banquet, then went back to her room to change" before returning to meet some friends at the Hilton. He did not note the time that Coughlin returned to the Hilton to *begin* her night of partying—about midnight, when every drunken party is at its peak. According to Lancaster, Coughlin changed into "casual, civilian clothes"—actually a denim miniskirt, a strapless bra, a shirt described variously by others as a "tube top" and a "tank top with thin shoulder straps," and "little black cowboy boots." (At the banquet, she had worn a "snazzy red silk dress" from Neiman Marcus.)[18] Lancaster depicted Coughlin walking unsuspectingly into a "youthful, clean-cut bunch of guys lounging" leisurely in the hallway, but Coughlin told investigators that when she got off the elevator it was already "loud and rowdy." Lancaster said Coughlin assumed that they were "pilots just like her." She apparently did not tell him that she had had an alcohol-fired argument about women in combat the night before with her fellow pilots. Lancaster did not mention allegations that Coughlin herself was intoxicated the night of her alleged assault. He did not tell us that Coughlin did not leave the party after her ordeal. He said that two of her attackers had been "positively identified," which was not true. No mention was made of Coughlin's difficulty in identifying her attackers. That information had been hidden in the investigation report's fifty-five missing pages, which also revealed contradictions in Coughlin's account of her assault.

Nothing in Lancaster's story made sense of Coughlin's comment that she is "not exactly the girl next door." Lancaster did quote her saying that she "worked [her] ass off" to prove herself in the Navy, but he didn't quote her saying repeatedly to her attackers, "What the fuck do you think you are doing?" Coughlin had a reputation in the Navy as quite a modern woman. According to her boyfriend, she had once shown up for a Navy "dining-in" carrying a large rubber dildo and wearing a black tuxedo jacket, short black miniskirt, black fishnet stockings, and high heels.[19] She had also attended the infamous 1985 Tailhook, the one that prompted Admiral Service's complaint to the Tailhook board. Yet Coughlin insisted she had never seen or heard of the gauntlet until September 1991.

By June 1992 Coughlin was most definitely on the defensive. The aviators under investigation had long known who she was, and they had begun to talk, alleging that Coughlin had willingly participated in the ribald revelries in both 1985 and 1992. Most damaging was the allegation made by Navy Lieutenant Rolando "Gandhi" Diaz, a Puerto Rican E-2C Hawkeye pilot who spent his time at Tailhook '91 in the VAW-110 suite giving free leg-shaves, asking only that his customers sign his banner. Diaz claimed he had shaved Coughlin's legs twice: once on Friday night while she was wearing her dress-white uniform jacket, and once again on Saturday night, when she was in civilian clothes. As thanks, claimed Diaz, Coughlin had written on his banner the blasphemous words: "You make me see God. The Paulster."[20]

Diaz's allegations had not yet been made publicly, but Coughlin was aware that she could not get away with the total innocent act and thus the admission that she was, well, not the girl next door.

Her words were intended for her fellow aviators and officers. The general public had no idea what she was saying. They had only read Lancaster's June 24 article in the *Post* or seen Coughlin's interview with Peter Jennings on ABC News that same night. The effect on the press and the public was entirely one-sided. The twenty-six victims now had a face and a name and a sympathetic audience.

Coughlin's going public was the *coup de grâce* for Larry Garrett. He had been taking on water since the Navy's failure to come up with culprits, and he had been sinking fast since his sighting in the Rhino Room, which torpedoed his integrity. With Barbara Pope apparently blackmailing the Bush administration in an election year, and Dick Cheney always ready to blow with the wind, it was just a matter of time. Two days after Coughlin's apotheosis, Garrett was forced to resign. In his resignation letter to President Bush, he insisted again that he "neither saw nor engaged in any offensive conduct" at the symposium. Nevertheless, he accepted responsibility for the "leadership failure" that made Tailhook possible.

The conventional wisdom in Washington was that if Garrett had taken responsibility for Tailhook in the beginning, "Tailhook would never have become the Navy's worst disaster since Pearl Harbor."[21] This facile lie ignored the political realities that kept fueling the controversy. Nearly two years after Garrett's departure, Tailhook was still bringing down the Navy's high and mighty. Nothing *that* powerful would have been stopped so easily. However blameworthy Garrett might have been, he was not responsible for the witch-hunt that followed it.

For a few short days after Garrett's resignation, his undersecretary, Dan Howard, a Cheney man, cracked the whip as acting secretary to bring the Navy to heel. In the Pentagon's auditorium, he lectured some 300 senior officers on their "stone age attitudes," explicitly denying that Tailhook was "just a problem with the integration of men and women." He ordered the entire Navy to "stand down" for one day to consider the problem of sexual harassment, and he proposed to the secretary of defense that sexual harassment be made a crime under the Uniform Code of Military Justice. But all his enthusiasm was not enough. On July 7 President Bush announced his choice of Sean O'Keefe, the Defense Department's comptroller, to be the next Navy secretary.

O'Keefe was a very unmilitary man. He was tall and handsome, with a big mustache that hid his lips, and a youthful, cocksure demeanor that showed little deference to his seniors. He was just thirty-eight and had never served in uniform, although his father had been a Navy civilian submarine engineer. O'Keefe was an accountant, first for the Naval Sea Systems Command, then for the Senate Appropriations Committee's subcommittee on defense, where he later became staff director. Cheney brought him to the Pentagon. He was just the kind of man that Cheney liked, suave and bright, politically astute, and utterly ruthless when it came to cutting the Defense budget and rooting out untimely attitudes and traditions.

Shortly after taking office, O'Keefe pulled the nominations for promotion of two admirals, Joseph Prueher and Jerry Tuttle. Prueher had offended Gwen Dreyer and her family when he was commandant of the Naval Academy two years earlier, and Tuttle had allowed an organizational newsletter to be published with a dumb joke comparing women to beer ("beer never has a headache"). O'Keefe also fired Vice Admiral Richard Dunleavy, chief of naval aviation, forcing him to retire as a rear admiral, on account of not having enough time-in-grade as a three-star, and without the usual fanfare for someone in his position: no flight-deck retirement ceremony, no fly-over by Navy jets, no brass band, no medals for long service, no printed program lauding his achievements, no bouquet of flowers for his wife.

In September, when the Defense Department's inspector general, Derek Vander Schaaf, submitted his first report on the handling of the investigation by senior Navy officials, O'Keefe announced the resignations of two more admirals, NIS chief "Mac" Williams and Navy Judge Advocate General Ted Gordon, and the reassignment of a third, George Davis, the Navy's inspector general. Gordon had been scheduled to retire November 1 anyway, but O'Keefe threw his name in for added effect. Williams, like Dunleavy, would be forced to retire early and therefore at a lower grade. Vander Schaaf had faulted him for shielding senior officers from investigation and for making insensitive comments that indicated bad faith on his part.[22] Both men were unrepentant and submitted lengthy rebuttals to Vander Schaaf's findings. Williams complained of being punished without due process.

Vander Schaaf had also recommended action against Dan Howard, Cheney's man in the Navy Department, but O'Keefe defended Howard. "These professionals failed him," O'Keefe said. "They did not give him the support and advice that he needed."

In announcing the resignations of Williams and Gordon, O'Keefe told the world:

There were quite a few good men caught up in the whirlwind of Tailhook.

> *I need to emphasize a very important message: We get it. We know that the larger issue is a cultural problem which has allowed demeaning behavior and attitudes toward women to exist within the Navy Department.... Sexual harassment will not be tolerated, and those who don't get that message will be driven from our ranks.*

It was an answer to Pat Schroeder's public complaint that Navy leaders "just don't get it." Now they did. Now nothing separated the views of the Republicans running the Pentagon from those of the most feminist member of the House of Representatives. Now it was Pat Schroeder's Navy, and the joke making the rounds among naval aviators was that Schroeder had gone to Europe for a sex change and came back as Dick Cheney.

In the next six months, the Defense Department inspector general set about investigating the Tailhook convention itself, sending a team of forty investigators out across the country to interrogate over 2,900 persons, 900 more than the Navy had interrogated. This time, undue command influence wasn't a concern. The high command wanted prosecutions, and the inspector general was out to get them. For their adolescent behavior, aviators found themselves hounded like vicious criminals. Officers reported being threatened with punishment or dismissal or with having their names leaked to the media if they did not cooperate. One Marine officer claimed that he was threatened with an IRS audit and subsequently endured one. Some were offered immunity in exchange for incriminating testimony. Others were ordered to take polygraphs. Agents asked suspects probing questions about their sex lives such as whether they masturbated. They even attempted to intimidate officers' wives at home to get information and in one case went undercover to obtain evidence.

In one case, a Defense Department agent tricked a civilian nurse in Las Vegas into signing a statement alleging that Navy Lieutenant Cole V. Cowden had sexually assaulted her by pressing his face against her chest, even though the woman repeatedly said that she did not consider Cowden's actions an assault or herself a victim. The woman later signed an affidavit to that effect, which Cowden's attorney used at his court-martial. In cross-examining the agent, the attorney took each statement in turn:

> Q: *That first statement by Ms. M., who wrote that?*
> AGENT: *I did, sir.*
> Q: *Did she tell you that she didn't consider that an assault?*
> AGENT: *Yes, sir.*
> Q: *Did she tell you that she didn't appreciate the government telling her whether or not she's been assaulted?*
> AGENT: *That I don't remember, sir.*
> Q: *You explained it to her that it was an assault whether or not she considered it to be an assault. Correct?*
> AGENT: *That's correct, sir.*
>
> ❈   ❈   ❈
>
> Q: *Have you read her subsequent statement that she provided?*
> AGENT: *Yes, sir.*

Q: *It's a lot different than her first statement.*
AGENT: *Yes, sir.*
Q: *So, the statement that you wrote out constituted an assault even though the woman clearly told you that she had not been assaulted?*
AGENT: *Yes, sir.*
Q: *Now, looking at the second statement, it's pretty clear that she hasn't been assaulted. Correct?*
AGENT: *In her view, yes, sir.*
Q: *Whose view is important here, the view of the victim or the view of you?*
AGENT: *Well, I would answer that question, sir, by saying that—*
Q: *No, the question was whose view is important. If you're talking about an assault, a woman has been assaulted, whose view is important?*
AGENT: *In this instance, the government.*[23]

By such methods, the inspector general's henchmen identified 140 suspects who were referred to their services for disciplinary action for assault, indecent exposure, conduct unbecoming an officer, dereliction of duty, lying under oath, and impeding an investigation. One hundred nineteen were Navy officers and twenty-one were Marines. Half of these officers were never prosecuted because of a lack of evidence. Most of the rest accepted nonjudicial punishment, called a captain's or admiral's mast in the sea services. A handful were exonerated but most received fines and the loss of leave time. Five Navy officers and one Marine refused nonjudicial punishment, opting instead for courts-martial.

No women were prosecuted, although the inspector general heard testimony that female officers participated in leg-shaving, belly shots, indecent exposure, and other unbecoming conduct. "The agenda of the Pentagon inspector general did not include looking at the misconduct of women," a senior naval officer told Greg Vistica of the *San Diego Union-Tribune*. "It was a conscious decision to punish male aviators for misconduct. That was the direction, and investigators were not going to get sidetracked by the misconduct of women."[24]

One female Navy lawyer who spent much of one evening topless was allowed to resign, however, and a female ensign was disciplined for making false accusations. During the investigation, the ensign had accused Lieutenant Cowden and several unnamed others of attempted rape. She admitted later that she had lied to keep her fiancé from finding out about her own misbehavior, which included having her legs shaved, serving belly shots, cavorting in public in a lace teddy, and consensual sex.

Paula Coughlin was never charged with unbecoming conduct, and neither was Rolando Diaz, who claimed to have shaved her legs. Instead, the Navy charged Diaz with failure to obey a direct order allegedly issued by his commanding officer forbidding leg-shaving above the midthigh. But Diaz's lawyer threatened to make an issue of The Paulster's signature on his banner, and the Navy backed off and dropped the charge.

Coughlin also escaped prosecution for publicly aiding Senator John McCain's bid for reelection in 1992, an obvious violation of the Hatch Act, which prohibits military personnel from participation in political activities. At the height of the Tailhook hysteria, McCain's opponent began making much of the senator's attendance at earlier Tailhooks. To protect himself, McCain requested and received a letter of endorsement from Coughlin. The Navy's congressional liaison office even acted as intermediary. When the matter was brought before Sean O'Keefe as secretary of the Navy, he declined to take action.[25]

Coughlin later left the Navy and became the subject of a flattering television movie by ABC entitled "She Stood Alone: The Tailhook Scandal." In 1995 she won a $6.7-million verdict against Hilton Hotels for failing to provide adequate security during her late-night visit to the third floor.

The case against Cole Cowden was dismissed when a Navy judge determined that the prosecutor had "become too personally involved" and "exceeded the permissible bounds of his official role as legal adviser" to Vice Admiral J. Paul Reason, commander of Naval Surface Forces Atlantic, who was assigned authority over all Navy Tailhook cases. The case against Cowden had always been weak, and Reason's previous legal advisor had, in fact, recommended dropping all charges.

The Marine Corps's prosecution of Captain Gregory Bonam collapsed during pretrial hearings, which convinced the Corps's counsel that the case was unwinnable. Several witnesses contradicted Coughlin's identification of Bonam as the man who had sexually assaulted her in the gauntlet, so Lieutenant General Charles C. Krulak ordered all charges dropped. Coughlin, still receiving kid-glove treatment from the Navy Department, was flown from Norfolk to Quantico, Virginia, to hear the decision from Krulak in person, before Bonam himself had been told. Afterwards she told reporters, "My impression was [Krulak] took it all seriously. But the outcome of the meeting was, he felt better and I didn't. Nobody's prosecuted. Everybody walked."[26]

The lawyers of three officers—Commander Thomas R. Miller, Lieutenant Commander Gregory E. Tritt, and Lieutenant Dave Samples—joined forces to file a motion for dismissal on the grounds that the Navy leadership, from Admiral Kelso on down, had exerted undue command influence that could only prejudice the cases. On February 8, 1994, a Navy judge, Captain William T. Vest, Jr., finally handed down his decision granting the defendants' motion for dismissal. After reviewing more than 1,000 pages of statements and testimony, Vest found that Admiral Kelso was present on the third floor patio on both Friday and Saturday nights, witnessed misconduct, did nothing to stop it, repeatedly lied under oath, and "manipulated the initial investigative process" to protect himself and others.

Kelso had no choice now but to retire early. Before he did so, female legislators, led by Senator Barbara Boxer of California, mounted a campaign to force him to retire without two of his four stars. The Senate by a narrow vote allowed him to keep them all.

More than a dozen admirals were reprimanded or censured for their involvement in Tailhook. Some were relieved of their duties or prematurely retired, while others were denied further promotion. Nearly three hundred naval aviators suffered serious blows to their careers. Among them was the hapless Captain Ludwig, the Tailhook Association's president. Once a rising star in naval aviation, Ludwig received much of the blame for the Tailhook affair. The Navy leadership tried to hold him accountable as the man in charge of the symposium, while junior officers blamed him for spilling the beans with his incriminating letter. While on cruise in the South Pacific on the carrier *Kitty Hawk*, Ludwig suffered a nervous breakdown and was confined to the psychiatric ward of a hospital in Singapore. His career was finished.

Another victim was Commander Robert E. Stumpf, a fighter pilot of star quality. Stumpf had commanded the Navy's demonstration squadron, the Blue Angels, and was a veteran of air action off Libya and in the Persian Gulf, where in twenty-two missions he won the Distinguished Flying Cross. He attended Tailhook '91 to receive the prestigious Estocin Award as commanding officer of the best F/A-18 squadron in the fleet. After accepting the award, Stumpf was invited that night to attend an impromptu party in a room on the 28th floor of the Hilton. While he was there, two strippers showed up to entertain the guests. One tried to draw Stumpf into her act, but he waved her off. He left before they finished their act, and before a stripper performed fellatio on a naval aviator from a different squadron. Stumpf was later exonerated of any wrongdoing by a Navy board of inquiry, but when he came up for promotion to captain, the Senate Armed Services Committee asked the Navy to remove his name from the list. A new procedure instituted by the committee placed all officers who had attended Tailhook under special scrutiny when up for promotion. Although the Navy first tried to change the committee's mind, Stumpf was never promoted, and he retired as a commander in 1996.

Not all of the victims of Tailhook attended the gathering. Some fell victim to the hysteria that followed. In the summer of 1992 the fighter jocks at Miramar Naval Air Station assembled for their annual "Tomcat Follies," another customary occasion for ribald behavior. There were no reports of assault, but there was some obscene humor at Pat Schroeder's expense in several of the skits. Schroeder was not the only enemy the aviators had in Washington, and not the only government official lampooned by the skits, but she was the one they most hated. One skit used a contraption to spell out the words "Hickory, dickory, dock, Pat Schroeder can suck my cock." Another skit produced the words "Pat, don't be a —" whereupon a picture of Dick Cheney appeared. Still another unfurled a banner that declared: "Pat Schroeder Sucks!"

The skits reportedly received standing ovations from the aviators present, but the Navy leadership was not amused. Taking no chances, Kelso himself informed Schroeder of the insults and offered the Navy's apologies. Schroeder pretended to laugh it off, and then had her staff call Vistica at the *Union-Tribune* with the story. Shortly thereafter, the commander-in-chief of the Pacific Fleet, Admiral Robert Kelly, sacked five squadron commanders at Miramar. Although two were later reinstated, the other three wrote scathing letters to senior officers denouncing the hypocrisy of the top brass. They had been fired for not stopping the offending skits, but Kelly himself and many other admirals had not (yet) been fired for not stopping the abuses at Tailhook.

Months later, Admiral Kelly was reported to have told a dirty joke at a staff meeting attended by three female officers, but was spared punishment by Admiral Kelso. One admiral who was not spared in the summer of 1992 was Vice Admiral Jack Fetterman, who was relieved of his post as chief of naval training and education for allegedly obstructing the investigation of a chief petty officer on his personal staff, who was accused making homosexual advances to other sailors. The charge had nothing to do with Tailhook, but the Navy brass was in an unforgiving mood and few of his peers sympathized with his circumstances. He had been an outspoken proponent of women in naval aviation, and his punishment allowed feminists once again to blame the Navy, this time for carrying things too far. "He's one of the good guys," moaned a female aviator to the press.

There were quite a few good men caught up in the whirl-wind of Tailhook, men who were expert in performing their military missions, men on whom the Navy had spent hundreds of millions of dollars to train, men with decades of experience, who had been tested in combat, and who had offered their lives in the service of their country. Not all were opposed to women in the Navy, and some of the men who suffered had "a good track record concerning women." But that's what happens when the governing principle is fear—fear of being burned for not burning others. Only accusers survive. Everyone else is a suspect.

Before the Pentagon's inspector general had completed its investigation, both statutory restrictions on women in combat had been repealed. Dissent from Pentagon policy was not regarded as a difference of political opinion, but as the unwelcome persistence of pernicious "attitudes" assumed to inspire criminal behavior:

> At the root of sexual harassment is a series of cultural
> beliefs, attitudes, and perceptions about women. Unless we
> can change stereotypical thinking, sexual harassment train-
> ing programs will likely prove ineffective.

The memo from which these words are taken, issued in July 1992 by the House Armed Services Committee, likens traditional beliefs about men and women to racial bias and drug abuse and recommends that the military apply a similar corrective to eradicate the evil.

Tailhook was a political purge. In the end, to the Navy's enemies, it mattered less that those responsible for outrageous conduct were disciplined than that the traditional culture of the military services, and indeed the traditional culture of the American people, had been condemned and outlawed.

Chapter 13

ASSORTED VICTIMS

It was a "freak tragedy with no larger lessons."

—OFFICIAL COAST GUARD COMMENT
ON THE SUICIDE OF CAPTAIN EDWARD BLANCHARD

ON FEBRUARY 10, 1993, the *Washington Post* ran a long article (over 1,300 words) on a pillow fight at the United States Naval Academy. Two female midshipmen were ambushed in their room at night by four male midshipmen, who blinded them with flashlights and then assaulted them with pillows. One woman received a black eye; the other was bruised. The men received demerits and were restricted to the academy grounds for one month. Why weren't they dismissed, the *Post* wanted to know? "Unless you can prove some sort of malice, dismissal is not the way to handle young people," said a spokesman. The attack was a familiar prank at the academy, known as a "Mack truck." The injuries were "incidental and not intentional."[1]

The *Post* wrote that the incident "reflects the sexism that has persisted at the male-dominated institution since women were admitted 17 years ago." The attack was intended to "send a message" to one of the victims, who was widely disliked for complaining of discrimination and harassment. An unidentified male mid was quoted as saying the woman was "like a lot of women here who say, 'We can do whatever we want because we're females, we're privileged.... She wasn't all that popular. Most people would put this in the category of DSAF—Did Society A Favor." Her roommate was apparently an innocent bystander who didn't deserve the pillowing. As one mid said, "She's a good Christian girl."

Two weeks earlier, a male midshipman had been accused of indecent assault for slipping into bed with a sleeping female classmate and trying to caress her. The previous month, two civilian professors had complained that they were unfairly denied tenure, and three months before that a former academy professor, in an article in *The New Republic*, had denounced the "obscene and misogynistic songs" and other "anti-female practices" she had encountered during her eight years at the school. Such things, wrote the *Post*, "suggest that the hostility women encountered when they were first admitted remains a problem today, despite a series of formal investigations, changes and sensitivity classes at the 147-year-old institution."

It was a tired old song that the *Post* knew by heart. But the rest of the media had more trouble than the *Post* taking a pillow fight so seriously. Most certainly the timing wasn't right. With the inauguration of Bill Clinton, the issue of women in the military was assumed to be settled. The new social revolution to be pushed on the military was the administration's desire to sanction homosexuality.

THE NEXT STEP

The campaign to repeal the military's longstanding ban on homosexuals in service actually began nearly two years earlier. When the media declared the participation of women in the Gulf War a smashing success, gay activists began calling for an end to the military's ban on homosexuals, arguing that if mixing men and women in the military didn't reduce readiness, how could mixing gays and straights? They had a point. The military had pretended for many years that sex was a trivial matter, nothing that a little leadership couldn't keep in line. Sexual harassment, fraternization, hostility within the ranks, and the resulting effects on morale were all problems the military claimed it could handle, but only when they were caused by women. When gays caused the same problems, they were booted out.

In August 1991, at a hearing of the House budget commit-tee, Congressman Barney Frank, a proud homosexual who had been reprimanded by the House in 1990 for allowing his male companion, Steve Gobie, to run a prostitution ring out of Frank's home, asked Defense Secretary Dick Cheney why the military still denied security clearances to avowed homosexual civilians. Cheney answered that he had "inherited a policy that has been in the department now for many years" and that the idea that homosexuals posed a security risk was "a bit of an old chestnut."[2] Cheney's defense of the ban on homosexuals in the military was so weak that Frank later commented, "I must say that if the normally articulate Secretary of Defense defended America as forcefully as he defended this policy, we would have lost nine States to Cuba sometime around 1988."[3]

Cheney's comments unleashed a torrent of editorials in newspapers across the country calling for an end to both the denial of security clearances to gay civilians and the ban on gays in the military. The *New York Times, Washington Post, Los Angeles Times, Seattle Times, Detroit Free Press, USA Today,* and many others joined the chorus. Even the privately pub-lished *Army Times* and *Air Force Times* chimed in in favor of repeal, lending the movement a special air of respectability, based upon the erroneous assumption that the service papers understood the military even if the rest of the media didn't. In fact, the three papers, *Army Times, Navy Times,* and *Air Force Times,* are largely written and edited by nonveterans who share the leftist leanings of their journalistic colleagues elsewhere.[4]

It was no accident that the drive for gays in the military fol-lowed so closely the successful drive for women in combat, or that feminist champions like Pat Schroeder and Barbara Boxer lined up in support of gays. The advocates of both movements shared the same values and used the same arguments. Both began with a demand for equality; both insisted that the ability

282 • WOMEN IN THE MILITARY

to "do the job" was all that mattered and that everything else was irrelevant; and both were determined to use the military to revolutionize American society.

The media portrayed the issue as a simple matter of letting good gay service members stay in service, but gay activists wanted much more. A coalition of pro-gay groups, including the ACLU, the American Psychological Association, and the National Lawyer's Guild called for a Defense advisory committee on homosexuals and bisexuals modeled on DACOWITS; mandatory annual reports to Congress from the secretary of defense on the progress of integration; and reeducation programs at all levels for all service members, specifically chaplains, with "didactic and experiential opportunities addressing prejudice, stigma, and discrimination," similar to those actually inflicted upon personnel assigned to Washington, D.C., under the Clinton administration.[5]

Bill Clinton had promised as early as March 1992 that if elected he would repeal the military's ban on homosexuals in service. By that time, senior military officers were beginning to speak up in defense of the ban. In February General Colin Powell, chairman of the Joint Chiefs of Staff, told the House budget committee that homosexual behavior was "inconsistent with maintaining good order and discipline." In May he sent a letter defending the ban to Pat Schroeder, who had written to him arguing that sexual orientation was no more relevant to military service than race. Powell wrote, "Skin color is a benign, nonbehavioral characteristic. Sexual orientation is perhaps the most profound of human behavioral characteristics. Comparison of the two is a convenient but invalid argument...."[6] Here was Powell arguing that sexual orientation—which, of course, includes the attraction of men and women to each other—is "the most profound of human behavioral characteristics," while presiding over a military that denied that it had any bearing on military readiness outside the combat arms.

Despite Clinton's promise, the issue of gays in the military was a sleeper throughout the presidential campaign. The Bush campaign never mentioned it, afraid as always of "divisive" social issues. Then, too, the Bush folks were hardly in a position to make Clinton's promise an issue since a key female advisor in the White House had actively sought homosexual support for Bush, and Bush's secretary of defense, Dick Cheney, had himself lit the fire for repeal of the ban. Cheney also had brought two homosexuals with him to the Pentagon to fill positions of considerable importance. One was responsible for screening candidates for other positions. The other was the Pentagon's chief spokesman, Pete Williams, the assistant secretary of defense for public affairs, who was "outed" in 1991 by *The Advocate*, a national gay and lesbian magazine. Williams never denied the charge, and Cheney, when asked if he would fire Williams even if he were gay, answered, "Absolutely not."

The issue plagued Clinton's first few months in office and ended in a partial defeat. Feminists had repeatedly succeeded in forcing the military to accept changes it didn't like, but they had done so gradually. Keeping Clinton's promise on homosexuals fully was going too far, too fast. The revolutionaries had over-reached themselves. In the end, the White House and the Pentagon settled on a compromise policy dubbed "don't ask, don't tell," whereby no inquiries would be made concerning a service member's sexual orientation but the services retained the right to dismiss members if their homosexuality became a problem.

Even this was too much for Marine Major Charles B. Johnson, an eighteen-year veteran who resigned in protest immediately after the policy was announced. Johnson was an exceptional officer. As a young captain in 1983, he became a national hero of sorts when he single-handedly stopped a column of Israeli tanks rolling into Lebanon by climbing onto the lead tank and putting his .45 in the tank commander's face. Later in his career, he earned a doctorate in education and policy analysis under the guidance of Charles Moskos and served as deputy director of research for the Presidential Commission on the Assignment of Women in the Armed Forces. A devout

284 • WOMEN IN THE MILITARY

Roman Catholic, Johnson regarded the new policy on homosexuals as an affront to fundamental morality. By resigning, he gave up a retirement that was just two years away, but he kept his conscience clear, which is more than many admirals and generals can claim.

TAILHOOK'S AFTERMATH

Another devout Christian who fell victim to the feminist revolution in the military was Navy Lieutenant Commander Kenneth Carkhuff—Naval Academy graduate, helicopter pilot, husband, and father of five. His fitness reports described him as a "community superstar" with "unlimited potential... destined for command and beyond." But in August 1994, just before his squadron was to be mobilized for combat duty in Haiti, Carkhuff told his commanding officer that he believed that exposing women to combat was morally wrong on religious grounds. One week later, his commanding officer informed him that if he did not submit his resignation within twenty-four hours, he would be forced out as soon as possible. Carkhuff submitted his resignation the next day with the understanding that he would be allowed six months to leave the Navy. When he later withdrew his resignation upon the advice of counsel, his commanding officer moved to have him separated "for cause," charging him with "substandard performance" and "failure to demonstrate accceptable qualities of leadership required of an officer." A special fitness report, written to justify his ouster, stated, "Carkhuff's stated beliefs are NOT COMPATIBLE WITH FURTHER MILITARY SERVICE."[7] (Emphasis in the original.)

Service members do not have all the civil rights of civilians. In fact, they have only the rights the military wants them to have, in accordance with the doctrine of "military necessity." Military necessity was invoked by the services to defend the ban on homosexuals, but while the Navy was still preparing its case against Carkhuff, military boards of inquiry voted to allow two admitted homosexuals—Navy Lieutenant Zoe Dunning and Air Force Airman 1st Class Prentice Watkins—to remain in service.

At Carkhuff's board of inquiry in May 1995, the Navy focused on Carkhuff's membership in Promise Keepers, a loose affiliation of evangelical Christian men who promise to uphold their responsibilities to God, church, family, and community. The seven promises to which Promise Keepers commit themselves are all rather innocuous, but many in the movement believe that men have a special responsibility to provide leadership in church, at home, and in society. Some Promise Keepers even teach the biblical doctrine that "the man is the head of the woman" (1 Cor. 11:3, Eph. 5:23) and that wives, being subject to them, are obliged to obey their husbands (Eph. 5:22-24, Col. 3:18, Titus 2:5, 1 Peter 3:1-7). Such beliefs were portrayed by Navy prosecutors as equivalent to the racist "attitudes" of white service members before the military's racial integration in 1948. Carkhuff's executive officer testified that he had tried to identify other Promise Keepers in the squadron, concerned about the influence of their subversive views. Carkhuff himself never refused an order or failed to do his duty, but his commanding officer testified that he had lost confidence that Carkhuff would serve as sworn. The board voted 3 to 0 to cashier Carkhuff.

With Bill Clinton's inauguration, the issue of women in the military was assumed to be settled.

Carkhuff's cause was taken up by Robert Maginnis at the Family Research Council, a subsidiary of James Dobson's Focus on the Family, and by Elaine Donnelly, who publicized his plight through the newsletters of her Center for Military Readiness, a small nonprofit corporation supported largely by retired flag officers alarmed by the repeal of the combat exclusions and the Clinton administration's efforts to force the military to accept homosexuals. Well connected in Washington and in the services, Donnelly nevertheless often stood alone against her feminist foes in the White House, Congress, the Pentagon, and the mainstream media. For the conservative media, the Center for Military Readiness became the chief source of information and argument against the feminist party line put forth by the Pentagon. Donnelly's appearance with Carkhuff on a Christian radio show hosted by Dobson provoked a national outpouring of support for Carkhuff from outraged Christians. In response, Navy Secretary John Dalton decided to allow Carkhuff to remain in service. But he was removed from flying duties, and it remains to be seen whether he will be promoted to commander. If not, he may leave the Navy anyway.

Lieutenant Larry Meyer was not so fortunate. As a helicopter instructor pilot, Meyer made insensitive comments to a student of his, Lieutenant Rebecca Hansen, who had him disciplined and discharged. According to Gregory Vistica, who wrote *Fall from Glory*, an exposé of Tailhook and other Navy follies, Meyer had criticized Hansen's appearance, suggesting that she dye her hair and wear blue contact lenses. When Hansen complained that her friction control knob was stuck, Meyer replied, "Isn't that just like a woman to complain about friction?" and he ended one flight with the words, "Come on, wench." Hansen was not one to take such things lightly. Even Vistica admits she was a "problem student," prone to argue with her instructors and resist correction. She also lacked the situational awareness required of good pilots and was washed out of a later stage of aviation training.[5]

Nevertheless, Hansen demanded an investigation to determine whether her earlier complaints about Meyer had been one of the reasons she was dropped from the program. Not satisfied with the Navy's negative response, she complained to Minnesota Senator David Durenberger, who asked the Navy for an explanation. Congressional inquiries prompted by complaints from constituents are not uncommon in the military and are never taken lightly. In this case, the Navy investigated and concluded that Hansen had been dropped for just cause. The report of the investigation was even approved by the vice chief of naval operations, Admiral Stanley Arthur, before it was delivered to Senator Durenberger. Still the senator was not satisfied. In retaliation, he placed a hold on Arthur's nomination to become commander-in-chief of all U.S. forces in the Pacific, the most prestigious operational command an admiral could hold.

The matter then fell to Admiral Boorda, Bill Clinton's pick to succeed Admiral Kelso as chief of naval operations. Scrupulously correct when it came to social politics, Boorda was appointed to keep the Navy on a politically correct course. Not a typical member of the Navy brass, Boorda, just five-foot-five, the son of Jewish Ukrainian immigrants, readily confessed that he joined the Navy to escape his father and a troubled upbringing.

Arthur, by contrast, was a much admired "operator"—not a politician like Boorda—a decorated combat veteran with a no-nonsense reputation. Although an aviator, he was untainted by Tailhook. If Arthur said Hansen wasn't qualified to fly, everyone in the Navy believed just that.

Boorda's task was to convince Durenberger that Arthur was right. Durenberger was claiming publicly that he just wanted answers, but Arthur had learned through personal meetings and correspondence that nothing would satisfy him. In a letter to the *Wall Street Journal*, Durenberger accused the Navy of stonewalling, but the Navy thought Durenberger was grandstanding, posing as the great defender of women for the folks back home.

Never one to cross the power-brokers on Capitol Hill, Boorda withdrew Arthur's nomination, which effectively ended Arthur's career. To add insult to injury, Boorda reversed the decision to discharge Hansen and traveled to the Great Lakes naval training depot to meet with her personally. Hansen presented Boorda with an impossible list of demands, including that the Navy send her to law school and assign her to work on women's issues. Boorda instead offered her a job on his staff, just as he had done for Paula Coughlin. Hansen declined and left the Navy.

The Navy's admirals, both active and retired, were scandalized. Former Navy Secretary James Webb put their contempt in writing in the *New York Times*. Boorda's abandonment of Arthur "raises serious questions about Admiral Boorda's fitness to be Chief of Naval Operations," wrote Webb, who also faulted Boorda for unfairly firing Rear Admiral Jack Snyder, Paul Coughlin's boss. In Webb's words, Boorda's actions were "seriously deficient" in that he had shown "disloyalty to deserving subordinates" and "faulty judgment."

In a very short time, Boorda realized he was all alone. He later confessed to regretting his abandonment of Arthur, but the admirals never forgave him.

THE DEATH OF KARA HULTGREEN

In the spring of 1993, in the midst of the furor over homosexuals in the military, the nation hardly noticed when President Clinton's new secretary of defense, Les Aspin, formerly chairman of the House Armed Services Committee, submitted legislation to repeal the statute barring women from assignment aboard combat vessels. The legislation passed quickly through Congress and was signed by the president. The Navy then spent $1.3 million to reconfigure the berthing spaces aboard the carrier *Dwight D. Eisenhower* to accommodate 500 women in its 5,000-man crew. A year later, when the *Ike* returned from a six-month Mediterranean cruise, the Navy reported that at least thirty-nine women (probably more) left the *Ike* before or during the cruise because of pregnancy. The Navy, of course, insisted that the departures had no negative effect on readiness, prompting an editorial in the *Washington Times* to ask, "If removing these sailors from active duty does not hurt readiness, what were they doing on board in the first place?"

Another immediate act by Aspin was to order the services to begin training women for combat aviation. The Navy, still under the gun for Tailhook, raised no objection to either change. The chief of naval operations, Admiral Kelso, even directed that women be given priority in the aviation training pipeline, moving them ahead of male officers already waiting for coveted training slots.

Among the first female officers to volunteer for combat aviation was Navy Lieutenant Kara Hultgreen, a twenty-eight-year-old Texan already qualified to fly the EA-6B Prowler, the electronic warfare version of the A-6 Intruder bomber. Nearly six feet tall, with long brown hair and an air of invincibility, Hultgreen was at once deliberately sexual and daringly tough. At the infamous 1991 Tailhook symposium, Hultgreen had shown up in a short black blazer, black leather miniskirt, and high heels, leading some to mistake her for a prostitute.[9] She was standing talking to two male aviators in one of the hospitality suites when the drunken Australian exchange officer tried to put his hand up her skirt. Hultgreen grabbed him by the collar, shoved him up against the wall, and told him she was a naval aviator and did not wish to be touched. The Australian wandered off, but then returned moments later and sank his teeth into her buttocks. More annoyed than offended, Hultgreen responded with a swift jab of her elbow that knocked the Australian to the floor. "Do that again and you're dead," she scowled. The Australian crawled out of the room.

Hultgreen's lifelong ambition was to be an astronaut, and the surest way to become one, she figured, was to become a Navy fighter pilot. She was selected to fly the F-14 Tomcat, a twin-engine supersonic fighter with a reputation as the most difficult aircraft then in the Navy inventory. She herself had described flying the F-14 as like "dancing with an elephant." But if any woman could do the dance, surely it was Hultgreen, or so the Navy assumed. She was the "Incredible Hulk" to her female colleagues, the great female barrier-breaker, "an airborne white female equivalent of Jackie Robinson whom fate had appointed to shoulder others' hopes and fears as she climbed into the cockpit."[10]

In April 1994, before Hultgreen had finished training, the journal *Proceedings*, published by the quasi-official U.S. Naval Institute, ran an article entitled "Who's to Blame When Women Don't Measure Up?" raising serious doubts about the Navy's treatment of female aviators. The article's author was Lieutenant Ellen Hamblet, a Navy reservist and former airborne intelligence officer, who was concerned that the Navy was not holding female pilots to standard. Hamblet claimed that women were "being allowed to carrier qualify, although they didn't meet the required standards." She told of "a woman near the bottom of her class being allowed to continue at the training command... because the commanding officer needed to keep a female instructor." One female pilot who blew a tire and ran off the runway was "praised by top leadership for keeping her wits about her but the general consensus among junior officers was that if a male pilot had done the same thing, he would have been severely disciplined." According to Hamblet, stories of mishaps involving male aviators often ended with the words "so he lost his wings," but similar stories involving women often ended with "and can you believe she is still flying?"

Hultgreen herself seems to have been concerned about standards. "Guys like you have to make sure there's only one standard," she told Rear Admiral Robert Hickey, for the benefit of the press. "If people let me slide through on a lower standard, it's my life on the line. I could get killed."

On the afternoon of October 25, 1994, Kara Hultgreen was attempting to land her F-14A on the deck of the carrier *Abraham Lincoln*, fifty miles off of San Diego. The weather was clear and calm, but for some reason Hultgreen swung wide on her approach, taking her too far to the right of the centerline on the flight deck below. In her attempt to correct her misjudgment, the plane yawed too far to the left. The landing safety officer on the *Abe* ordered her to "wave off." "Wave off! Wave off!" he yelled when she didn't respond. "Power! Raise your gear!" He flashed the warning lights on deck. Low on air speed and losing lift, the plane banked steeply, about to roll over. "*Eject! Eject!*" yelled the LSO. Hultgreen's radar intercept officer, Lieutenant Matthew Klemish, riding in the back seat, initiated the ejection procedure, which sent him out over the water, just high enough for his chute to deploy before he hit the surface with only minor injuries. Hultgreen's ejection followed automatically half a second later, but by that time the plane was upside down. Ejecting rocketed her straight into the water, knocking her unconscious if not breaking her neck. A Navy salvage team found her three weeks later, still strapped in her ejection seat, in four thousand feet of water, ninety yards from the wreckage of her aircraft.

The day after the crash there was already speculation that Hultgreen had caused her own death. Two Tomcat pilots phoned into a radio talk show in San Diego to say that pilot error was responsible for nearly all carrier landing accidents, and that Hultgreen had a poor record as an F-14 pilot. She was "an accident waiting to happen, every one of her squadron mates knew it, but they could not speak up for fear of reprisal," according to an anonymous fax received by the San Diego station. Others told the *San Diego Union-Tribune* that Hultgreen had had trouble before with carrier landings and had failed in her first attempt at "car-quals," or "carrier qualification," in April 1994.

The Navy was just as swift to defend Hultgreen. Two days after the crash, Captain Mark Grissom, commander of the Pacific Fleet's fighter forces, told the *San Diego Union-Tribune* that Hultgreen had indeed failed to qualify on her first attempt, but that this was not unusual in the F-14. "It's a difficult airplane to fly aboard the carrier and it happens quite often that somebody does not qualify," said Grissom. "On the second attempt, she did extremely well. She had excellent grades and VF-213 was very happy to receive her on board, and she performed extremely well in VF-213 subsequently in carrier operations aboard Abraham Lincoln."

The Navy routinely declines comment on the cause of aviation accidents until a formal Mishap Investigation Report (MIR) can be completed, but in Hultgreen's case Navy officials directly responsible for Hultgreen's performance were quick to suggest that engine failure might have caused the crash. As early as November 19, three months before the MIR was completed, Grissom was speculating publicly on the engine failure suspicion. A few weeks later, Vice Admiral Robert J. "Rocky" Spane, commanding officer of the Pacific Fleet's naval air forces, confirmed the suspicion, telling reporters that a video-tape of the attempted landing showed a trail of exhaust coming from the starboard engine only.

To quiet persistent rumors about Hultgreen's poor perfor-mance, Hultgreen's mother released her training records, which the Navy had given her. The records stated that Hultgreen was fully qualified to fly the F-14 and an "average to above average" pilot. According to the records, Hultgreen scored 3.22 in day landings on the carrier, with a boarding rate (successfully catching the arresting wire) of 89 percent, putting her first in her class of seven. Her night grade on the carrier was 2.82, with a 71 percent boarding rate, putting her sixth in the class of seven. Her overall score was a 3.10, just above the mean score of 2.99 for all pilots attempting to qualify, ranking her third in her class of seven, all of whom qualified. According to Grissom, the records "establish that this girl was not given spe-cial favors…. She did not qualify with marginal grades. She was in there swinging with the best of them."[11]

What Grissom did not point out was that this was Hultgreen's second attempt at qualifying, and her scores were below average for pilots attempting to qualify for the second time. Nor did he mention Hultgreen's difficulties in training, which were not included in the records her mother released to the press. Those difficulties fueled rumors of Hultgreen's poor performance, but it was months before they came to light in a credible form.

Male pilots who are lost at sea in depths are routinely aban-doned, along with their planes, but the Navy spent $100,000 to recover Hultgreen's body and plane. And she was given a hero's funeral at Arlington National Cemetary.[12]

The Navy obviously had a special interest in Hultgreen. It had once blamed a sailor for a fatal naval disaster, in the turret explosion aboard the battleship *Iowa*, and it was not about to repeat its political mistake by blaming Hultgreen for her own death. Only by exonerating Hultgreen could the Navy avoid yet another congressional inquisition led by Pat Schroeder and

Barbara Boxer, and the likes of John McCain and David Durenberger.

No one was surprised when the Navy announced the results of its investigation on February 28, 1995, at a press conference at North Island Naval Air Station in Coronado, California, across the bay from San Diego. "Engine failure" was responsible for the Hultgreen crash. A "mid-compression bypass valve" had caused her port engine to stall, resulting in a loss of both power and control.

"The Navy's report and officials' comments clearly blame the engine failure for the fatal crash," wrote Pat Flynn, a reporter representing the *San Diego Union-Tribune* at the press conference. The reporters were not shown the actual MIR, but they were given a much shorter "JAG manual" report, with three letters of endorsement from Navy admirals, each one spinning the report toward the "engine failure" conclusion. At the press conference, Rear Admiral Jay B. Yakeley III defended Hultgreen's record as a pilot, saying, "I knew her. She was qualified and a darn good pilot.... For those who say otherwise anonymously, I find that cowardly." While admitting that Hultgreen might have survived if she had acted differently, he insisted that only more experienced pilots would have responded correctly. Asked by Lloyd Billingsley of the Center for the Study of Popular Culture whether Hultgreen had any "downs" in her training record, indicating serious errors in performance, Yakeley appeared startled and then answered that "she had one down in her record, as many other pilots have." A down is an error so bad that it risks the "safety of flight."

The next day, headlines across the nation announced that Hultgreen was not to blame. She, too, was a victim, of engine failure. Worried feminists sighed with relief and then crowed their satisfaction. "So it was the engine after all. Not the pilot,"

> Advocates of gays and women in the armed forces were determined to use the military to revolutionize American society.

wrote columnist Ellen Goodman. "Lt. Kara Hultgreen did not die on the altar of 'political correctness' or 'preferential treatment' or 'reverse discrimination.' She died because the F-14 Tomcat stalled as it approached the aircraft carrier."[13] When conservative columnist Linda Chavez, writing for *USA Today*, doubted "that any honest investigation into Hultgreen's tragic death is even possible," Senator Barbara Boxer was incensed and demanded publicly that Chavez "withdraw the scurrilous and irresponsible charges made about women in the military."

Reporters who looked beyond the letters by admirals to the JAG report itself found ample evidence to justify Chavez's doubts. In one passage, Hultgreen's squadron commander, Michael Galpin, even admitted that pilot error, and not mechanical failure, might have caused the crash: "Whether the engine stall was brought on by an overly aggressive pilot using rudder to remedy a dynamic overshoot, or a failed or closed MCB [mid-compression bypass] valve and/or unknown additional causal factors will never be definitively determined." The rest of the report was filled with veiled references to Hultgreen's errors. Notice what is not said in the following excerpts:

> *A delay in recognition of the extremis condition, either due to preoccupation with correcting the overshooting start, or the timing of the stall warning system…. Subsequent pilot technique permitted Angle of Attack to increase to a point where rudder effectiveness began to be reduced to nil and departure from controlled flight was imminent…. the window of opportunity for a successful recovery was missed. Finally, inexperience prevented the crew from recognizing the point at which recovery was impossible and ejection the only alternative.*[14]

The missing word in each sentence above is the pilot's name. *Hultgreen* was late in recognizing the extremis condition. *Hultgreen* was preoccupied with correcting the overshooting start. *Hultgreen's* technique permitted the plane's angle-of-attack to increase to a point where the rudder became ineffective. *Hultgreen* missed the window of opportunity for a successful recovery. And finally, *Hultgreen's* inexperience prevented her from recognizing the point at which recovery was impossible and ejection the only alternative.

Before long, other details leaked out that cast doubt on the Navy's public version. The independent newspaper *Navy Times* reported that two messages sent by the *Abraham Lincoln* immediately after the accident were strongly critical of Hultgreen, but both were later withdrawn. When the Navy later claimed that simulator tests had shown that few pilots could recover from the same situation, unidentified sources accused the Navy of rigging the tests by instructing male pilots "flying" the simulation not to follow mandatory procedures to avert a crash. In time, however, the MIR itself was leaked to the press, falling first into the hands of Gregory Vistica, then at *Newsweek*:

> This Mishap Investigation Report spelled out in clear and direct language Hultgreen's many mistakes that led to her death. The bluntness of the findings was in direct contrast to the shortened version of the JAG report handed out to reporters by the Navy at the press conference. Some officers in the chain of command at Spane's headquarters in San Diego had warned Washington of this and said if it leaked the Navy would appear to be covering up.[15]

Newsweek reported that the MIR pulled no punches in blaming Hultgreen, explicitly stating that the failed bypass valve could not explain the stalled engine. Instead, the stall was caused by Hultgreen's erratic handling of the aircraft, which deprived the port engine of air. The controversial simulator test merely assumed Hultgreen's erratic handling and thus tested only pilot response to the resulting emergency.

The Navy did all it could to discredit the MIR. The Navy's chief of information, Rear Admiral Kendell Pease, sent out a memorandum advising reporters to "please allow Navy public affairs an opportunity to help avoid the errors of fact evident in some recent news reports." Admiral Boorda and Rear Admiral J.S. Mobley, commander of the Naval Safety Center, both protested that the MIR's release was a high crime that threatened Navy safety. "Unauthorized disclosures really damage the system," said Boorda, while Mobley fumed that he was "angry," "disappointed," and "concerned."[16] As Vistica notes, the campaign succeeded in discouraging several major news organizations from even reporting the MIR's findings.

But Robert Caldwell, an editor at the *San Diego Union-Tribune*, was not discouraged, and he reported that the MIR "documented enough pilot error to make an irrefutable case that it was a major contributor and perhaps the primary cause of Hultgreen's fatal crash."[17] Caldwell questioned the integrity of the Navy's leadership, namely Vice Admiral Spane, prompting a lengthy written reponse from Spane himself. In writing to address "perceived discrepancies" between the MIR and the shorter JAG report, Spane dismissed the MIR as little more than hearsay: "The JAG discusses facts and bases opinions on these facts. Just as in a court of law, hearsay, innuendo and conjecture are not allowed." The MIR, on the other hand, consists of "[f]acts, opinion (whether or not substantiated by fact), guesses, possible causes, ideas, etc." Furthermore:

> *The JAG defines what we know and the logical conclusions and opinions based on those facts.... The MIR, on the other hand, contains facts, conjecture, as yet unproven theories and opinions, some of which are not rigidly based on fact. This is appropriate for an MIR but should not be used as the definitive cause of the accident nor to malign the pilot.*[18]

All of this came as quite a shock to naval aviators, who knew that in every other accident, the MIR was the last word. Spane's article was answered by another article in the *San Diego Union-*

Tribune, written by Gerry Atkinson, a retired Navy captain and computer science professor. Atkinson wrote:

> *Spane states that the JAG report is more reliable than the MIR. Again, not so! The JAG investigation is based on a legal model, adversarial in nature. Consider the O.J. Simpson trial. The legal model does not have a goal of ascertaining the truth, only winning a judge and/or jury over to one view, not in actually revealing the truth [for the purpose of setting] policy to avoid recurrence of the accident, the purpose of the MIR.*
>
> *An officer of Spane's rank knows the differences between the JAG report and the MIR. The MIR is the only complete and ruthlessly, scrupulously truthful account of an aircraft accident. Period.*

As for the MIR's unauthorized release:

> *Unauthorized release of the privileged MIR to the public had to have been undertaken purposely by active duty personnel who were trying to send the American people a signal: "What you were reading in the national press is not the truth, and something is terribly awry at the highest levels of naval leadership."*[19]

Besides wishing to avoid feminist ire and again blaming the victim, Admiral Spane and the rest of the Navy leadership were desperate to deny that they themselves had contributed to Kara Hultgreen's death by not allowing her to fail. Around the debate over pilot error versus mechanical failure swirled endless rumors and suspicions that Hultgreen would never have made it if she had been a man.

Many military men believed the rumors; they had seen it themselves. Boorda's abandonment of Stanley Arthur for merely concurring with the decision to fail Rebecca Hansen had sent a powerful message to the fleet: Women were trouble, and failing them or even criticizing them could quickly end careers. Vistica tells of a female helicopter pilot who was allowed to keep her wings after Rocky Spane overruled a safety panel's recommendation that she lose them. This woman had been assigned as an instructor pilot at North Island, but when she arrived she failed a routine check ride. Vistica writes:

> *A performance review followed and found that the woman had panicked on numerous occasions while airborne with passengers aboard. One time, her copilot had to land the aircraft because the woman had become incapacitated. On the ground, medics had to revive her with oxygen and take her away on a stretcher.*[20]

Instead of taking away her wings, Spane reassigned her to an air-traffic-control unit, which meant that she could later be reassigned to flight duties.

Gullible journalists of a standard feminist outlook had bought the Navy's story on Kara Hultgreen's carrier landing scores, and as long as her training records stayed with her mother, the truth remained a secret. As early as December 1994, however, a second copy of Hultgreen's training records had been delivered by a confidential source to Elaine Donnelly of the Center for Military Readiness. On January 16, 1995, after consulting with several retired aviators on the records, Donnelly sent a nine-page letter to Senator Strom Thurmond, the new chairman of the Senate Armed Services Committee, detailing specific events, low scores, and major errors alleged by the documents. Thurmond then requested the Navy to answer Donnelly's allegations.

In February and March, Donnelly met once with Admiral Boorda and three times with Admiral Arthur, who was then still vice chief of naval operations. At her third meeting with Arthur, Donnelly and an aide from Senator Spence Abraham's office were shown a report by Rear Admiral Lyle G. Bien, which Arthur and Rear Admiral Kendell Pease, chief of information, insisted disproved Donnelly's principal allegation that Hultgreen and another female pilot, identified as "Pilot B," received preferential treatment in scoring and evaluation.

The Bien report had been completed two months earlier and was based largely on interviews with the Navy officers responsible for training the two women, including Captain Tom Sobieck, commanding officer of the Replacement Air Group, the last stop before a pilot joins an operational squadron. Sobieck had been burned for his involvement in Tailhook and was reportedly under pressure to prove his bona fides by guaranteeing the success of the first women entering combat aviation.[21] Worried by Donnelly's allegations, Sobieck twice phoned Donnelly to try to convince her that everything he had done for Hultgreen and Pilot B had been perfectly reasonable, but to no avail. The Bien report nevertheless accepted the word of officers like Sobieck that all was in order.

Donnelly and the aide were not allowed to take a copy of the Bien report with them, but what they read on the first page confirmed that the allegations in her letter to Senator Thurmond were "largely accurate." Three major allegations were substantiated:

- Kara Hultgreen was retained in the F-14 program and graduated to the fleet despite low scores and four major "downs" on her record, two of which were similar to mistakes made in her fatal landing attempt.
- Pilot B earned even lower scores and an astonishing seven downs, the last of which was later reclassified as just a "warm-up" so that she could be sent to the fleet.
- The Navy had taken no action since Hultgreen's death or since Donnelly made her allegations to change the way the training commands treated women or the status of Pilot B.

A month after the Bien report had been delivered to Admiral Spane, Rear Admiral Yakeley lied to all Americans when he said at the February 28 press conference that

Hultgreen had only one down on her record. With the Navy unwilling to set the record straight, Donnelly decided she had no choice but to publish the records in her possession.

She did so in April 1995, issuing a document with twenty-three pages of text and over one hundred pages of photocopies from the actual training records. The records showed that in March 1994 an instructor observed Hultgreen "making power corrections that were erratic and unpredictable," just the behavior she exhibited on that fateful day in October. As for Pilot B, in her first attempt at car-quals, she received the worst night score in the history of the training squadron. During tactics training, her instructor noted that she "seemed to have lost her grasp of basic tactical concepts: positioning, mutual support, visual responsibilities, weapons employment, engaged communications and maneuvering."

Neither Hultgreen nor Pilot B ever went before a Field Naval Aviator Evaluation Board, despite four downs for Hultgreen and seven for Pilot B. After one down, a pilot usually goes before an evaluation board, which will decide whether the pilot may continue with training or be dropped. Two downs are usually enough to wash a pilot out, especially in F-14 training.

The Navy refused to comment on Pilot B's records, but continued to insist that Hultgreen was a "fully qualified naval aviator." Experienced "airedales" knew better. Kara Hultgreen might have been a fully qualified *EA-6B* aviator, but she never really mastered the F-14.

The *San Diego Union-Tribune*'s Robert Caldwell asked five former naval aviators, three with experience flying the demanding F-14, to review Hultgreen's training records. One pilot told him, "Neither of these two women should have been in the cockpit. I feel strongly about that." Another aviator told him, "It's crystal clear to me that they moved Hultgreen out to the ship too quickly. She wasn't ready and they overlooked a number of shortcomings. She clearly got special treatment."[22]

If Hultgreen's records were bad, Pilot B's were even worse. One aviator told Caldwell that Pilot B had "the worst flight records I've ever seen, the worst [training] scores in the Replacement Air Group (RAG) I've ever seen.... Yes, some pilots are late bloomers, OK. But this was just bad, unacceptably bad." Another said he was "astonished" at the number of downs Pilot B received without being dropped from F-14 training or at least being called before a formal review board.

Two months after the publication of her training records, Pilot B's name was revealed to the public, not by Donnelly but by *Navy Times*, which reported that a Field Naval Aviator Evaluation Board had recommended that she be relieved of flight duties for poor performance. The woman's name was Lieutenant Carey Dunai Lohrenz. She has since sued Donnelly's Center for Military Readiness, the *Washington Times*, the *San Diego Union-Tribune*, and assorted "John Does 1–100," charging them with publishing "false and defamatory" allegations of double standards in Navy training that cost Lohrenz her wings and her career. Lohrenz received a sympathetic profile, à la Dreyer, à la Coughlin, in an NBC *Dateline* segment, which portrayed her as the "victim" of "gossip" and sex discrimination, totally ignoring the Center for Military Readiness report.

Navy leaders were desperate to deny that they themselves had contributed to Kara Hultgreen's death by not allowing her to fail.

Donnelly never revealed Lohrenz's name, and she had nothing to do with Lohrenz losing her wings; she may even have saved her life. Yet she is now being sued, proving that when it comes to careers, feminists are once again pro-choice as opposed to pro-life.

Lohrenz's lead attorney is Susan Barnes, founder of WANDAS, or "Women Active in Our Nation's Defense, their Advocates and Supporters," a feminist group that needs help in the names department. Barnes's objective is nothing less than the criminalization of open opposition to feminist ideology in the civilian world, as it already is in the military. In the parlance of revolutionary legal theory, Lohrenz's filing is a "SLAPP suit."

SLAPP stands for "strategic litigation against public participation." The objective of SLAPP suits is not to win in court (they rarely do) but to silence political opposition by draining the opposition of funds.

Lohrenz recently returned to flight status, but only for shore-based aircraft. An investigating panel composed by the Navy inspector general concluded that she was properly removed from flight status for failure to obey the directions of landing safety officers. Her commanding officer had also faulted her for a lack of motor skills and poor motivation, but the inspector general's panel faulted him for not being more understanding of the stress she was under.

The inspector general's panel rejected claims that Lohrenz had received preferential treatment in training, despite testimony to the contrary from the instructors responsible for her training. One instructor told the panel, "the instructors at VF-124 wanted to see the females succeed, and I believe we went to some extraordinary lengths to have them do so." Another said, "I honestly believe that if Lt. Lohrenz was a male, that she may not have made it through the tactics syllabus."

As for the Bien report, it disappeared for two years immediately after Donnelly formally requested a copy under the Freedom of Information Act, which makes it a federal crime for executive agencies like the Navy to withhold documents from the public. For a while during those two years, the Navy even insisted that no such document ever existed. Then, lo and behold, it appeared again in January 1997, and Donnelly finally received her copy. A critique of the Bien report documenting the accuracy of Donnelly's claims was published by the Center for Military Readiness in March.

THE BIGGER THEY ARE...

In October 1995 Everett L. Greene, rear admiral (select), became the highest ranking Navy officer since World War II to face a court-martial. Greene stood accused of sexually harassing two female officers who had worked under him two years earlier. By 1995 quite a few admirals had fallen under the ax for having committed or condoned one of the many new crimes of gender. Most had gone quietly, knowing they could never expect a favorable hearing anywhere—not in the Navy, not in Congress, and certainly not in the press. A few groused publicly about their punishment, but none demanded their day in court. Greene did. Greene was black, and his accusers were white, and when he was alleged to have committed his heinous deeds, he was heading the Navy's office on equal opportunity.

Greene was an academy graduate and Navy SEAL who was being pushed along the career ladder by Admiral Boorda in the interest of diversity. He was accused of showing unrequited romantic interest in both women, writing them letters, cards, and poems of a deeply personal nature. One said, "What you offered to do with me was very special, very precious. I wanted you just as much, if not more, than you wanted me." Although he never touched them, his attentions made the women uncomfortable enough to complain. Their complaints were initially handled informally, to the apparent satisfaction of all. But with Greene scheduled for promotion to admiral and already serving in a prominent position as the Navy's Special Operation Command, the Navy was afraid that the leniency it had shown him would come back to haunt them. All it would have taken was for one of the women to take her story to the press. Admiral Stanley Arthur, vice chief of naval operations, wanted Greene to stand for admiral's mast, a nonjudicial proceeding that would allow the Navy to say later that Greene had been held accountable, even if he received only light punishment.

But Greene maintained that he was innocent and that his attentions to the women were just his way of giving encouragement and showing gratitude. He also believed that he was being lynched by white admirals in retribution for his equal opportunity work. He opted for a court-martial, which, unfortunately for the Navy, forced the whole issue before the public. It was a no-win situation for the senior sea service. The Navy was caught between competing interests—the desire to improve its record

on minorities by promoting more blacks to flag rank, its need to
protect itself from charges of favoritism for admirals, and its
internal pressure to be tough on sex discrimination and harassment by aggressive prosecution. Whatever it did, it was vulnerable to another bout of abuse. Greene was acquitted in the
court-martial but lost his promotion. The press did not rally to
his flag of race as he had hoped.

Coast Guard Captain Ernest Blanchard's case was more
clear-cut. At a Coast Guard banquet on January 10, 1995,
Blanchard, the Coast Guard's chief of public affairs, made jokes
that some women found objectionable. This had happened
once before, and the Coast Guard took no action. The second
time, it initiated criminal proceedings. Blanchard was a thirty-
year veteran who had joined the Coast Guard at the age of sixteen. He was married and the father of two teenagers, but the
Coast Guard was his family. When word got around that he had
committed an unpardonable sin, friends and colleagues began
avoiding him. Blanchard became despondent. On March 10 he
offered to retire immediately if the Coast Guard agreed to drop
its investigation, but the Coast Guard turned him down. Four
days later, Blanchard killed himself with a shot to the head,
leaving no suicide note. Coast Guard spinmasters called his suicide a "freak tragedy with no larger lessons," but a Navy psychological review concluded:

> [H]is style seemed consistent with someone whose duty it
> was to shoulder the burden and assume responsibility, even
> as that style clouded his ability to keep his situation in per-
> spective. The emotional pain and shame that Captain
> Blanchard felt he had brought upon himself and the Coast
> Guard led him to choose suicide as a solution.[23]

After Mike Boorda abandoned Admiral Stanley Arthur to
the political wolves, who demanded his hide for not reinstating
a washed-out female helicopter pilot, Boorda also found himself shunned by friends and colleagues. On April 25, 1996,

Boorda's severest critic, James Webb, expressed his outrage at the Navy's lack of leadership, in an address at the Naval Academy. Lamenting the loss of moral courage, Webb asked:

> When the acting secretary of the Navy, who had never spent a day in uniform, called a press conference and announced that the antics of one group of aviators at Tailhook were an indication that the Navy as a whole had a cultural problem—cultural, as in ethos, as in the overall body of traits that constitute an institution's history and traditions—how could the chief of naval operations stand next to him and fail to defend the way of life he had spent a career helping to shape?
>
> When Paula Coughlin's commanding officer, who had previously received dual honors as the Navy's outstanding fighter squadron, was relieved of his command based on a letter she wrote, without being given so much as five minutes to explain his own actions in her case to the admiral who summarily dismissed him, who dared to risk his career by taking Jack Snyder's side?
>
> When one of the finest candidates for commander in chief of the Pacific in recent times, a man who flew more than 500 combat missions in Vietnam and then, in the Gulf War, commanded the largest naval armada since World War II, was ordered into early retirement by the chief of naval operations because one senator asked on behalf of a constituent why Stan Arthur as vice chief of naval operations had simply approved a report upholding a decision to wash out a female officer from flight school, who expressed outrage? Who fought this? Who condemned it?
>
> When a whole generation of officers is asked to accept the flawed wisdom of a permanent stigma and the destruction of the careers of some of the finest aviators in the Navy based on hearsay, unsubstantiated allegations, in some cases after a full repudiation of anonymous charges that resemble the worst elements of McCarthyism, what admiral has had

the courage to risk his own career by putting his stars on
the table, and defending the integrity of the process and of
his people?[24]

As soon as he had finished, former acting Navy secretary Dan Howard, taking Webb's words as a personal attack, stormed up to the podium to denounce the speech as "fiction." When Howard tried to grab the microphone away from Webb, Webb told him, "You want a rebuttal? Write an article. That's what I do. Were you invited to this podium?"

Three days later, the *Washington Post* printed the text of Webb's speech, slightly edited for length, and a few days after that, an anonymous letter appeared in *Navy Times* declaring that Boorda had lost the respect of the entire officer corps and that his fellow admirals even privately referred to him as "Little Mikey Boorda."

None of this, even all together, would have been enough to drive Mike Boorda to "punch out," as the airedales say. It would take a much deeper blow to his personal integrity, something that went to the very core of who he was as a man.

It is difficult for military men to explain to those who have never served the appalling significance of the charge of wearing unauthorized decorations. Decorations are not merely lines on one's résumé, and wearing unauthorized decorations is not merely "résumé enhancement." People lie on their résumés to deceive others. They wear unauthorized decorations to deceive themselves. When a man pretends to be something he's not, he does so out of deep dissatisfaction with the man he actually is. When a military man is discovered to have worn decorations he did not earn, it tells other military men not so much that he is dishonest, but that he is crazy, or deeply disturbed to say the least.

For years, Admiral Boorda wore decorations he did not deserve, two tiny "V devices" (V for valor) indicating combat service. Boorda had never served in combat. He had served on a destroyer in the South China Sea during the Vietnam War, but his ship did not see action. Boorda never received orders authorizing him to wear the devices, nor did his service record ever indicate that he deserved them. No one else pinned them on his uniform; he did that himself, but only after he made rear admiral, many years after he supposedly earned them.

Boorda was twice informed privately before 1996 that he was not authorized to wear the V devices, once in 1987 and once again after Boorda had assumed the top post in the Navy, chief of naval operations. After the second time, he took them off, but by then thousands of photographs had been taken of the admiral wearing the unauthorized decorations. Eventually a member of the press noticed, a reporter for the tiny National Security News Service, who requested a copy of Boorda's service record under the Freedom of Information Act and then compared the records with the photographs. The tip was then passed to David Hackworth, a retired Army colonel writing on military matters for *Newsweek*. Hackworth requested an interview with Boorda.

On the day of the interview, Boorda discussed it with Kendell Pease, chief of information. Pease told reporters later that Boorda asked, "What should we do?" He then immediately answered his own question: "We will tell them the truth." Even this was a lie, for Boorda would not tell the truth. He had planned to have lunch in his office, but changed his mind and drove himself home to his quarters at the Washington Navy Yard. In his study, he wrote two notes, one to his wife and one to "my sailors," then he went into the garden and shot himself through the heart.

The pols plastered over the death with more lies about how he was a "sailor's sailor," much loved in the fleet, and about how he had given his life to atone for the Navy's many sins. The truth was far more personal and not at all heroic. The approval of others and the glory of rank and office were everything to Mike Boorda. Without the world's approval, he had no reason to live, and he could not bear to see his glories taken away in shame.

Chapter 14

SCHOOLS FOR SCANDAL

Hell hath no fury like a woman scorned.[1]

—WILLIAM CONGREVE

EVENTS FOLLOW FAST, with one scandal after another. In November 1996 the Army held a press conference to announce that it was charging five soldiers assigned to the Ordnance School at Aberdeen Proving Grounds, Maryland, with various sex crimes including rape, adultery, sexual assault, fraternization, and sexual harassment. Shortly thereafter the Army shifted into high gear to show that it had learned from the Navy's experience not to take such things lightly. Soldiers worldwide were ordered to undergo another round of sexual harassment training, and victims were encouraged to call the Army's new twenty-four-hour harassment hotline, which in its first twelve weeks logged nearly 7,000 calls and 1,074 allegations of sexual abuse. Before long, multiple prosecutions sprang up at Fort Leonard Wood, Missouri; Fort Jackson, South Carolina; Fort Bliss, Texas; Fort Sam Houston, Texas; and Darmstadt, Germany. The old threat to "drop a dime" on someone had taken on a whole new danger.

In the nation's capital, a tribunal of twelve congresswomen interrogated four Army generals on their failure to eradicate sexism and sexual harassment. "There are procedures that the

310 • WOMEN IN THE MILITARY

Army has in place, but while that looks good on paper, something has gone wrong. What are the causes of that? Is there a
climate that allows this to happen?" wondered Congresswoman
Rosa DeLauro of Connecticut. The women were pleased,
though, with the Army's vigorous response, which Pat
Schroeder said "has been very thorough."

But just to make sure the Army stayed on the tribunal's
good side, Army Secretary Togo D. West, Jr., announced the
formation of a Senior Review Panel on Sexual Harassment,
headed by retired Major General Richard S. Siegfried and
including noted feminists such as Sara Lister, a veteran not of
the Army but of the Carter administration, now assistant secretary of the Army for manpower and reserve affairs; retired
Brigadier General Pat Foote, who returned to active duty to
serve as an assistant to West; Major General Claudia Kennedy,
assistant chief of staff for intelligence; Professor Mady Segal of
the University of Maryland; Holly K. Hemphill, DACOWITS
chairwoman; and Professor Madeline Morris of Duke
University.

Also on the list was the Army's senior enlisted man,
Sergeant Major of the Army Gene C. McKinney. When his
appointment was announced, a female sergeant major, Brenda
L. Hoster, came forward to accuse him publicly of assaulting
her by making a pass at her in a hotel room in Hawaii in 1996.
There were no witnesses, and there was no evidence, but under
pressure from female members of Congress, the Army relieved
McKinney of his duties pending an investigation.

In Aberdeen it was a young recruit named Jessica Bleckley
who sparked the investigation with her complaint of sexual
assault. Bleckley, by her own admission, acquiesced to having
sex not once but twice with a male drill sergeant, Staff Sergeant
Nathaniel Beech, because she "thought she had to," according
to the *New York Times*. The *Times* quoted the young woman
saying, "When he got through [the second time], he was like:
'Get out. Don't get in my face.'" The *Times* viewed Bleckley as
an innocent young soldier ("solidly built... with a firm jaw") vic-

timized by a predatory superior and the Army's sexist culture. Diane Sawyer of ABC saw her in the same light. A military jury, more experienced with young recruits, proved less gullible and voted for Sergeant Beech's acquittal. Bleckley, it turned out, had a history of difficulty with the truth.

Military justice is swift. In a matter of weeks, the Army had produced convictions, but also more acquittals—of a staff sergeant at Fort Leonard Wood, Missouri, acquitted of all charges of sexual misconduct; of another staff sergeant at Fort McClellan, Alabama, acquitted of all similar charges; and of a West Point cadet acquitted of raping another West Point cadet after a drunken beach party. In the latter case, Army investigators recommended against a court-martial (both male and female witnesses supported the defense), but the Army chose to try the cadet for rape rather than appear insufficiently sensitive to women. The Aberdeen investigation also produced one more suicide—Private Alan M. May, an Army reservist who was accused of raping a female reservist in his unit. May hanged himself in the bathroom of his quarters on January 7, 1997.

Many of the accused soldiers avoided court-martial by pleading guilty to lesser charges like fraternization and sexual misconduct, involving consensual sex. For all the talk about rape, there was very little evidence of it. Five women lined up and publicly accused Army investigators of trying to blackmail them into making *false* accusations of rape, and threatening to charge them with fraternization and sexual misconduct if they did not cooperate. As in the Tailhook investigation, the government exaggerated the grievances of the supposed victims themselves.

Rape charges against Staff Sergeant Vernell Robinson, Jr., were dropped when it turned out his victim went to quite a lot of trouble to be raped, keeping assignations off post by wearing a beeper.

In the end, the charge of rape stuck against only one soldier, drill sergeant Delmar Simpson, who was convicted of eighteen counts of rape involving six young female soldiers in his charge at Aberdeen. Only two of the six women actually accused Sergeant Simpson of using physical force. The other four claimed that Simpson simply ordered them to do things and they did as they were told. "One even testified that Simpson could not have known she did not want to have sex with him," wrote Hanna Rosin for *The New Republic.* "Many of the women who testified described themselves as being in a sort of hypnotic state, frozen by fear and incapable of resisting. Their passivity often lasted for months, through several rapes."[2]

The Uniform Code of Military Justice does not require physical force to define rape; it is sufficient that the perpetrator applied "constructive force," i.e., abusing one's status and authority to obtain consent. Rosin faulted the Army for embracing a "definition of rape cribbed from radical feminist theory: rape is what happens when a man has sexual intercourse with a woman who is in a subordinate position to him." But the definition of rape applied in Simpson's case was not all that different from the civilian definition of *statutory* rape, in which the consent of the victim is all but assumed. The major difference is that statutory rape in the civilian world carries a much lighter penalty than forcible rape. Simpson faced the possibility of life in prison for each of his eighteen counts.

One "victim," whom witnesses called a "compulsive liar," had sex with Simpson five times in one month. Another testified that she gave Simpson sex in return for his help in having charges dropped against her for a minor infraction. She also testified to giving him nothing but encouragement both times they had sex:

> QUESTION: *It's fair to say that Staff Sergeant Simpson could have gotten the perception from you that you wanted to have sex with him?*
> ANSWER: *Yes, sir.*
> QUESTION: *Isn't it in fact true that you didn't want him to know you didn't want to have sex?*
> ANSWER: *Yes.*

None of Simpson's victims complained of being raped until questioned by Army investigators. Several had sex with him on more than one occasion, and at least one woman testified that she not only had sex "willingly," but that investigators pressured her into accusing Simpson of rape. Even so, he was convicted of raping her.

Minutes after the verdicts were announced, Drill Sergeant Mariana Shorter, a colleague and friend of Simpson, told CBS News, "I was a private once [and] there's no way you could rape me eight times and me not telling anybody.... These are not innocent young ladies. These women are very forceful and very, very aggressive. They're not children, young innocent children that they portrayed themselves to be."[3]

To Sergeant Shorter as well as to Sergeant Major McKinney, the investigations and prosecutions appeared to be racially motivated. Shorter, McKinney, Simpson, Beech, and most of the accused were black, whereas almost all of the victims were white. As in the case of Navy Captain Everett Greene, the white women ultimately won.

> Five women publicly accused Army investigators of trying to blackmail them into making false accusations of rape.

THE KELLY FLINN AFFAIR

No sooner was Simpson's punishment announced than the media were off to an even more sensational story: the first female bomber pilot in the history of the U.S. Air Force was being drummed out of the service for adultery.

As the Air Force's first female bomber pilot, First Lieutenant Kelly Flinn was treated like an aviation princess. Senior civilian and military officials from around the country showed up in Minot, North Dakota, to visit her. The media were enamored. Flinn was always in the spotlight. As a joke, Flinn's fellow crew members donned name tags that identified themselves merely as members of her crew: Kelly's Navigator,

Kelly's Crew Chief, Kelly's Bombardier, etc. Flinn was a graduate of the Air Force Academy. She was tops in her class in flight
training. She was blond and beautiful. She was a feminist dream
girl. She was also The Victim.

The way her story played in the media and in Washington is
a textbook example of feminist victimology, the clearest demonstration yet of how feminists identify The Victim in any circumstance. Only two things count: The Victim must serve the cause
of feminism, and The Victim must fit the image of the high-
flying woman brought down by low-lying men. Kelly Flinn served
the cause, and Kelly Flinn fit the image. Gayla Zigo did neither.

Gayla Zigo was a lowly airman who moonlighted behind the
front desk of the local Holiday Inn. The few times she was pic-
tured by the press, she was wearing a shapeless Air Force–issue
skirt and a plain blue uniform blouse, in contrast to Flinn's
dashing Nomex flight suit and leather flight jacket.

Some details of the case are in dispute, such as just how
Flinn met Gayla's civilian husband Marc Zigo and whether
Flinn knew that Marc Zigo was still married. Flinn swore that
Marc Zigo had told her he was legally separated. But witnesses
swore that Flinn was introduced to the Zigos as husband and
wife, that both Zigos had joined her for a barbecue at her quarters, and that she had visited the Zigos in their home.

Otherwise, the facts involved in the five charges leveled
against Flinn by the Air Force are not in doubt. (1) Flinn was
charged with adultery for her acknowledged affair with Marc
Zigo. Maximum penalty: one year in prison. (2) She was
charged with making a false official statement, in that she
denied to another officer that anything "intimate or sexual has
ever occurred" between herself and Zigo. Maximum penalty:
five years in prison. (3) She was charged with disobeying a
direct order, continuing to live with Marc after being ordered
to stay at least one hundred feet away from him by her
commanding officer. Maximum penalty: six months in prison.
(4) She was charged with conduct unbecoming an officer,
bringing disgrace upon the Air Force by committing adultery.

Maximum penalty: one year in prison. (5) She was charged with fraternization, because she had also had sexual relations with an unmarried enlisted man a few months before shacking up with Zigo. Maximum penalty: two years in prison. For all five counts, she could have gone to prison for nine and a half years.

Somehow this adulterous, dishonest female officer became a *cause célèbre* for journalists and politicians. According to Tucker Carlson, who writes for *The Weekly Standard*, the man responsible was Todd Ensign, editor of a leftist journal aimed at the military called *Citizen Soldier*. Over the years, Ensign has pushed a variety of subversive issues on the military like unionization and gay rights. "I'm on the left," he told Carlson. "I believe that a lot of these militaristic policies come from the domination of the military of our foreign policy."[4] *Citizen Soldier* has never had much impact on the military itself, but mainstream journalists who don't know any better, and who are often sympathetic to Ensign's leftist views, have tended to pay it more attention, and so Ensign's portrayal of Kelly Flinn as a victim of sex bias in military prosecutions for adultery ended up in *USA Today*. There wasn't any evidence to support the allegation of sex bias, but Ensign had said it was so, and that's all the media needed.

There followed sympathetic profiles of Flinn in the "Style" section of the *Washington Post* and on the front page of the *New York Times*, and not one but two interviews with a sympathetic Morley Safer for CBS's *60 Minutes*, one of which was humorously described by Carlson. After reading from Air Force evaluations describing her as an "aggressive" and "incredibly sharp professional warrior," Safer asked how she was holding up under the circumstances:

> *"You're a tough woman, yes?" he asked. The aggressive*
> *professional warrior looked down, lower lip quivering.*
> *"Yes," she replied, her voice barely audible. Then she started*
> *to cry.*

According to Carlson, Flinn showed even less control in private, throwing tantrums and becoming "hysterical," in the words of his source. Carlson concluded:

> *The fact that someone as psychologically fragile as Kelly Flinn had been put in command of a B-52 bomber with a nuclear payload was powerful evidence of the Air Force's determined, even reckless, effort to install women in positions of leadership.*

Flinn cried often in her interviews, playing two roles at once for the media: gung-ho Air Force team-player and helpless heartbroken young girl. She claimed she had been sexually assaulted at the Air Force Academy but hadn't reported it. She claimed she had been unfairly suspected of lesbianism because she would not date officers in her squadron for professional reasons. She claimed she had been deeply hurt by the special name tags and that she disliked all the attention. She claimed she had been offended by the questions investigators asked about her sex life. She claimed she had been manipulated by Marc Zigo, "a real con artist," in her words. She claimed she had been abused by Zigo while they were living together. She claimed she had wanted to leave him, "but I didn't know how."

Flinn also showed little or no remorse for her own actions. "It's not like I committed treason or murder or robbery or this heinous crime," she told Tamara Jones of the *Washington Post.* "I fell in love with the wrong man." (The *Post* gave her the usual star treatment: a full-page story with a large flattering photo on page 1 of its "Style" section and two more photos inside.)

The explanation Flinn gave for her actions changed over time. When Safer asked her why she lied and disobeyed orders, Flinn answered that she was young and confused and concerned for her career. Later, on *Good Morning America*, she said she had just found out she might have cancer and was confused and wasn't thinking about the investigation. Carlson was told by another reporter that the cancer scare had come weeks after she had lied and disobeyed orders. (Another Air Force officer had already used the same excuse to explain her own adultery, saying she was "lonely, vulnerable."[5]) Much of Flinn's defense rested on her claim that Marc Zigo had lied to her about being separated from Gayla. But when both were questioned separately by investigators, Marc Zigo did not support Flinn's story.

Such details did not affect the way the story was reported. The "story" that impressed the media, after all, was that the military was targeting women for prosecution for the archaic crime of adultery. The Air Force responded defensively, with General Ronald R. Fogelman, Air Force chief of staff, telling the Senate Armed Services Committee, "this is not an issue of adultery. This is an issue about an officer entrusted to fly unclear weapons who lied. That's what this is about."

Nobody stood up for Gayla Zigo or argued that dashing young officers shouldn't be allowed to swoop down and carry off the spouses of enlisted personnel. Many press reports, including an early front-page *Washington Post* story, did not even mention that Marc Zigo was married to an enlisted woman. He was a "married civilian," not a military dependent. Even after Gayla entered the story, she did not receive much sympathy. To feminists, Gayla was the enemy. Ellen Goodman wrote, "That battered and betrayed ex-wife managed to turn her rage on the other victim of Marc's attentions. I leave her and her self-deception to Ann Landers."

Politicians like Senators Slade Gorton and Trent Lott were indignant on Kelly Flinn's behalf but seemed not to notice Gayla Zigo. One could expect feminist pols like Republican Nancy Johnson and Democrat Carolyn Maloney to weigh in on Flinn's side. But Gorton, a former Air Force lawyer, actually wrote to Air Force Secretary Sheila Widnall to demand that the charges against Flinn be dismissed. Lott's support for Flinn came off the cuff, and it showed. After admitting that he did not know much about the case, Lott declared on camera:

*I think it's unfair. I don't understand why she is being sin-
gled out and punished the way she is. I think at the minimum she ought to get an honorable discharge. And I've got
a lot of other questions about why the Air Force hasn't
stepped up to this issue and dealt with it better. I'll tell you,
the Pentagon is not in touch with reality on this so-called
question of fraternization. I mean, get real. You're still dealing with human beings. And the way she has been treated
really disturbs me greatly.... My wife has a good question:
Where's the guy that was involved in this deal? I don't
understand all this. And I think it's very unfair.*[6]

The *New York Times* praised Lott for his "sound civilian
advice," but it is hard to see how the Air Force could have acted
on it without ceasing to make dishonesty, disobedience, and
conduct unbecoming an officer no longer punishable under
military law. Lott, of course, had never been in the military; he
had spent the Vietnam War as a cheerleader for Ole Miss. It
appeared his major interest in the case was pandering to
women voters. Columnist George Will called Lott a "media-
driven nonleader" who was "sounding like a Valley Girl doing an
impression of former Congresswoman Patricia Schroeder." *The
Weekly Standard's* William Kristol wrote that he sounded
"Clintonian."

Opinion polls, however, showed that most Americans saw
Flinn just the way Lott did. Flinn's commanding officer still
wanted to see her court-martialed and convicted, but Secretary
Widnall was under pressure to let her resign instead. The trouble was that Flinn, encouraged by the sympathy she had
received, refused to resign with anything less than an honorable
discharge, which the Air Force's uniformed leadership opposed.
An honorable discharge would have allowed her to keep her veterans benefits and remain in the Air Force Reserve, and the Air
Force wasn't about to trust Flinn to fly again.

Events turned against Flinn when Gayla Zigo wrote to
Secretary Widnall to urge against an honorable discharge. In

her letter, Airman Zigo complained that "less than a week after we arrived to the base, Lt. Flinn was in bed with my husband having sex." Flinn visited their house several times, "always in her flight suit flaunting the fact that she was an academy graduate and the first female bomber pilot.... How could I compete with her?"

Widnall refused Flinn's request for an honorable discharge, and just before going on trial, Kelly Flinn gave in to the pleas of her family that she accept a general discharge instead. Even the *Washington Post* conceded defeat in an editorial admitting that Flinn had manipulated the press and that "Lt. Flinn wasn't singled out for her gender."

For Flinn it was over, but for the military the ordeal was still alive, as later cases demonstrated. A lesser-known case occurred in the summer of 1997 involving one of Flinn's former Air Force Academy classmates, Lieutenant Crista Davis. Davis filed racial and sexual discrimination charges against the service, although she herself had had an affair—and a child—with a married superior officer and had boasted about this in sexually explicit letters to the officer's wife. At one point, Davis faced fifty-five years in prison on charges including willful dereliction of duty, conduct unbecoming an officer, absence without leave, willfully disobeying a superior officer, and making false official statements. The case was eventually heard in a nonjudicial administrative hearing rather than a court-martial. Davis was reprimanded and fined $2,000 after she was found guily of conduct unbecoming an officer for the affair and for writing the sexually explicit letters.

> Somehow Kelly Flinn—this adulterous, dishonest female officer—became a *cause célèbre* for journalists and politicians.

The military's moral standards were now being openly questioned. They were too high, according to the know-it-all nonveterans in the media and in Congress. Congressman Barney Frank submitted a bill to move consensual sexual behavior beyond the military's regulatory reach, another ploy to win approval of homosexuality. At the same time, the services were more obligated than ever to prosecute men for the slightest sexual infraction. In the spring of 1997 the Army relieved two general officers of their duties for having affairs with civilian women, and days after Kelly Flinn capitulated, Air Force General Joseph Ralston was forced to withdraw his name from nomination as the next chairman of the Joint Chiefs of Staff, on account of an affair he had with a civilian woman ten years after having been separated from his wife.

Normally such affairs would never have been noticed, but the twenty-four-hour sexual harassment hotline made anonymous accusations easy and effective. And normally such infidelities would never have been prosecuted unless they were believed to disrupt official duties. But the military had lost all ability to discriminate, to tell the difference between adultery with the spouse of a helpless airman and adultery with a divorced civilian secretary. Once again, fear had made a reasonable response impossible.

THE BOYS OF SYRACUSE

If the Flinn case turned out relatively well, with Flinn's misdeeds ending her career, another case involving the New York Air National Guard produced opposite results without attracting the interest of Mr. Safer or *USA Today* or the rest of the journalistic herd. No case better illustrates the power of one woman to work the political system to her own advantage than the case of Major Jacquelyn S. Parker. Parker literally destroyed a fighter squadron with her accusations of a "hostile environment" and "disparate treatment," escaping any blame for her own alleged transgressions and shortcomings.

The trouble began when Defense Secretary Les Aspin finally gave the go-ahead for the training of female fighter pilots. Eager to be the first to admit women, the New York National Guard went "barnstorming" for female candidates. The 174th Fighter Wing in Syracuse, New York, came up with five candidates and hired one, Sue Hart Lilly, through the normal screening process. State Guard headquarters sent them another, Jackie Parker, who had been slated originally for a fighter squadron in Niagara that was subsequently selected for conversion to tankers. Parker was a C-141 pilot who boasted of having once been an Air Force test pilot and a NASA flight controller, and of having finished college at an early age with a degree in computer science. While on active duty, she had caught the attention of General Michael Hall, the adjutant general of New York, whose support secured her slot in the F-16 program.

Both Parker and Lilly passed the initial training phase at Wichita, Kansas, learning to fly the F-16C Falcon, a multipurpose, supersonic, single-engine, single-seat fighter. In the next phase, conducted by the 174th Fighter Wing, they would learn to fly tactically in order to qualify as combat fighter pilots. The wing commander, Colonel David Hamlin, had actively encouraged the search for female candidates and had expressed to others his ambition that the 174th could write the manual on how to integrate women. At the same time, Hamlin was aware that State Guard headquarters was especially interested in the women's progress, Parker's in particular. In one of the many irregularities of the case, Parker was neither assigned nor officially attached to the 174th. Instead, Parker filled a headquarters billet, although the 174th was expected to train her.

The combat qualification program required pilots to complete eight "rides," successfully demonstrating their ability to perform the various combat missions the squadron might be called upon to execute. It was not unusual for new members to require many more rides to master the missions. New members were often coming off active duty, converting from another type of tactical aircraft to the F-16 while at the same time learning their new civilian jobs as airline pilots.

Parker had no civilian job and would have been available for training full-time, except that she spent a considerable amount of time in Washington, D.C., being celebrated as one of the first female fighter pilots. In the year she was with the 174th, Parker was honored by First Lady Hillary Clinton at the White House and by the commanding general of the Air Combat Command. Such events took priority over her training and would have extended the time needed to qualify even if her performance had been outstanding—but it wasn't. After ten months of training, Parker had still not qualified despite as many as fifty-two rides. She repeated one mission nine times before receiving a passing score. On one practice bombing mission, she missed the target five out of six times, even after having it marked by her wingman. One of her misses landed two kilometers away, in the wrong valley, far enough off target to pose a danger to friendly forces in the area.

Her several instructor pilots all held civilian jobs and rarely saw each other, but before long their concern for her performance prompted them to compare notes. The trends were obvious. A small woman, just five-foot-three or -four, she had a tendency to black out when pulling G's. Her instructors advised her to work out at the gym to develop the upper-body strength necessary to maintain consciousness. One recommended that she undergo remedial centrifuge training, which she had already done and could not repeat. Parker also never mastered the "switchology" of the aircraft. She took too long to find the right switch for what she needed to do. Most distressingly, she lacked sufficient "situational awareness," a critical faculty for fighter pilots. She often lost track of her flight lead. She was easily overwhelmed with the demands of flying the aircraft, tracking targets, and executing maneuvers in a changing environment. It was a deficiency that nearly proved fatal in training and ultimately ended her attempt to qualify for combat.

The fateful last ride came in June 1995, the day before the 174th was scheduled to deploy to Turkey for Operation Provide Comfort, a mission in support of relief efforts for Kurdish refugees in northern Iraq. This was not long after a U.S. Air Force fighter had shot down a U.S. Army helicopter in northern Iraq, having mistaken it for an Iraqi helicopter violating the Allied no-fly zone. To prevent such mistakes in the future, the pilots of the 174th were required to qualify for the low-altitude intercept mission. If Parker could do so, she would deploy with the wing as the first female fighter pilot to see combat service. The New York Air National Guard intended to disregard one requirement of the Air Force tasking for the mission, which specified that only operational combat pilots deploy. Parker was not in an operational billet, but the Guard was not about to deny her, on a technicality, the honor of being the first female pilot to see combat.

Parker's attempt at qualifying was graded by Major Jeffrey "X" Ecker, the wing's weapons-and-tactics officer, a "Top Gun" in Navy terms, specially trained to train other pilots in tactical maneuvers. The test mission involved two F-16s intercepting two A-10 "Warthogs" flying a known route at an altitude of just 500 feet. On her first attempt, Ecker led the way, with Parker following as his wingman. Upon spotting the A-10s, Ecker descended from 3,000 to 500 feet and engaged the Warthogs. Parker, however, made no calls to indicate that she had made radar contact or spotted the Warthogs, made no descent, and did not fire a shot.[7]

For her second attempt, Ecker suggested a different tactic. This time, they would separate, fly parallel, and then converge on the Warthogs from different directions, in a maneuver called a "split" or "bracket." All Parker had to do was watch for Ecker to turn and descend, but once again she failed to follow, making no calls, no turn, no descent, no attempt to engage.

On her third ride, Ecker put Parker out in front flying the same simple intercept course as her first ride, but this time Parker flew right by the Warthogs without seeing them, so they shot her.

Ecker and Parker had to refuel before trying again. On her fourth ride, Ecker tried to make the mission even easier. The plan was to fly a bracket again, but instead of engaging the enemy on the first pass, they would take advantage of their superior speed to dash past the A-10s for a positive identification before turning back to engage. Once again, Parker made no calls to indicate that she had spotted the Warthogs. Ecker zoomed past them and then turned back and descended to give chase. After engaging the lead Warthog, he saw Parker approaching straight ahead, still at 3,000 feet. When she at last spotted a turning A-10 much closer to the ground, she banked sharply, nearly flipping completely over, and started to dive in on her target, a maneuver called an "oblique slice." It might have worked at a higher altitude, but from 3,000 feet it would have killed her. "Knock it off!" Ecker yelled into the radio. The command was used to stop pilots from executing unsafe maneuvers. In response, Parker immediately rolled out of her deadly dive, and Ecker called off the exercise.

Back on the ground, Ecker sent Parker to the debriefing room to relax. Then he went to consult with two superiors. He knew that if he flunked her, she would not go to Turkey and would miss her famous first. It had not bothered him before or during the exercise, but he wondered how the Guard would handle her failure. "You have to call it like you see it," one officer told him. The other concurred. Should he fail her after four attempts and a life-threatening mistake? "Absolutely" was the answer.

As one of her principal instructors, Ecker had flown with Parker many times before. He knew that she was often defensive in critiques, making excuses for her faults and arguing against criticism. She sometimes told instructors her in-flight video recorder of radar and cockpit displays didn't work, to avoid having to replay her mistakes. She had always seemed to Ecker to be more interested in "playing the part" of the tough fighter pilot than in actually becoming one. She didn't study; she didn't work out; she didn't even seem all that eager to fly.

This time, however, he found her drained and white, clearly shaken, with the familiar "Casper-the-Ghost look" of a pilot who has just escaped death. She did not question his critique, which he couched in careful, technical terms that faulted a "dangerous set-up" that almost "put her aircraft in a position that no one could have converted." On a scale of 0 to 4, he gave her an unsatisfactory 1, but the grade didn't seem to phase her. She seemed too frightened at that time to care. "I think she knew then she was in over her head," said Ecker. That same day, she quit.

Days after quitting, Parker blamed her failure on a "hostile environment" in the wing that had resulted in "disparate treatment" in the form of biased evaluation of her performance. Her complaint prompted a board of inquiry headed by Brigadier General Johnny Hobbs, a lawyer who was deputy commander of the New York Air National Guard.

The basis of Parker's complaint was Colonel Hamlin's handling of rumors about Parker's relationship with Lieutenant Colonel Robert A. "Snake" Rose, commander of the wing's operations group and one of Parker's instructors. Parker and Rose, a married man, were known to have spent time together socially, sailing, rock-climbing, dining, and drinking. Both insisted that their relationship was strictly platonic, a

> Jacquelyn Parker's deficiencies nearly proved fatal in training and ultimately disqualified her for combat.

"mentor-student" relationship that supported her training. Other officers in the wing saw evidence of more, as Rose and Parker seemed entirely too tight. Rose was suspected of inflating her scores. Five of her nine 3's she owed to Rose. (She never received a top score of 4 and never received a 3 on a first try.) In December 1994 some of the pilots got together and gave Rose a mock award for the "most disgusting guardsman" of the year. It was their way of putting him on notice.

Hamlin also warned Rose about the appearance of impropriety and advised Rose to stay away from Parker. Hamlin was later quoted as saying, "I asked Rose to kindly put his relationship on a professional basis. In my mind, that wasn't taking away a mentorship. It was telling him not to go sailing and drinking wine." Finally in May 1995, after three previous warnings, Hamlin relieved Rose of his duties. According to Parker, Hamlin's actions encouraged the hostility of the other pilots in the wing, making them unfairly critical of her performance.

For their part, the pilots of the 174th at first assumed that Parker's long documented history of poor performance would disprove any charge of bias, but before long it became apparent that the investigation was headed in other directions. Parker's three principal instructors, including Ecker, were never even interviewed by investigators. Other pilots were instead questioned on what they had heard about her performance. Interviews with Sue Hart-Lilly and the squadron's only black pilot were brief and superficial, as neither provided evidence to support Parker's accusations.

Colonel Rose was the second person to be interviewed, immediately after Parker. When he was questioned about his relationship with Parker, he twice asked for legal counsel, but the investigating officer, a JAG lieutenant colonel named John Clark, misled him into thinking he was not entitled to counsel. The questioning went as follows:

> ROSE *[for the second time]: I'd like a lawyer present before I answer that, because it borders on things outside the unit that I consider personal and not work-associated. If I have that right. If I don't, I'll answer it truthfully, if I don't have that right for legal counsel.*
>
> LTC CLARK: *I'm not treating you as a suspect. I haven't read you your Miranda rights.*
>
> ROSE: *Okay.*
>
> LTC CLARK: *So I'm going to ask you the question again, and you are required to answer it.*
>
> ROSE: *Okay.*[8]

The investigating officer knew that any competent legal counsel would have shut Rose up tight, possibly preventing Rose from incriminating others. At the same time, since the investigator had no intention of prosecuting Rose, he was not concerned with securing testimony that could be later used against Rose in court. By such tricks, the investigator obtained the testimony that served his purpose, later leading the witness through the following questions:

QUESTION: *And that association [between Rose and Parker] was a professional association and a friendship, was it not?*

ANSWER: *Yes. Uh-huh.*

QUESTION: *It was never more than that, was it?*

ANSWER: *No. It wasn't.*[9]

The same tactics were used in the Tailhook investigation to pump accusations out of alleged victims who might otherwise have needed to protect themselves from self-incrimination. The rest of the interview focused not on Rose's relationship with Parker but on the alleged abuse that Rose and Parker had suffered as a result of what others thought of their relationship.

Parker, of course, had earlier denied anything inappropriate in her relationship with Rose:

> He did come into my room a few times.... but it was never overnight. Nothing like that.... Basically what I'm saying is if I have lunch with someone, it's not unusual for me to hear about it later that I have been suspected of having some sort of romantic relationship with someone.... I made sure to tell Col. Hamlin and Col. [Thomas] Webster that they must know nothing happened. And they didn't care, really. That wasn't the point. The point was they had told Snake not to do it; and he had hung out with me; and that the perceptions were that we were having an affair, and that was really what was important, were the perceptions, not what really happened. I expressed that I think their perceptions should be changed, that there was a lot more underlying this than my relationship with Snake and that they were succeeding in ostracizing me.[10]

On August 30, 1995, before the results of the investigation had been announced, Brigadier General John H. Fenimore V, adjutant general of New York, informed Colonel Hamlin by letter that he was removing Hamlin's name from the promotion list, and delaying his promotion to brigadier general on account of the interim report of the investigation, which Hamlin had not seen. Three weeks later, Fenimore went all the way by relieving Hamlin of his command and requesting his resignation. Hours later, the results of the investigation were announced in a nationally televised press conference. Investigators had concluded that Parker had indeed suffered disparate treatment in a hostile environment. They found Hamlin responsible as wing commander, faulting him for not squelching rumors against Parker and Rose and for unfairly interfering with their mentor-student relationship.

Hamlin's second in command, Colonel Thomas Webster, was also relieved and reassigned to another unit, and two other officers were to receive Article 15s, a form of nonjudicial punishment. Captain Anthony Zaccaro was accused of sexually harassing Parker, while Major Theodore Limpert was faulted for having a lawyer friend call Rose on the telephone posing as a reporter to inquire about their relationship. Both were removed from flight status. (Zaccaro later filed a $2 million lawsuit against Parker, accusing her of sexually harassing him.)

The next day, Rose himself was quietly asked to retire. In the preceding weeks, Colonel Brent J. Richardson, the State Guard's director of operations, had told General Fenimore that Rose had confided to him privately that he had indeed carried on a "sustained and intimate personal relationship" with Parker.[11] This allegation was not included in the 500 copies of the investigation report distributed to the press, as investigators continued to base their conclusions on the assumption that both Rose and Parker were telling the truth in their sworn statements. It was, however, deemed sufficiently credible to hasten Rose's retirement. At the end of his tour, Richardson himself was not selected for continued service and was forced to retire.

The pilots of the 174th were incensed at the treatment of their commanding officer and fellow pilots and at the public humiliation of their unit and the viciousness of the system's response. Still believers in the system, they decided to do what they could to set things right.

On November 4 Major Ecker and another instructor met with Fenimore's personal legal advisor and another lawyer who had been involved in the investigation. Perhaps not being pilots and without having interviewed Parker's principal instructors, they just didn't understand how bad Parker was in the cockpit. Afterward, Ecker came to believe that they had known all along and that his naive attempt to explain things had only identified him as a non-team-player.

On November 14 another experienced pilot, Lieutenant Colonel John M. Whiteside, took the matter to the Air Force Office of Special Investigations (OSI) and to the office of the secretary of the Air Force. That same day, his new wing commander threatened him with a psychiatric evaluation. One week later the OSI investigation was called off on orders from the Air Force office that oversees the air national guards.

Two weeks later the 174th was grounded for "safety concerns" and "good order and discipline," and four weeks after that, when the grounding was lifted, eight pilots, including Ecker and Whitehead, were notified that they were being removed from flight status and reassigned to nonexistent maintenance jobs with the stated excuse of "career broadening." All eight had complained to the Air Force, members of Congress, state legislators, Governor George Pataki's office, or the press. Notifications were made by certified letter. Padlocks were cut off of the pilots' lockers to force them to clear out as soon as possible. Whiteside was barred from the base for being out of uniform (he was accused of wearing a nonstandard name-tag). Others were ordered to submit to testing for drugs. Rumors were circulated that the boys of Syracuse were a bad lot—crazy, dishonest, and, of course, sexist.

Then on January 16, 1996, Robert Rose signed an affidavit admitting to an intimate sexual relationship with Parker. Torn by guilt at what was happening to his unit, Rose confessed three days before he retired:

> *I did have a strong, emotionally supportive personal
> relationship and on a number of occasions it did include
> engaging in touching [and] kissing, which was conduct that
> would be considered unprofessional. We never had and I
> never intended to have sexual intercourse, but I did on one
> occasion spend the night in the same bed with Parker.
> There were also other times when I visited Parker at her
> apartment.*
>
> *Col. Hamlin appropriately advised me on several occas-
> sions to end my unprofessional relationship with Parker. I
> had also conveyed the nature of my relationship with Parker
> to both Col. Hamlin and Col. Richardson. I offered to con-
> vey the information directly to B[rigadier] G[eneral]
> Fenimore.*[12]

Rose's confession directly contradicted Parker's sworn statement and invalidated the main findings of the State Guard
investigation. As a result, Governor Pataki on February 1
ordered a second investigation of the first investigation, to be
conducted by the state inspector general, Roslan Mauskopf.
Then in June 1996 the Air Force inspector general opened a
whistle-blower investigation to examine allegations of retaliation against those pilots who complained.

"Justice delayed is justice denied." At this writing, the New
York State inspector general has yet to complete its investigation of the Parker affair, although it has been twenty months
since the investigation was ordered. The whistle-blower investigation was also still pending. The politics of the issue are too
dangerous for anyone in the New York State government or the
Department of the Air Force to move swiftly and courageously.
Who, after all, would want to risk his career standing up for a
handful of successful, upstanding white males?

Whatever the results of the two investigations, the 174th
will never be the same. There is talk now of disbanding the unit
and closing the base. A highly effective combat unit has already
been destroyed. Millions of tax dollars invested in the training

of combat-experienced pilots has been lost. The faith of pilots throughout the Air Guards in the organizations they serve has been shaken. Once again, the integrity of senior military officers has been impugned.

"Maybe we were old and naive, but we actually thought we could maintain standards," says one former 174th pilot. Once again the principal victims were not narrow-minded traditionalists opposed viscerally and ideologically to the advancement of women, but forward-thinking, fair-minded men willing to give a competent woman a chance.

They just didn't understand how things work in the real world, how powerful sex is, how craven some men are, and how spiteful and manipulative some women can be.

Chapter 15

EXPOSING THE LIES

It will avail us little if the members of our
defeated force are all equal. History will treat us
for what we were: a social curiosity that failed.

—PROFESSOR RICHARD A. GABRIEL
ST. ANSELM'S COLLEGE

IN THE WAKE OF THE ABERDEEN SCANDAL, *The New Republic*, a venerable magazine of neoliberal opinion, published a cover story by Stephanie Gutmann entitled "Sex and the Soldier." Under a previous editor who was an avowed homosexual, *The New Republic* had endorsed not only women in combat but gays in the military. With Gutmann's cover story, the magazine executed a surprising about face.

"Sex and the Soldier" took a wry look at the various problems afflicting the integrated military—the lack of physical strength among women, the double standards, the softening of co-ed training, the persistent problems with fraternization and harassment, the pregnancy and nondeployability, the resentment and hostility of men, the contradictions inherent in official policy, and the ideological silliness and dishonesty of senior leaders. The outlook, overall, was not good:

> *In a military that is dedicated to the full integration of women,*
> *and to papering over the implications of that integration as*
> *best it can, sex and sexual difference will continue to be a dis-*
> *ruptive force. And regulating sex will become an ever more*
> *important military sideline, one whose full costs in money,*
> *labor and morale we will not really know until the forces are*
> *called on to do what they are assembled to do: fight.*[1]

Gutmann stopped just short of calling for a return to an all-male military. She wrote not one word of praise for women in the military, made no specious distinction between combat and noncombat, and conceded no military role for women even in the most limited sense.

No doubt because she was a woman writing in *The New Republic*, Gutmann inspired a bout of soul-searching among the self-appointed guardians of the nation's conscience. After a few weeks filled with more revelations, acquittals, and convictions, Richard Cohen of the *Washington Post* finally spoke up. "Whatever comes out of the Aberdeen mess ought not be pre-ordained by an ideological commitment to the status quo," he wrote. Comparing his own experience in the Army with the new reality described by Gutmann, Cohen concluded, "In some ways, the military has become the most politically correct institution in the country. The question is whether that has affected its fighting ability." He wrote:

> *[The military is] not the place where an ideology, unproved*
> *no matter how worthy, should be imposed so that the rest of*
> *society will follow.... [It is possible] the [Aberdeen] scandal*
> *is a warning to both the brass and the civilian leadership*
> *that they are attempting the impossible—a fight not against*
> *a few bad men but against a more formidable foe: human*
> *nature.*[2]

Cohen was having second thoughts about feminist assurances of success in the military, and he was not alone. Even members of Congress began speaking up with uncharacteristic forthrightness. At the outbreak of the Aberdeen scandal, Congressman Robert Livingston of Louisiana said on *Good Morning America*:

> *There were 70 pregnancies in the last year in Bosnia; some 500 women a year get pregnant on ships. And then you have all these incidents of rapes, which no one can defend. The point is that we've gone to a unisex environment. We expect young men and women to live together in the military without any distinction between the sexes. And we've lost all common sense.*[3]

On the floor of the Senate, Democratic Senator Robert Byrd of West Virginia declared, "I think the scandals which we are seeing... must be taken as a danger sign that sexual integration complicates an Army's fighting capabilities." In the House, Congressman Roscoe Bartlett of Maryland proposed a bill that would have forced the services to resegregate basic training, ostensibly to protect young, impressionable female recruits from predatory drill sergeants. The bill would not have protected the women at Aberdeen Proving Grounds, which is not a basic training post, neither would it have made an appreciable difference in the overall problem, but it would at least have been a step in the right direction, which Congress had been unwilling even to consider in the previous years.

Before long, doubting the success of integration was no longer forbidden. In April 1997 Anna Simons, a female assistant professor of anthropology at UCLA, defended the exclusion of women from combat units in the *New York Times* on the grounds that women would inhibit "male bonding" and unit cohesiveness.[4] Later, in June, *The New Republic* ran another article decrying the injustice of the Aberdeen trials, this time by Hanna Rosin. That same month, Edward Luttwak, senior fellow of the Center for Strategic and International Studies, told the *New York Times Magazine*:

So long as men and women are in the Army together, lines
of power will get entangled with sexual lines. The attempt to
prevent this is ridiculous. It's a fantasy, not to mention a
grotesque puritanical hypocrisy. The Army can't do some-
thing that eluded the Franciscans. It can't run a mixed
monastery.[5]

And Jonathan Steinberg, an American historian at Cambridge
University, lamented the unreasonableness of the American
demand for a type of social justice not shared by the rest of the
world. He told the *Times*, "We're utopian perfectionists. If
we're going to have gender equality, we're damn well going to
have it all the way."

Some feminists seemed to realize the hopelessness of their
cause, the frustrating elusiveness of success at actually integrating men and women on an equal footing anywhere without continuing conflict. "The more men and women blend, the more
we clash. The more we talk to each other, the less we understand each other," despaired the *Washington Post*'s Maureen
Dowd. Linda Bird Francke, author of the recently published
book *Ground Zero: The Gender Wars in the Military*, sadly
admits the irreconcilable differences between feminism and
the male military culture, and declines even to suggest how to
combine the two. "The resistance to women will not go away
because it can't," she writes. "Instead of drawing the genders
together, the dynamics of work in the military culture often
force them apart."[6]

By and large, though, feminists stuck with their familiar alibis. Senator Olympia Snowe, a Maine Republican, called
Cohen's column "uninformed and inaccurate," then ventured
the outdated argument that women are "absolutely essential to
meeting the force requirements under the current voluntary
service system." At the high point of Kelly Flinn's popularity, the
Washington Post spoke up in defense of sexual licentiousness,
condemning the military for its "unrealistic" demands that service members eschew fraternization and adultery. (The military

has no regulation against fornication.) "This dilemma isn't really about women in the military, though it's often presented that way," the *Post* protested. "It's about drafting the rules so that expectations are relevant to the essential functioning and well-being of the organization...." It was another outdated argument: that the right rules, the right policies, the right words on paper would bring the whole of human nature under control.

Less abashed feminists continued to blame everything on the masculine nature of the military itself. Of the Aberdeen scandal, NOW's Karen Johnson, a retired Air Force officer, told the *Baltimore Sun*, "They cannot get a handle on this problem because of a military culture that is macho, that uses women as sexual objects."

> The ideology of "equal opportunity" trumps our military needs and our national security.

About the same time as the Gutmann article, *The Weekly Standard*, a neoconservative version of *The New Republic*, published a cover story by James Webb entitled "The War on the Military Culture," which received rave reviews in conservative circles, usually timid on issues involving women. Webb's thesis was that the military was being destroyed by its ideological enemies, who were "actively interested in undoing the military's historic culture," not principally to provide more opportunity for women, but to annihilate a power structure that oppresses civilian society. The drive for equal opportunity for both women and homosexuals was merely a means to an end, a way to subvert the military from within.

The principal butt of Webb's logic was Madeline Morris, professor of law at Duke University, appointed to the Army's Senior Review Panel on Sexual Harassment by Army Secretary Togo D. West, Jr. Morris had served as a "special consultant" to West since publishing a 130-page treatise in the *Duke Law Journal* entitled "By Force of Arms: Rape, War, and Military Culture," in February 1996. In this work, Morris focused on the "rape differential." Its seems that crime rates are lower in the military for everything except rape. This suggested to Morris

that something in the "masculinist military construct" enhanced
the "rape propensity" of male service members. She wrote,
"The socialization of the hypermasculine male may script him
to overvalue a definition of masculinity as tough and unfeeling,
violent and exploitative of women." According to Morris, the
services had reason to fear that a "critical mass of potential
rapists" could cause periodic outbreaks of violence against
women. She concluded, "there is much to be gained and little
to be lost by changing this aspect of military culture from a masculinist vision of unalloyed aggressivity to an ungendered
vision...."

When Morris's ideas became known, Secretary West
attempted to dissociate himself from her, but there was nothing
unusual about Morris's thesis, nothing that the Army and the
other services had not already succumbed to many years ago.
Feminists have long blamed the services for "the encouragement of a 'macho' male image" which supposedly contributes to
the problem of sexual harassment,[7] and they have always
insisted that masculinity is an accidental characteristic of military service, not essential to the military's mission. As early as
1979, a West Point study group on the integration of women
was arguing:

> There is nothing inherent in what the Army does that must
> be done in a masculine way; therefore, women must be
> offered the opportunity to be feminine and nothing should
> be done to deny women opportunities to be feminine.[8]

The actual experience of women in the military has proved
otherwise—those who are most masculine are most successful
leading men, and those who retain their femininity receive the
least respect. "People just don't give you commands [of units]
when you're pregnant," complained a female West Point graduate. "They want you in the staff someplace."[9]

Feminists, nevertheless, have always insisted that the attri-
butes of a leader are neither masculine nor feminine, that

virtues traditionally considered masculine or feminine can be found in both sexes, and that the military should look for an androgynous or "ungendered" model of leadership not based upon the ubiquitous male model. Some feminists, indeed, hold androgyny to be the ideal for both sexes. They seek to make the words *masculine* and *feminine* meaningless, except in reference to genitalia. Most feminists, however, being women, continue to favor traditionally feminine characteristics.

Attempts by the services to reconcile a masculine military and a feminist philosophy have produced strange results. Service women here and there have become somewhat more masculine, but in general the military has been thoroughly feminized. The modern military has trivialized combat as incidental to military service and relegated readiness to secondary status behind the more pressing concern for equal opportunity. The dictum "every Marine, a rifleman" is no longer true. The Army's Basic Combat Training is now just Basic Training, with many of the more rigorous drills gone and self-esteem more important than physical fitness. The Army, after all, is a "caring" organization:

> We want soldiers, of all ranks, feeling they belong to a "family".... Building the "family" requires a professional sensitivity toward and caring for one another.... We want these professional, caring relationships because they are necessary to build the vertical bonds which tie leader to led.[10]

In 1986 the Army published a definition of the "warrior spirit" that said nothing about combativeness, aggressiveness, an eagerness to fight, a willingness to die, or the courage to kill. Instead, even under Reagan, soldiers were told that military values mirrored "the ethic of our people which denies any assertive national power doctrine and projects a love and mercy to all."[11] The military existed to protect the "supremacy of the individual" and therefore needed leaders "who embrace a value system that places the individual soldier and citizen at the center of society."[12]

340 • WOMEN IN THE MILITARY

Such nonsense preceded Morris by more than a decade. During that time, the revolutionaries intent upon destroying the military have spoken more and more boldly. Their leading critics meanwhile have marshalled arguments only against the lost cause of women in combat, conceding the good of having women everywhere else in the military. Never mind that every single argument against women in combat roles can also be made against women in so-called noncombat roles. Never mind that the distinction between combat and noncombat is entirely arbitrary, that it existed only to provide a place for women, and that it served only to expand their participation continually. Never mind the fundamental absurdity of a "noncombat military" that requires discipline, efficiency, and optimum effectiveness only of its withered combat arm.

No one, it seems, is courageous enough to approach the issue of women in the military as one would any other issue, analyzing it with cold rationality in the simple terms of costs versus benefits. The problem, of course, with weighing the pluses and minuses of using women in the military is that there are too many minuses. A partial list would include higher rates of attrition, greater need for medical care, higher rates of nonavailability, lower rates of deployability, lesser physical ability, aggravated problems of single-parenthood, dual-service marriages, fraternization, sexual harassment, sexual promiscuity, and homosexuality, all of which adversely affect unit cohesion, morale, and the fighting spirit of the armed forces.

Against these many disadvantages, women offer the military one single advantage: they are better behaved. They lose less time for disciplinary reasons and are less prone to drug and alcohol abuse. And even this is not true for the Air Force, where men are as well behaved as women.

From a strict cost-benefit standpoint, the military use of women makes sense for only a handful of jobs, largely in the medical professions, where the military's need for doctors, nurses, and medical specialists well outweighs any difficulty of using women. For all other military jobs, the only reason to use women is not a military reason. It is a political reason driven by an ideology that is hostile to the military, according to which the advancement of women, under the euphemism of "equal opportunity," trumps the needs of the military and the cause of national defense.

With all the accumulated evidence of the past quarter of a century, the nation's top military leaders have no excuse for pretending that the presence of women in the military has been for the good of the armed forces. Initially they went along with this ruse for fear that without women the all-volunteer armed forces would not be able to meet its requirements. It is debatable whether this was ever true. The All-Volunteer Force was never allowed to work without women. At the start, its architects resorted to greater use of women without considering the possibility that an all-male military, with its distinctly masculine appeal, might attract more young men than a more feminine force.

Women are no longer needed in the military, and their presence is destroying the military's body and soul.

Now, however, with a military that is a full 30 percent smaller than it was ten years ago (down from 2.1 million members in 1988 to 1.5 million members at the end of 1996), no one can seriously argue that the military must recruit women to make up for the lack of men. During the drastic downsizing of the post–Cold War age, the military was forced to go easy on women and expand their percentage in the ranks (from 10.3 to 13.5), while simultaneously discharging many good men, many of them involuntarily and some just prior to retirement.

The simple facts are that women are no longer needed in the military and their expanding presence is destroying the military's body and soul. Without doubt the worst effect of integration on the armed forces is "the general retreat of honor and integrity" prophesied in *Weak Link*, my first book on this subject. The widely known but unaccepted truth is that most of what our senior civilian and military leaders tell us about women in the military is a lie.

It is a lie that military women are meeting the same standards as men. The truth is that women enjoy preference and protection in a variety of forms. Nowhere are women required to meet the same physical standards as men, and nowhere are women subjected to the military's sternest trials of mind and body that many men face. Promotions and assignments are governed by quotas, theoretically illegal but nevertheless universally used and never admitted. Pregnancy remains the only "temporary disability" that gives a service member the option of breaking a service contract without penalty. It is also the only disability for which service members cannot be punished for deliberately inflicting upon themselves. Applying the same standards to men and women has repeatedly proved to be impossible, for it conflicts with the overriding political and ideological interest in advancing women over men.

It is a lie that the presence of women has had only a positive effect on military readiness. The truth is that the overall effect of integration has been a general softening of military service. Conditions and performance requirements that aggravate attrition among women and expose their limited abilities have been systematically eliminated. The "LaBarge Touch," with its myopic focus on getting recruits through training instead of preparing them for wartime service, has cheated the field and fleet of the highly trained and capable manpower needed to fight and win. The modern military's emphasis on self-esteem and "positive motivation," inspired by the need to protect women from the harshness of military life, has led the military to an excessive reliance upon leadership and a potentially fatal neglect of discipline.

It is a lie that the victimization of women is a product of a patriarchal culture that distinguishes male from female and orders them appropriately. The truth is that women are most victimized where they are most liberated. It is the modern world that sets the sexes at odds, that teaches boys to muscle girls on the court and on the field, that forces men to see women only as competitors and opponents. In the patriarchal world of old, the strong were obliged to serve the weak. Men and women strove to be gentlemen and ladies. Men were taught to protect women, to bear a woman's burdens, and to watch their language in her presence. Chivalry honored women with care and safety if not with freedom, at least not the freedom to be men. Today, women are free to live as coarsely and as brutally as men, while men are "desensitized" to the suffering of women in training. Yet, somehow, when women discern the slightest offense, the old ways are always to blame.

These are the lies that our military today lives by. These are the lies that our officers force upon their subordinates with Soviet slavishness. From the top down, the example to follow is one of cowardly, self-protective deceit.

Duty in the American military means doing as one is told. Obedience to civilian control is the supreme law. Defying that control, even publicly protesting it, is unthinkable. The American military has no tradition of honorable dissent, of standing upon principle against official policy. Its officers do not fall on their swords for anything. The lessons they learn early in their careers are "get with the program," be a "team player," "go along to get along," "cooperate and graduate." They follow orders even if it means acting contrary to conscience, even if it means saying things in public that they do not personally believe, even if it means punishing the innocent and rewarding the undeserving.

The feminization of the American military is no longer a story of reluctant admirals and generals forced to do things against their better judgment by unsympathetic politicians. After more than two decades of political correctness, the military men and women who have survived to become today's admirals and generals are themselves either true believers in the military's unmaking or unprincipled opportunists who enthusiastically persecute the men under them to protect and advance their own careers, who will not put their stars on the

344 • WOMEN IN THE MILITARY

table to see justice done and the defense of the nation assured. Sworn to defend the Constitution, they in fact defend nothing but the status quo, the powers that be, the corrupt regime of which they are a part. They believe in nothing else. They know no other god. They serve only themselves and their careers.

The single greatest lesson of the late twentieth century is that lies so contrary to nature cannot live forever. Half of the world once lived under communism until, finally, that lie lost its power. Without terror to maintain it, it became a joke, and then it died.

In the second thoughts and open doubts lately expressed in odd corners, we may be seeing the lie of integration turning into a joke. Let us hope the joke spreads before the American military is reduced to a cowardly and corrupt institution, a high-tech danger to free peoples at home and abroad.

Appendix

TESTIMONY OF BRIAN MITCHELL

Before the Presidential Commission on the Assignment
of Women in the Armed Forces

MAY 4, 1992

I'D LIKE TO THANK the Commission and its staff for inviting
me here today. I certainly hope I can assist the Commission in
making sense of the issue.

There are just two ways to see this issue, and two sides to
take in the debate. One side believes that men and women are
fundamentally different and will always remain so; the other
side believes that men and women are pretty much the same
and that their differences are either insignificant or eradicable.
One side wants society to remain much as we have always
known it; the other wants revolutionary change, with an utterly
androgynous society as a result.

The one side generally argues against expanding the role of
women in the military on the basis of military effectiveness; the
other side argues for expanding the role of women in the military in the interest of equal opportunity.

Those are our choices, but before choosing sides, let's get
one thing straight: The latter choice is not really for equal
opportunity, but merely for opportunities for some women. It's
not equal opportunity when the services are forced to pay more

to employ women—more for medical care, for higher attrition rates, and for lower rates of availability. It's not equal opportunity when standards are "gender-normed" to get women into jobs for which they are otherwise unqualified. It's not equal opportunity when quotas are used in promotions and assignments to advance and protect women against men.

If you have any doubt about the use of illegal quotas by the military, I recommend to you two articles, one of which appeared last January in *Army Times*, the other of which appeared last year in *Military Law Review*. As a result of these two articles, a lawyer here in town—a former head of the Army Judge Advocate General's very own litigation division—is now preparing a class-action lawsuit charging the Army with discrimination against literally tens of thousands of servicemen because of their race and gender.

No, the policy that we have today in the military is not equal opportunity, but deliberately unequal opportunity. That's what the revolutionaries demand and that's what the military is giving them.

It will surprise no one that I reject this injustice and the arguments used to advance it. I reject the notion that the differences between men and women are insignificant. The evidence is plain and plentiful that they are not. I also reject the notion that there exists some overriding moral imperative that requires us to provide a place for women in the military, regardless of the differences. No God that I know requires it. Even our Constitution, which some (for their own purposes) would make a god, requires no such thing.

We don't owe anyone a military career. Everyone serves as he is needed, to be dismissed when he is needed no longer. That is what it means to serve. To obligate the military to employ certain people is to make the military the servant of its members, a complete reversal of the natural relationship between the service and the serviceman.

I also reject the canard that ties full citizenship to military service. Citizenship has never depended upon military service.

Our military today includes many members who are not citizens, and the vast majority of our voting public are not veterans. Our nonveterans include the present secretary of defense and several major presidential candidates.

We do have a moral imperative to obey in this business, but it is to provide for the best defense of the nation. Military effectiveness, with few exceptions, should therefore be our only concern. The question we must ask ourselves repeatedly is: Does a policy enhance or degrade the ability of the military to fulfill its purpose?

In answering this question, I recommend that we avoid all debate on the issue of combat versus noncombat. It is a great waste of words. The distinction between combat and noncombat is purely descriptive and never definitive. The only reason it is made at all is to say where women may serve or where they may not serve. The line between the two is always drawn arbitrarily. Even the Army's elaborate combat probability coding is nothing more than a pseudo-scientific disguise for arbitrariness.

The services are, *in toto*, combat organizations. They exist to do combat. Anything that degrades their efficiency or readiness, degrades their ability to do combat. Support units that operate less efficiently hinder the operation of the units they support. Resources expended to accommodate women in support units are resources that could have been used to enlarge combat capability. Our approach to the military use of women must therefore be comprehensive. We must consider all things, every inconvenient item that bears upon the military's overall effectiveness.

Very often the revolutionaries will attempt to limit the debate to the ability to do the job, ignoring every other consideration. If a woman can "do the job," they argue, the military should then spare no expense to allow her to do it. Notice, however, that this is an appeal to ideology—to the notion that we owe qualified women a place in the military. There is no military reason why our debate should be so limited.

Often the same people will point to similarities between men and women and invite us to marvel at how much alike the sexes are, and at how much women can accomplish when given the chance. This is nothing but a ploy to divert our attention from the very real differences between the sexes. And the differences are all that matter. The similarities are of no account. When we weigh the relative merits of using men and women in the military, the similarities are neutral. They tell us nothing we need to know, except that we must look elsewhere for the differences.

To avoid such distractions, I suggest re-phrasing our question in terms of substitution: if we substitute a woman for a man, will the military be helped or hindered?

The present draw-down in forces has made answering this question much easier by eliminating completely the argument that women are needed, despite their disadvantages, "to make the All-Volunteer Force work." Today we can get all the men we need. The question of whether to employ women instead of men is therefore reduced to a simple matter of advantages versus disadvantages.

The disadvantages of substituting women for men are many. I will name just a few, without argument:

- higher rates of attrition
- greater need for medical care
- higher rates of nonavailability
- lower rates of deployability
- lesser physical ability

I would add to this list a number of problems that are aggravated if not caused by substituting women for men:

- single-parenthood
- in-service marriages
- fraternization
- sexual harassment
- sexual promiscuity
- homosexuality

A few disadvantages are harder to observe and measure, but should not be discounted. They include the deleterious effects of the presence of women on unit cohesion, the fighting spirit, and loyalty and respect that servicemen feel toward their service.

Don't be misled by the services' claims to have solved this or that problem. Most of their solutions merely involve shifting the burden of the problem from one account to another. The military "solves" the problem of the greater need for medical care among women by hiring more gynecologists and obstetricians. It "solves" the problem of separating mothers from their children during wartime by granting servicewomen deferments from war. The bottom line of such solutions is inevitably increased costs and decreased readiness.

Even drastic solutions, such as discharging women who become mothers or single parents, are really no solution at all, because they would greatly aggravate attrition rates, thereby reducing the military's return on its recruitment and training investment. As attrition goes up, the justification for recruiting women goes down. The only way to truly solve these problems is to not recruit women.

What of the advantages of using women? There is only one: women are better behaved than men. They miss less time for disciplinary reasons and are less prone to drug and alcohol abuse. This is much less of an advantage today than it once was. As the Defense Department will tell you, proudly, drug and alcohol abuse and disciplinary problems aren't nearly as bad today as they were in the late 1970s. They should be even less of a problem in the 1990s, as the shrinking military becomes more choosy about whom it recruits. At present, I hardly think this one advantage outweighs the many disadvantages.

I'll say again that the ability of many women to perform many military jobs just as well as men is not an advantage. It is not a reason to replace a man with a woman. It becomes an advantage only when the woman can perform the job much better than the man. It becomes a reason to replace the man only if the woman's performance is so much better that it outweighs all of the disadvantages of employing women.

Following my line of reasoning, one would have to conclude that the service in which it makes the least sense to employ women is, surprisingly, the Air Force. Why? Because Air Force enlisted men are much better behaved than enlisted men in the other services, so that women present only disadvantages to the Air Force, no advantages. At least two Air Force studies have documented these disadvantages, and one of those went so far as to conclude that increasing the number of women in the Air Force necessitates significantly increasing the Air Force's end strength and personnel budget.

Is there a place at all for women in the military? There is, in fact, even if one's only concern is the good of the military. Women are desperately needed as military doctors and nurses, for the very reason that the military cannot get enough doctors and nurses, male or female, as it is. There may be other jobs for which the need justifies the cost. Those jobs ought to be open to women.

For all other jobs, however, we must admit that there are simply no compelling military reasons to fill them with women instead of men. "This is a hard saying. Who can bear it?" And yet simple logic forces us to that conclusion. Any other answer, any attempt to "balance" the interests of military effectiveness and opportunities for women, is a compromise and a sure sacrifice of national security to an unworthy end.

Of course, many will say that only a compromise is politically possible. In response, I would say that if the American people want a compromise, then they should be fully informed of the seriousness of the sacrifice. So far, they have been fed a line about how the inclusion of large numbers of women in the military doesn't degrade readiness in the least. If this commission does nothing else, it should set the record straight and give the American people an honest choice.

NOTES

NOTES ON THE INTRODUCTION

1. Rowan Scarborough, "Top Army woman: Marines 'extremist,'" *Washington Times,* November 13, 1997.

2. Sandra L. Beckwith, "Teaching Women to Soldier: The LaBarge Touch," *Army,* March 1982, 44.

3. Paul Richter, "Boot Camp Kicks Its Harsh Image," *Los Angeles Times,* October 26, 1997.

4. Jackie Spinner, "The New Drill Sergeant," *Washington Post,* August 14, 1997.

5. An analysis of the historical use of women by the militaries of countries other than the United States is beyond the scope of this book. For more on Israel, see Chapter 9.

NOTES ON CHAPTER 1

1. U.S. Marine Corps, History and Museums Division, "The Legend of Lucy Brewer," 1957. This report lists a number of objections to Lucy's claim, the only basis for which is a series of pamphlets Lucy wrote and published after the war. Among the report's objections: the similarity between some of Lucy's accounts of the *Constitution's* naval engagements and contemporary newspaper reports; the unlikelihood that Lucy, as an inexperienced marksman, would have been assigned as a sharpshooter in "the fighting tops," as she claimed she was; her accounts' overabundance of technical detail, of which a Marine at his post in the topsails would have had no knowledge; and the fact that Marine Corps regulations at the time required all Marine recruits to strip, bathe, and don a Marine uniform in the

presence of their commander, who would have been derelict in his duties not to ascertain the physical condition of the men in his charge. Among those who have perpetuated the myth of "the first girl Marine" are Martin Binkin and Shirley Bach in *Women and the Military* (Washington, D.C.: Brookings Institution, 1977), 5, and Jeanne Holm in *Women in the Military: An Unfinished Revolution* (Novato, Calif.: Presidio Press, 1982), 3.

2. WAC strength peaked at 99,000 in April 1945. The WAVES, SPARS, and Women Marines peaked in September 1945 with 83,000. The remainder of the 266,000 were Army and Navy nurses.

3. Robert R. Palmer et al., *The Procurement and Training of Ground Combat Troops* (Washington, D.C.: Historical Division, Department of the Army, 1948), 41. Between August and November 1943, the Army alone discharged 55,000 men as ineligible for overseas assignment because of such things as missing teeth, hernia, perforated eardrums, and excessive nervousness.

4. Palmer, 212.

5. U.S. Navy, Bureau of Naval Personnel, "History of the Women's Reserve," an unpublished draft manuscript produced in 1946, 153. Navy units, particularly medical units, reported that men bore up much better under the strain of being overworked, while women suffered inordinate rates of stress-related breakdown working the same hours as the men.

6. Mattie E. Treadwell, *The Women's Army Corps* (Washington, D.C.: Office of the Chief of Military History, Department of the Army, 1954), 711–712. Treadwell, herself a WAC veteran, produced this thorough history of both the successes and failures of the WAC nine years after the war's end. The Navy's unpublished history of the WAVES was written within the first year after V-J day and is entirely too self-congratulatory to give an adequate appraisal of the WAVES's record.

7. Treadwell, 460.

8. Quoted by Holm, 159.

9. Quoted by Holm, 182.

10. Officers of all services hold pay grades numbered 1 to 10 in increasing seniority. Each grade has a corresponding rank, though ranks vary depending upon the service. An O-3 in the Army is a captain, but a captain in the Navy is an O-6. An O-6 in the Army, Air Force, and Marines is a colonel. Admirals and generals are O-7s, 8s, 9s, or 10s and are often called flag officers.

11. Flag officers are still sometimes asked to take reductions in rank to accept certain positions. When General Andrew J. Goodpaster took over as superintendent of the U.S. Military Academy at West

Point, he accepted a reduction to lieutenant general, the highest rank authorized for the superintendency. Prior to 1967 the women's components were, in a sense, miniature armies. The system for managing women's promotions and assignments therefore resembled the way promotions and assignments are managed by smaller foreign armies, in which an officer must resign, retire, or die before another can move up.

12. Holm, 199.

13. Margaret Eastman, "DACOWITS: A Nice Little Group That Doesn't Do Very Much," *Army Times*, Family Supplement, March 15, 1972, 11.

14. Thomas D. Morris, assistant secretary of defense for manpower. Statement before the House Armed Services Committee on a proposal to remove restrictions on female officer promotions.

15. The same House report admitted: "It is recognized that a male officer in arriving at the point where he may be considered for general and flag rank passes through a crucible to which the woman officer is not subjected—such as combat, long tours at sea, and other dangers and isolations."

16. Holm, 197.

17. Quoted by Holm, 192.

NOTES ON CHAPTER 2

1. National Advisory Commission on Selective Service, *In Pursuit of Equity: Who Serves When Not All Serve?* (Washington, D.C.: GPO, 1967).

2. Richard M. Nixon, "The All-Volunteer Armed Force," address given over the CBS Radio Network on Thursday, October 17, 1968.

3. President's Commission on an All-Volunteer Armed Force, *The Report of the President's Commission on an All-Volunteer Armed Force* (New York: The MacMillan Company, 1970).

4. U.S. Comptroller General, *Additional Cost of the All-Volunteer Force* (Washington, D.C.: GPO, 1978), ii.

5. *Congress and the Nation* (Washington, D.C.: Congressional Quarterly, Inc., 1973), III, 510. In arguing against exemptions from combat, Bayh minimized the likelihood of just what he was arguing for, a common tactic among radical reformers. He said, "There is an extremely small likelihood that any [women] will really reach combat service."

6. Among them were Senators Howard Baker of Tennessee and Robert Dole of Kansas. The defeat of the military service exemptions made the ERA unacceptable to more Americans.

7. Report 92-51 of the Special Subcommittee on the Utilization of Manpower in the Military.

8. Central All-Volunteer Task Force, *Utilization of Military Women* (Washington, D.C.: Department of Defense, 1972).

9. Martin Binkin and John D. Johnston, *All-Volunteer Armed Forces: Progress, Problems, and Prospects* (Washington, D.C.: GPO, 1973), 3.

10. Martin Binkin and Shirley Bach, *Women and the Military* (Washington, D.C.: Brookings Institution, 1977).

11. *Frontiero v. Richardson*, 36 L.Ed. 2d 583 (U.S. Supreme Ct. 1973). Noting that the Equal Rights Amendment, then before the states, would have accomplished the same effect as Brennan's characterization of sex as "inherently suspect," Powell argued that "the Court has assumed a decisional responsibility at the very time when state legislatures, functioning within the traditional democratic process, are debating the proposed Amendment." Brennan's opinion therefore did not show the proper "respect for duly prescribed legislative processes."

Rehnquist agreed with the District Court's ruling that the military would have required all members to prove dependency of a spouse, as it required all members to prove dependency of other adults, if that were administratively feasible. Because it was not, the military was simply trying to curb the excess of benefits on the basis of probability. It was highly probable that the wives of servicemen were in fact dependent upon their husbands for primary support, but it was unlikely that the husbands of servicewomen were primarily supported by their wives. Probability, not sex, therefore, was the determining factor. See *Frontiero v. Laird*, 341 Federal Supplement 201 (U.S. Dist. Ct. 1972).

12. "Sex Equality: Impact of a Key Decision," *U.S. News & World Report*, May 28, 1973, 69.

13. *Schlesinger v. Ballard*, 42 L.Ed. 2d 610.

14. Hébert's first claim to fame was as city editor of the *New Orleans Times-Picayune* when the paper broke the Huey Long scandals in 1939.

15. Defense Advisory Committee on Women in the Services, "Recommendations made at the 1974 Spring Meeting," April 25, 1974, 2.

16. Albert P. Clark, "Women at the Service Academies and Combat Leadership," *Strategic Review,* Fall 1977, 67.

17. Hearings before the House Armed Services Committee, 94th Congress, "Eliminate Discrimination Based on Sex for Admission to the Five Federal Service Academics" (Washington, D.C.: GPO, 1974), 165.

18. Ibid, 137.

19. Ibid, 256.

20. Ibid, 265.

21. Judith Hicks Stiehm, *Bring Me Men and Women: Mandated Change at the U.S. Air Force Academy* (Berkeley, Calif.: University of California Press, 1981), 38.

NOTES ON CHAPTER 3

1. The rumor that "Bring Me Men" was later removed is not true.

2. Office of Institutional Research, "Women in the Classes 1980–1990: The First Decade" (Colorado Springs, Colo.: U.S. Air Force Academy, September 1986). The Air Force Academy Class of 1986 was the only other class where male attrition exceeded female attrition, 35.9 percent to 32.1 percent. It was also the only other academy class where the female rate was below 40 percent. The only classes with male rates above 40 percent were 1980 and 1982, with 44.4 and 42.3 percent, respectively.

3. Judith Hicks Stiehm, *Bring Me Men and Women: Mandated Change at the U.S. Air Force Academy* (Berkeley, Calif.: University of California Press, 1981), 99.

4. At the time, only 5 percent of Air Force officers were women, but expecting a higher rate of attrition among female cadets and an increased requirement for women officers in the future, the Air Force decided that 11 percent of the Class of 1980 would be female.

5. Lois B. DeFleur, Dickie Harris, and Christine Mattley, "Career, Marriage and Family Orientations of Future Air Force Officers," 20. DeFleur and William Marshak, "Changing Attitudes Toward Women's Roles and Women in the Military at the U.S. Air Force Academy," 13.

6. Lois B. DeFleur, Frank Woods, Dick Harris, David Gillman, and William Marshak, *Four Years of Sex Integration at the United States Air Force Academy: Problems and Issues* (Colorado Springs, Colo.: U.S. Air Force Academy, August 1985), 168.

7. One might extend this analysis to the entire experience at the academy BCT would be the rite of separation, four years of education and training would serve as the rite of transition, and the rite of incorporation would be the commissioning of new Air Force second lieutenants.

8. Lois B. DeFleur, David Gillman, and William Marshak, "The Development of Military Professionalism Among Male and Female

Air Force Academy Cadets," 168. Upon entry, cadets were given physical aptitude tests. Males averaged eleven pull-ups. Females averaged 24.1 seconds of the "flexed arm hang."

9. Lois B. DeFleur, David Gillman, and William Marshak, "Sex Integration of the U.S. Air Force Academy: Changing Roles for Women," *Armed Forces and Society*, August 1978, 615.

10. David Gillman and William Marshak, "The Integration of Women into a Male Initiation Rite: A Case Study of the USAF Academy," 16.

11. Ibid, 15.

12. Ibid, 18, 23.

13. *Four Years of Sex Integration at the United States Air Force Academy: Problems and Issues*, 168.

14. Stiehm, 264.

15. *Four Years of Sex Integration at the United States Air Force Academy: Problems and Issues*, 167.

16. This particular cadet finished her academic exams for the year but did not participate in "Hell Week," a final week of harassment before doolies became third-classmen. Hell Week was traditionally the week before final exams, but for the Class of 1980 it was the week after exams, a variation intended to ensure that the stress of Hell Week did not interfere with the women's performance on final exams.

17. Stiehm, 83.

18. Quoted by Stiehm, 257–259. In a 1988 interview, Allen said integration "went very well" and cited as proof the praise the Air Force Academy received from Congress, the press, and the Carter administration. He insisted that male and female cadets were held to the same standards, which were merely "applied differently."

19. Lois B. DeFleur and William Marshak, "Changing Attitudes Towards Women's Roles and Women in the Military at the U.S. Air Force Academy," 13.

20. "Air Force Academy Has Inevitable First—Pregnant Cadet Quits," *Denver Post*, March 11, 1977, 3.

21. "So Far, So Good: A Report Card on Coeducational Military Academies," *U.S. News & World Report*, July 11, 1977, 30.

22. "Female Cadets: a rough start," *Science News*, September 15, 1979, 182.

23. With an actual male attrition rate of 44 percent, the Class of 1980 graduated 798 men and 97 women, for a total of 895. If the male attrition rate had been 35 percent, the average rate of previous classes, the Class of 1980 would have graduated 933 men alone. If the

number of women had stayed the same, the graduating strength would have been 1,030.

NOTES ON CHAPTER 4

1. "So Far, So Good: A Report Card on Coeducational Military Academies," *U.S. News & World Report*, July 11, 1977, 26. West Point officials had been warned by female drill sergeants at Fort Knox, Kentucky, and Fort McClellan, Alabama, that female recruits often took advantage of male drill sergeants, who tended to treat them less roughly than they treated the men.

2. Kathleen P. Durning, *Women at the Naval Academy: The First Year of Integration* (San Diego, Calif.: Navy Personnel Research and Development Center, 1978), 20.

3. Department of Behavioral Sciences and Leadership, *Project Athena: Report on the Admission of Women to the U.S. Military Academy* (West Point, N.Y.: U.S. Military Academy, June 1, 1979) Vols. I–IV.

4. Helen Rogan, *Mixed Company: Women in the Modern Army* (New York: G.P. Putnam's Sons, 1981), 199.

5. Lieutenant General Sidney B. Berry, "Women Cadets at West Point," Address to the Defense Advisory Committee on Women in the Services, Washington, D.C., November 16, 1976.

6. *Project Athena*, Vol. IV, 48.

7. Rear Admiral William P. Lawrence, letter published in *The Washingtonian*, January 1980.

8. James H. Webb, Jr., "Women Can't Fight," *The Washingtonian*, November 1979.

9. James Feron, "West Point '78 Closing Book on Cheating '76," the *New York Times*, June 5, 1978, D9. The General Order of Merit was not so sinister as it was made out to be. The last man to graduate in each class was honored as the "goat" at West Point, the "anchorman" at the Annapolis, and "Tail End Charlie" at the Air Force Academy. Tradition held that the last man received a dollar from each of his classmates. Famous goats include George A. Custer, George E. Pickett of "Pickett's charge," and one superintendent of the academy.

10. See John P. Lovell's "Modernization and Growth of the Service Academies: Some Organizational Consequences," in *The Changing World of the American Military*, Franklin D. Margiotta, ed. (Boulder, Colo.: Westview, 1978). Lovell says that prior to World War II, the academies were essentially "military seminaries," run faithfully as they had been since founding, with knowledge of the fourth-class

system passed from class to class. The growth of the military bureaucracy in America forced the academies to codify their policies, taking control of the class system out of the cadets' hands and putting it into the hands of the academy administrators.

11. Rogan, 188. Rogan says that Berry almost resigned rather than accept the mission of integrating West Point. In an interview, Berry said he might have mentioned resigning in an off-hand remark but he never seriously considered it.

12. James A. Salter, "It's Not the Old Point," *Life*, May 1980, 76. Salter is a 1945 graduate of West Point.

13. Feron, "West Point '78 Closing Book on Cheating '76."

14. James Feron, "West Point Concedes Some Hazing Tactics Have Been 'Sexist,'" *New York Times*, November 10, 1979, 25.

15. In the first case, the academy dropped the charges and allowed the cadet to graduate with his class to avoid a court ruling that might have had far-reaching effects on the cadet honor system. In the second case, Alexander had first requested that Goodpaster simply review the case before taking action. Goodpaster did so and concurred with the honor committee's recommendation for dismissal. Alexander then overruled Goodpaster's determination on the basis of an unstated "collateral issue." The cadet was reinstated with a lesser punishment.

16. Committee on the Integration of Women into the Cadet Wing, "Recommendations: Report on the Integration of Women into the Cadet Wing," U.S. Air Force Academy, July 1984, 13–15. Oddly, after months of interviews and surveys, the committee produced no written findings, only thirty pages of recommendations.

17. Committee on the Integration of Women into the Cadet Wing, 12–18, 27.

18. Salter, 76.

19. General Douglas A. MacArthur, "Duty, Honor, Country," Address to the Corps of Cadets of the United States Military Academy on May 12, 1962.

20. Lawrence, 18.

21. *Project Athena*, Vol. III, 12.

22. Feron, "West Point '78 Closing Book on Cheating '76."

23. Committee on the Integration of Women into the Cadet Wing, 1.

24. Lois B. DeFleur, Frank Woods, Dick Harris, David Gillman, and William Marshak, *Four Years of Sex Integration at the United States Air Force Academy: Problems & Issues* (Colorado Springs, Colo.: U.S. Air Force Academy, August 1985).

25. Committee on the Integration of Women into the Cadet Wing, 23. The committee also recommended making miniature academy class rings unavailable to anyone but female cadets. For decades, "miniatures" have been given as engagement rings to fiancées and as special gifts to mothers. The committee deemed this a devaluation of identical rings worn by female graduates, but the academy rejected the recommendation.

26. Jerome Adams, *Project Proteus* (West Point, N.Y.: U.S. Military Academy, 1984), Vol. II, 3-19 and 3-20.

27. Esther B. Fein, "The Choice: Women Officers Decide to Stay In or Leave," *New York Times Magazine*, May 5, 1985, 45.

28. Adams, 3-38.

29. C.H. "Max" Freedman, "Navy Valedictorian and Feminism Stole Male Cadet's Award," *New York Tribune*, June 1, 1984, 2B.

NOTES ON CHAPTER 5

1. Office of the Assistant Secretary of Defense for Manpower, Reserve Affairs, and Logistics, *Use of Women in the Military* (Washington, D.C.: Department of Defense, May 1977). Binkin and Bach estimated saving as much as $6 billion annually.

2. Martin Binkin and Shirley Bach, *Women and the Military* (Washington, D.C.: The Brookings Institution, 1977).

3. Office of the Assistant Secretary of Defense for Manpower, Reserve Affairs, and Logistics, *Background Review: Women in the Military* (Washington, D.C.: Department of Defense, 1981), 144.

4. Memorandum from the Commanding Officer, USS *Sanctuary*, to the Chief of Naval Operations, "Evaluation of Women Aboard the USS *Sanctuary*," November 19, 1973, 13.

5. *Final Report: Evaluation of Women in the Army* (Ft. Ben. Harrison, Ind.: Department of the Army, 1978), 1–18.

6. George Gilder, "The Case Against Women in Combat," *The New York Times Magazine*, January 28, 1979.

7. Quoted by Seth Cropsey in "The Military Manpower Crisis: Women in Combat," *The Public Interest*, Fall 1980, 66.

8. Hearings before the Military Personnel Subcommittee of the House Armed Services Committee, November 13–16, 1979 and February 11, 1980, 232.

9. Hearings, 238.

10. The Coalition Against Drafting Women included, among others: Sen. Jesse Helms, Rep. Marjorie Holt, Rep. Richard Ichord, Marine Corps Gen. Lewis W. Walt, Army Lt. Gen. Daniel O. Graham, Army Maj. Gen. Henry Mohr, Army Maj. Gen. John K. Singlaub,

Rabbi Herman N. Neuberger, Dr. Bob Billings, Dr. Gregg Dixon, Dr. Bill Pennell, the Rev. Jerry Falwell, and representatives of the National Council of Catholic Women, the American Security Council, the Conservative Caucus, Young Americans for Freedom, Family America, and the Moral Majority. All of the military men were retired.

11. Senators Sam Nunn, Jake Garn, Roger Jepsen, and John Warner had led the fight against inclusion. Among those who voted to register women were Senators John Glenn, Howard Metzenbaum, William Proxmire, and Bill Bradley. Senators Edward Kennedy, George McGovern, Frank Church, and Joseph Biden, though reliable supporters of feminist causes, did not vote.

12. *Rostker* v. *Goldberg*, 69 LEd 2d 478.

NOTES ON CHAPTER 6

1. Office of the Assistant Secretary of Defense for Manpower, Reserve Affairs, & Logistics, *Background Review: Women in the Military* (Washington, D.C.: Department of Defense, October 1981), 7. See page 81 for data.

2. Office of the Deputy Chief of Staff for Personnel, *Women in the Amry Policy Review* (Washington, D.C.: Department of the Army, November 12, 1982), 4–9.

3. *Final Report: Evaluation of Women in the Army* (Ft. Ben. Harrison, Ind.: Department of the Army, 1978), 1–18.

4. Before either the MEPSCAT or the categorization of an MOS could be trusted to predict accurately a recruit's ability to perform in an MOS, the entire system required "validation." To ensure accuracy, the system would be validated by both the Army Research Institute and a commercial research contractor with extensive experience in the study of physical performance but no previous involvement in the WITA project. The validation process was expected to take more than a year. It had just started when the WITA review group released its final report in the fall of 1982.

5. Margaret Eastman, "DACOWITS: a nice little group that doesn't do very much," *Army Times*, Family Supplement, March 15, 1972, 11.

6. DACOWITS, Recommendations Made at the 1974 Spring Meeting, April 21–25, 1974, 2.

7. DACOWITS, Recommendations Made at the 1975 Spring Meeting, April 6–10, 1975, 2.

8. DACOWITS, Recommendations, Requests for Information, Commendations Made at the 1976 Fall Meeting, November 14–18, 1976, 1.

9. DACOWITS, Recommendations etc., 1976 Fall Meeting, 2.

10. "Women Can Do Anything Men Can Do," *Air Force Times*, November 29, 1976, 2.

11. "DACOWITS: 'Actions' Hurt Women's Morale," *Air Force Times*, November 30, 1981, 16.

12. M.C. Devilbiss, "'Women in the Army Policy Review'—A Military Sociologist's Analysis," *Minerva*, Fall 1983, 95. Believers in WITA have nothing to fear from this "analysis."

13. Mary Evelyn Blagg Huey, Letter to Caspar W. Weinberger, June 6, 1983.

14. Caspar W. Weinberger, Letter to Mary Evelyn Blagg Huey, July 27, 1983.

15. Caspar W. Weinberger, Memorandum for the Secretaries of the Military Departments, Subject: Women in the Military, July 19, 1983.

16. David C. Myers, Deborah L. Gebhardt, Carolyn E. Crump, and Edwin A. Fleishman, *Validation of the Military Entrance Physical Strength Capacity Test* (Bethesda, Md.: Advanced Research Resources Organization, 1984). The report concluded that the MEPSCAT was "a valid predictor of performance on physically demanding tasks," viii.

NOTES ON CHAPTER 7

1. Minutes to DACOWITS's Spring 1984 Meeting, 6.

2. Lawrence J. Korb, Statement to DACOWITS's Spring 1984 Meeting.

3. "Korb Says Women in Military 'Are Here to Stay,'" *Army Times*, May 14, 1984, 31.

4. Quoted by Senator William Proxmire in the *Congressional Record*, March 21, 1986.

5. Lawrence J. Korb, Statement to DACOWITS's Spring 1984 Meeting.

6. Caspar Weinberger, Statement to DACOWITS's Fall 1986 Meeting.

7. U.S. Air Force Special Studies Team, *An Analysis of the Effects of Varying Male and Female Force Levels* (Washington, D.C.: Department of the Air Force, August 9, 1985).

8. Sharon B. Young, "Need Told for Navy to Define Women's Sea Duty Clearly," *Navy Times*, January 13, 1986.

9. Tom Burgess, "DACOWITS Seeks Closer Look at Women's Role," *Air Force Times*, May 6, 1985, 30.

10. Sharon B. Young, "Navy Secretary Sees Chance of Women Having Greater Combat Support Roles," *Army Times*, November 10, 1986, 45.

11. Sharon B. Young, "Navy Fights Opening More Sea Billets to Women," *Navy Times*, March 23, 1987, 4.

12. Jacquelyn K. Davis, Letter to General Anthony Lukeman, August 26, 1987, subject: DACOWITS's 1987 WESTPAC Visit.

13. Mel Jones, "Gray's Tough Stand on His Responsibility Clarified," *Navy Times*, May 9, 1988, 4.

14. Ibid.

NOTES ON CHAPTER 8

1. See U.S. Army Research Institute for Environmental Medicine, *Incidence of Risk Factors for Injury and Illness among Male and Female Army Basic Trainees*, 1988.

2. Department of Physical Education, *Project Summertime* (West Point, N.Y.: U.S. Military Academy, 1976), 25–30. Differences between men and women were even greater before training, as the physical performance of men actually declined during the eight weeks of training in which little emphasis was placed on strength and power.

3. Martin Binkin and Shirley Bach, *Women and the Military* (Washington, D.C.: The Brookings Institution, 1977), 80.

4. Paul O. Davis, "Physical demands of ships' tasks are a factual matter," *Navy Times*, July 2, 1990. See D.W. Robertson and T.T. Trent, *Documentation of Muscularly Demanding Job Tasks and Validation of an Occupational Strength Test Battery (STB)*; Report No. 86-1, Naval Personnel Research and Development Center, San Diego, Calif., 1985.

5. Colonel R.W. Lind, Office of Assistant Secretary of Defense for Force Management & Personnel, Letter to Penny Pullen, State Representative, Illinois State Assembly, December 6, 1985.

6. Jay Blucher, "Mass Appeal," *Army Times*, July 6, 1987, 68.

7. Blucher, 68.

8. See memo from Colonel Ronald A. Redman, U.S. Air Force, to Dr. Mayer, subject: "The Health of Women in the Services," May 14, 1985; Anne Hoiberg, "Sex and Occupational Differences in Hospitalization Rates Among Navy Enlisted Personnel," *Journal of Occupational Medicine*, October 1980, 686; and Anne Hoiberg, "Health Care Needs of Women in the Navy," *Military Medicine*, February 1979, 109.

9. D.S. Nice and S.M. Hilton, *Sex Differences in Health Care Requirements Aboard U.S. Navy Ships*, report No. 90-2, Naval Health Research Center, San Diego, Calif., 1990.

10. See "Sex Differentials of Time Lost Due to Hospitalization, Male and Female Active Duty Army Personnel: Worldwide, CY 1976–1981," *Supplement to Health of the Army*, December 1983, 60–61; and Hoiberg, "Sex and Occupational Differences in Hospitalization Rates Among Navy Enlisted Personnel," 689.

11. Redman.

12. Quoted by Joyce Price, "Supply of Brain's Pain Killer Tied to Pre-menstrual Blues," *Washington Times*, June 29, 1987, A3.

13. Redman.

14. Ronald A. Redman, "The Feasibility of a Cohort Study on the Health Needs of Women in the Services," Health Studies Task Force, Office of the Assistant Secretary of Defense (Health Affairs), May 15, 1985, 6–7.

15. Office of the Assistant Secretary of Defense, *Military Women in the Department of Defense* (Washington, D.C.: Department of Defense, July 1987), 63.

16. Marjorie H. Royle, *Factors Affecting Attrition Among Marine Corps Women* (San Diego, Calif.: Naval Personnel Research and Development Center, 1985), vii.

17. Jeanne Holm, *Women in the Military: An Unfinished Revolution* (Novato, Calif.: Presidio Press, 1982), 293.

18. Letter from the Chief of Promotion, Separation, and Transition Division, Deputy Chief of Staff for Personnel, Department of the Army, to Department of the Air Force, April 23, 1970, quoted by Holm, 294.

19. Quoted by Holm, 300.

20. "Female GIs in the Field: Report from Honduras" (Evanston, Ill.: Northwestern University, 1985), 17.

21. Charlie Schill, "Navy's Unwed Pregnancy Rate 37%," *Navy Times*, November 28, 1988, 2. The figure of 12.5 percent was taken from the report of the Presidential Commission on the Assignment of Women in the Armed Forces, C-115, and applied to 1996 year-end female strength (197,118).

22. Office of the Assistant Secretary of Defense, *Background Review: Women in the Military* (Washington, D.C.: Department of Defense, 1981), 7.

23. *Background Review: Women in the Military*, 81.

24. Lt. Col. Steven M. Hinds, "Single Parents and the Marine Corps," *Marine Corps Gazette*, January 1989, 64.

25. Message from Commander, U.S. Army Intelligence and Security Command, to subordinate units, subject: "Married Army Couples," November 20, 1986.

26. Minutes, DACOWITS Spring Meeting, 1984, C-7.

27. Royle, vii.

28. Letter from the Adjutant General, U.S. Army, to all commands, subject: "Fraternization and Regulatory Policy Regarding Relationships Between Members of Different Ranks," November 21, 1986.

29. Letter from the Adjutant General.

30. Helen Rogan, *Mixed Company: Women in the Modern Army* (New York: G.P. Putnam's Sons, 1981), 154.

31. Rogan, 155.

32. Ibid, 156.

33. Quoted by Grant Willis, "More Women Than Men Discharged as Homosexuals," *Navy Times*, February 29, 1988, 3.

34. Moskos, 11.

35. Jacquelyn K. Davis, DACOWITS chairwoman, Memo to General Anthony Lukeman, USMC, subject: "1987 WESTPAC Visit of the DACOWITS," August 26, 1987.

36. Grant Willis, "'Witch-Hunt' for Lesbians Never Intended," *Army Times*, March 28, 1988.

37. Willis, "More Women Than Men Discharged as Homosexuals."

38. Quoted by Larry Carney, "Ono Hails Quality of Army's Newest," *Army Times*, June 15, 1987, 8.

39. Martin Binkin and Mark J. Eitelberg, "Women and Minorities in the All-Volunteer Force," in *The All-Volunteer Force After a Decade: Retrospect and Prospect*, ed. William Bowman, et al. (Washington, D.C.: Pergamon-Brassey's, 1986), 96–97. There was no difference on one test segment, word power. The Defense Department has recently added emphasis to the mathematic segments of the test battery and deemphasized the importance of certain clerical segments.

40. Moskos, 5.

41. *Background Review: Women in the Military*, 149.

42. Niel L. Golightly, "No Right to Fight," *U.S. Naval Institute Proceedings*, December 1987, 48.

43. Hoiberg, "Sex and Occupational Differences in Hospitalization Rates Among Navy Enlisted Personnel," 689.

44. John Money and Anke A. Ehrhardt, *Man and Woman, Boy and Girl: The Differentiation and Dimorphism of Gender Identity from Conception to Maturity* (Baltimore, Md.: Johns Hopkins University Press, 1972).

45. Scott Pengelly and James C. Benfield, "Handicapping the Battle of the Sexes," *Washington Post*, September 11, 1988, C3.

46. Eleanor Maccoby and Carol Jacklin, *The Psychology of Sex Differences* (Stanford, Calif.: Stanford University Press, 1974), 242–243.

47. George Gilder, *Men and Marriage* (Gretna, Louis.: Pelican Books Publishing Co., 1986), 33.

48. Allen Carrier, "Defense EO Chief Decries End of Army Coed Basic," *Army Times*, July 12, 1982, 28.

49. Moskos, 10.

50. Quoted by Theodore C. Mataxis, "How Realistic Are Female Test Scores?" *Army Times*, March 21, 1977, 15.

NOTES ON CHAPTER 9

1. Jean Bethke Elshtain, *Women and War* (New York: Basic Books, 1987), 231.

2. Panel discussion, in *Registration and the Draft*, Martin Anderson, ed. (Stanford, Calif.: Hoover Institution, 1982), 42. Michael Levin reported this inconsistency in *Feminism and Freedom* (New Brunswick, N.J.: Transaction Books, 1987).

3. Allen Carrier, "Defense EO Chief Decries End of Army Coed Basic," *Army Times*, July 12, 1982, 28.

4. Charles C. Moskos, "Female GIs in the Field: Report from Honduras," unpublished report, 1985, 17.

5. Michael L. Rustad, *Women in Khaki* (New York: Praeger Publishers, 1982), 219.

6. Helen Rogan, *Mixed Company: Women in the Modern Army* (New York: G.P. Putnam's Sons, 1981), 186.

7. William J. Gregor, "Women, Combat, and the Draft: Placing Details in Context," in *Defense Manpower Planning: Issues for the 1980s*, eds. William J. Taylor, et al. (New York: Pergamon Press, 1981), 39.

8. Mary Jo Salter, "Annie, Don't Get Your Gun," *The Atlantic Monthly*, June 1980, 83.

9. Kathleen Guest-Smith and Ellen Wilkinson, "Why Women in the Military," Statement presented to the Defense Advisory Committee on Women in the Services, November 14, 1976, 3.

10. Salter, 84.

11. Hearings before the Military Personnel Subcommittee of the House Armed Services Committee, Subject: Women in the Military, November 13–16, 1979, and February 11, 1980, 55–56.

12. *Minerva: Quarterly Report on Women and the Military*, Spring 1985, 95.

13. Lesley Hazelton, *Israeli Women: The Reality Behind the Myth* (New York: Simon and Schuster, 1977).

14. Ibid, 20.

15. Ibid, 139.

16. Lionel Tiger and Joseph Shepler, *Women in the Kibbutz* (New York: Harcourt Brace Jovanovich, 1975), 189.

17. Tiger, 204.

18. Hazelton, 139.

19. Judith H. Stiehm, "Women and the Combat Exception," *Parameters: Journal of the U.S. Army War College*, June 1980, 57.

20. Judith H. Stiehm, *Bring Me Men and Women: Mandated Change at the U.S. Air Force Academy* (Berkeley, Calif.: University of California Press, 1981), 2.

21. M.C. Devilbiss, "Gender Integration and Unit Deployment: A Study of G.I. Jo," *Armed Forces and Society*, Summer 1985, 525.

22. James Webb, "Women Can't Fight," *The Washingtonian*, November 1979, 144.

23. Brig. General Andrew J. Gatsis, Testimony before the Military Personnel Subcommittee of the House Armed Services Committee, November 13–16, 1980, 279.

24. "Women's Work," *Parade Magazine*, January 5, 1986, 17.

25. *Minerva*, Fall 1987, 33.

26. Lois B. DeFleur with Frank Woods, Dick Harris, David Gillman, and William Marshak, *Four Years of Sex Integration at the United States Air Force Academy: Problems and Issues* (Colorado Springs, Colo.: U.S. Air Force Academy, August 1985).

27. Stiehm, "Women and the Combat Exception," 57.

28. Rogan, 164.

NOTES ON CHAPTER 10

1. "Woman Leads G.I.'s in Panama Combat," *New York Times*, January 4, 1990.

2. Unpublished memorandum signed by Major James J. Woods, S-3 (Operations Officer) 5th Battalion, 87th Infantry, Subj: Just Cause

Lessons Learned (Initial). The memorandum and its draft are in my possession.

3. "Army clears female soldiers," *Washington Times*, January 24, 1990. Molly Moore, "Army: Female Drivers Did Not Disobey Orders," *Washington Post*, January 23, 1990.

4. "Soldier Boys, Soldier Girls," *The New Republic*, February 19, 1990.

5. Based upon interviews with officers of the 5/87th Infantry. As it happened, the executive officer of the 5/87th was a personal friend of mine, having been my company commander in the 82nd Airborne Division. See also my article "Women in Arms: What Happened in Panama," *Chronicles*, May 1990.

6. Grant Willis and Julie Bird, "Women-in-combat-units gets cool reception," *Navy Times*, April 2, 1990.

7. Ibid.

8. Sally Quinn, "Mothers at War: What Are We Doing to Our Kids?" *Washington Post*, February 10, 1991.

9. Transcript of Committee Meeting, Presidential Commission on the Assignment of Women in the Armed Forces, June 9, 1992.

10. Testimony before the Subcommittee on Military Personnel and Compensation, Committee on Armed Services, House of Representatives, February 19, 1991.

11. Genevieve Henderson, "Women endure desert life," *Colorado Springs Gazette Telegraph*, October 30, 1990. Before this article, several puff pieces about women in the Gulf had already appeared in the major media. After this article, the story changed and the focus of press reports followed the *Gazette Telegraph*.

12. Jane Gross, "Standoff in the Gulf: Needs of Family and Country Clash in Persian Gulf Mission, *New York Times*, December 9, 1990.

13. Henderson, op cit.

14. Gross.

15. Henderson, op cit.

16. Jack Anderson and Dale Van Atta, "When Soldiers Have Babies," *Washington Post*, March 8, 1991.

17. *Report to the President*, 57–58, and C-121. Women were less likely to have deployed with their units by a factor of 3.3 for the Army, 3.7 for the Navy, 3.5 for the Air Force, and 3.9 for the Marine Corps.

18. Anderson, op cit.

19. *Report to the President*, C-48, C-121.

20. Ibid, C-50. See U.S. GAO, *Nondeployable Personnel in the Persian Gulf*, GAO/NSIAD-92-208, August 31, 1992.

21. Henderson, op cit.

22. Testimony of Sergeant Lori L. Mertz, USAR, before the Presidential Commission on the Assignment of Women in the Armed Forces, July 15, 1992.

23. Testimony of Sergeant Mary E. Rader, USA, before the Presidential Commission on the Assignment of Women in the Armed Forces, July 15, 1992.

24. Judy Gerstel, "The military tells troops a thing or two about sex and the returning soldier," *Detroit Free Press*, May 20, 1991.

25. Testimony before the Presidential Commission on the Assignment of Women in the Armed Forces, June 25, 1992.

26. A pamphlet recently published by the Army warns commanders of this danger.

27. Quoted by a brochure entitled "Feminine Protection for Deployed Female Military Personnel" by International Forecasts and Analysis, Alexandria, Va.

28. *Report to the President*, C-51–C-52.

29. Ibid, C-52 and D-4.

30. *Washington Post*, August 8, 1992. Her macho comments prompted Wesley Pruden, editor of the *Washington Times*, to write, "Lucky for her she was sent to Iraq and not to a Tailhook party." ("How Flapping Lips Sink Navy Ships," *Washington Times*, June 29, 1992).

31. She also received the Prisoner of War Medal, the National Defense Service Medal, the Bronze Star, and the Purple Heart (her arms were broken in the crash). Her commanding officer had recommended her for the Air Medal with V device (V for valor), but with the approval of the army chief of staff, the Air Medal was upgraded to the Distinguished Flying Cross.

32. The recommendation would have passed without debate had it not been for Eunice Ray, a newly appointed member from Kentucky. As a concession to Ray, each member was allowed three minutes to speak. Only Ray and two other new members voted against the recommendation.

33. *Washington Times*, April 26, 1991.

34. "Republican Leaders Missing in Action," *Human Events*, June 29, 1991.

35. Republicans who opposed the amendment were Bob Stump (Ariz.), Duncan Hunter (Calif.), Robert Dornan (Calif.), Jim McCrery

(Calif.), and Joel Hefley (Colo.). The lone Democrat in opposition was, oddly, Ron Dellums (Calif.).

36. Letter of Christopher Jehn, assistant secretary of defense for force management and personnel, to Senator John McCain, May 7, 1991.

37. *Report to the President*, president of the Presidential Commission on the Assignment of Women in the Armed Forces, November 15, 1992, iii.

NOTES ON CHAPTER 11

1. Cheney's original slate included Heather Wilson, a former Air Force captain and National Security Council staff member who had lobbied Congress to repeal the ban on woman in combat aviation.

2. Transcript of Commission Meeting, November 22, 1992, 288.

3. Ibid, 287.

4. Ibid, 320.

5. Presidential Commission on the Assignment of Women in the Armed Forces, *Report to the President*, November 15, 1992, C-98.

6. Testimony of Lieutenant Colonel William Gregor, September 9, 1992.

7. Testimony of Lieutenant John Clagett, USN, August 6, 1992.

8. Detailed pilot attrition statistics were somehow omitted from the Commission's bound report, but a half-page statistical table was later inserted unbound at page C-138.

9. David Hackworth, "War and the Second Sex," *Newsweek*, August 5, 1991, 26.

10. Testimony of Lieutenant Colonel William Gregor, USA, September 12, 1992.

11. Capt. Donovan R. Bigelow, "Equal But Separate: Can the Army's Affirmative Action Program Withstand Judicial Scrutiny After *Croson?*" *Military Law Review*, Winter 1991.

12. Interview with the author, January 1992. See Brian Mitchell, "Army, Bush keep quotas, disregard law," *Army Times*, January 27, 1992.

13. Memorandum for deputy chief of staff for personnel, from Brigadier General Donald W. Hansen, acting judge advocate general, March 19, 1990, in the possession of the author.

14. Transcript of proceedings before the Honorable Jackson L. Kiser, Roanoke, Va., on April 8, 1991, in the United States District Court for the Western District of Virginia, Roanoke Division, Civil Action No. 90-0126-R, *United States of America* v. *Commonwealth of*

Virginia et al., page 489. This author served as a consultant to the attorneys for VMI.

15. Ibid, 527–528. The defense entered into evidence a memo Toffler himself had written in 1990 stating that more than half of female first-classmen and nearly half of male first-classmen felt that integration had not been successful.

16. Ibid, 537–540.

17. Captain Jamie Ann Conway, "Let Women Fly in Combat," *New York Times*, June 25, 1992.

18. Transcript of Commission Meeting, November 22, 1992, 316.

19. The commissioners could never agree on whether to use the phrase "military effectiveness," "military readiness," or the legal term "military necessity."

20. Transcript of Commission Meeting, November 3, 1992, 266.

21. Transcript of Commission Meeting, June 8, 1992.

22. Major John Bruce Jessen, USAF, transcript of Commission Meeting, June 8, 1992.

23. Transcript of Commission Meeting, June 26, 1992.

NOTES ON CHAPTER 12

1. Mary McGrory, "Closing Ranks Around Alibis," *Washington Post*, May 29, 1990.

2. *The Assimilation of Women in the Brigade of Midshipmen*, United States Naval Academy, April 1991.

3. At the press conference, Mikulski herself defended this unfairness by saying that head-shaving is too humiliating for women but not at all humiliating for men.

4. The Office of the Assistant Chief of Naval Operations for Air Warfare, who in 1991 was Vice Admiral Richard M. Dunleavy.

5. The Tailhook Association also published an excellent magazine, *The Hook*, featuring dramatic accounts of aviation endeavors in wartime and in peacetime.

6. *Report of Investigation: Tailhook 91—Part 2*, Inspector General, U.S. Department of Defense, February 1993, VI-3.

7. Ibid, VI-11. Others passed down the hall in this manner included a young male Air Force officer who foolishly showed up wearing his Air Force flight jacket.

8. Ibid, VI-13 and F-26.

9. Gregory L. Vistica, *Fall from Glory: The Men Who Sank the U.S. Navy* (New York: Simon & Schuster, 1995, revised 1996).

10. *Congressional Record*, October 29, 1992.

11. According to Vistica, Coughlin told investigators on November 1 that she had complained to Snyder much earlier, but that he had not pursued the matter. Snyder denied hearing about the assault before September 19, and Coughlin's first two statements to investigators made no complaint against Snyder. Vistica says that Coughlin later admitted to him, "I guess I didn't tell [Snyder] enough to make him realize what really happened to me," but she also later denied this admission. See Vistica, pages 339–341 with notes on page 454.

12. The Navy "frocks" officers selected for promotion, allowing them to assume their new rank before the promotion becomes legally effective. Snyder had been selected for promotion to rear admiral and frocked months earlier.

13. Like many aged gents, Goldwater had a soft spot for the ladies and was ever eager in his later years to live down his earlier association with "right-wing conservatives."

14. Vistica, 345.

15. Vistica, 344.

16. Vistica, 456. Vistica explains in a footnote that he found out about her interviews with the *Post* and with ABC News beforehand, and called to give her a chance to tell him about the interviews, but that she never mentioned them and made excuses for why she didn't grant him an interview for attribution. He writes, "We could have easily identified her by name before the *Post* or ABC did, but we didn't. I had promised not to identify her until she said okay. She may have lied to me, but I was not about to break my word as a journalist."

17. John Lancaster, "A Gantlet of Terror, Frustration: Navy Pilot Recounts Tailhook Incident," *Washington Post*, June 24, 1992. For some reason, the *Post* preferred the alternate spelling to the more common *gauntlet*.

18. David Horowitz and Michael Kitchen, "Tailhook Witch-Hunt," *Heterodoxy*, October 1993, 11.

19. Vistica, *Fall from Glory*, 356. Military dinings-in are formal dinners without spouses conducted according to a comic protocol.

20. David Horowitz and Michael Kitchen, "Tailhook Witch-Hunt," *Heterodoxy*, October 1993, 11. Curiously, Vistica quotes the words "You make me see God" in relation to Diaz's leg-shaving, but does not say where the words come from and what their significance is.

21. Vistica, *Fall from Glory*, 355. Among those who blamed Garrett for everything, Vistica names Barbara Pope and Richard Armitage, each of whom played a part in the Navy's disaster.

22. He had reportedly joked that any woman who used the F word as often as Paula Coughlin did would welcome the attention she received. He was also accused by one woman of referring to female Navy pilots as "go-go dancers, topless dancers, or hookers," but this was disputed by other witnesses.

23. Horowitz, op cit.

24. Gregory Vistica, "Is Tailhook punishing only males? Female misbehavior ignored, say lawyers," *San Diego Union-Tribune*, August 27, 1993.

25. O'Keefe's leniency was nothing new. Female officers had long been allowed to campaign freely in uniform for repeal of the combat exclusions, both in media and on Capitol Hill, while male officers did not assume the same freedom to defend even current law and policy publicly.

26. Barton Gellman, "Key Case in Tailhook Is Dropped; Identification of Pilot Ruled to Be Inadequate in Harassment Incident," *Washington Post*, October 22, 1993.

NOTES ON CHAPTER 13

1. Fern Shen, "4 Midshipmen Disciplined in Pillow Attack; Academy Orders Loss of Leave in Incident That Left 2 Female Classmates Bruised," *Washington Post*, February 10, 1993.

2. "Frank blasts anti-gay military," *Washington Times*, August 1, 1991.

3. *Congressional Record*, September 11, 1991.

4. All seven publications were produced in the same large newsroom by the Times Journal Company, which reverted to its original name, Army Times Publishing Company, before being sold to Gannett in June 1997.

5. Memorandum entitled "Recommendations for Accepting Homosexuals and Bisexuals into the U.S. Armed Forces," Gay, Lesbian, and Bisexual Military Freedom Project, February 1993.

6. Jim Wolffe, "Powell stands by gay ban," *Army Times*, May 25, 1992, 5.

7. *V.I.P. Notes*, Center for Military Readiness, May and June 1995.

8. Gregory Vistica, *Fall from Glory* (New York: Simon & Schuster, 1995, revised 1996), 388–389.

9. Vistica, 327.

10. K.L. Billingsley, "Dancing with the Elephant," *Heterodoxy*, March/April 1995.

11. Pat Flynn, "Pilot qualified, files show," *San Diego Union-Tribune*, November 20, 1994.

12. Dori Meinert, "Naval aviator comes to rest at Arlington," *San Diego Union-Tribune*, November 22, 1994.

13. Ellen Goodman, "So it wasn't pilot error after all—Kara Hultgreen's death tells us prejudice still exists," *San Diego Union-Tribune*, March 3, 1995.

14. Quoted by Billingsley.

15. Vistica, 396.

16. Ibid, 396.

17. Robert J. Caldwell, "Hultgreen Case: Were the simulator tests rigged?" *San Diego Union-Tribune*, April 9, 1995.

18. Robert J. Spane, "Anatomy of a plane crash—Evaluating, explaining the results of two different Navy investigations," *San Diego Union-Tribune*, April 13, 1995.

19. Gerald L. Atkinson, "Navy breaches integrity at the very highest levels," *San Diego Union-Tribune*, July 7, 1995.

20. Vistica, 393.

21. Billingsley.

22. Robert J. Caldwell, "Navy files cast doubt on gender neutral training," *San Diego Union-Tribune*, May 14, 1995.

23. *Time*, May 13, 1996.

24. Quoted from "The Navy Adrift," *Washington Post*, April 28, 1996.

NOTES ON CHAPTER 14

1. As commonly quoted from *The Morning Bride*, which reads: "Heaven has no rage like love to hatred turned,/Nor hell a fury like a woman scorned."

2. "Sleeping with the Enemy," *The New Republic*, June 23, 1997.

3. Elaine Sciolino, "Sergeant Convicted of 18 Counts of Raping Female Subordinates," *New York Times*, April 30, 1997.

4. Tucker Carlson, "The Making of a Feminist Hero," *The Weekly Standard*, June 9, 1997.

5. "Military on the Offensive Against Illicit Love Affairs," *Washington Post*, April 28, 1997.

6. Quoted by *The Weekly Standard*, June 9, 1997.

7. This account is based on the author's interview with Ecker, June 28, 1997.

8. Testimony of Lt. Colonel Robert Rose, July 24, 1995.

9. Ibid.

10. Testimony of Major Jacquelyn S. Parker, July 24, 1995.

11. Letter of Colonel Brent J. Richardson to Ms. Roslynn R. Mauskoph [*sic*], Office of Inspector General, New York State, January 29, 1997, copy in the possession of the author.

12. Robert A. Rose, affidavit sworn before Joanne Vandyke, January 16, 1996, copy in the possession of the author.

NOTES ON CHAPTER 15

1. *The New Republic*, February 24, 1997.

2. Richard Cohen, "Duty, Gender, Country," *Washington Post*, April 24, 1997.

3. *Good Morning America*, November 18, 1996.

4. Simons's novel contribution to the subject involved the importance of talking about sex to the Army's Special Forces soldiers she had studied. Talking about anything else, other than work, tended to create uncomfortable distinctions that divided soldiers from each other. She writes, "Only discussions about sex allowed the men to define themselves separately, while not challenging the group's unity." See "In War, Let Men Be Men," *New York Times*, April 23, 1997.

5. Quoted by Richard Rayner, "The Warrior Besieged," *New York Times Magazine*, June 22, 1997.

6. Linda Bird Francke, *Ground Zero: The Gender Wars in the Military* (New York: Simon & Schuster, 1997), 260.

7. Jacquelyn K. Davis, Memo to General Anthony Lukeman, August 26, 1987, subject: "1987 WESTPAC visit of the DACOWITS," 2.

8. Department of Behavioral Sciences and Leadership, *Project Athena: Report on the Admission of Women to the U.S. Military Academy* (West Point, N.Y.: U.S. Military Academy, June 1, 1979), Vol. III, 191.

9. Science Research Laboratory, *Early Career Preparation, Experiences, and Commitment of Female and Male West Point Graduates* (West Point, N.Y.: U.S. Military Academy, undated), 1–52.

10. Letter from the adjutant general of the Army, subject: "Fraternization and Regulatory Policy Regarding Relationships Between Members of Different Ranks," November 21, 1986.

11. John O. Marsh, Jr., secretary of the Army, "Soldierly Values: Vital Ingredients for a Ready Force," *Army*, October 1986, 15.

12. John O. Marsh, Jr., secretary of the Army, "On Values," *Soldiers*, November 1986, 2.

Index